Intertwined Worlds

Other books in English by this author:

Studies in Al-Ghazzālī (Jerusalem: The Magnes Press, 1975)

Some Religious Aspects of Islam: A Collection of Articles (Leiden: Brill, 1981)

Intertwined Worlds

MEDIEVAL ISLAM AND BIBLE CRITICISM

Hava Lazarus-Yafeh

PRINCETON UNIVERSITY PRESS
PRINCETON, NEW JERSEY

Published by Princeton University Press, 41 William Street,
Princeton, New Jersey 08540
In the United Kingdom: Princeton University Press, Oxford

Library of Congress Cataloging-in-Publication Data

Lazarus-Yafeh, Hava.
Intertwined worlds : medieval Islam and Bible criticism / Hava Lazarus-Yafeh.
p. cm.
1. Bible. O.T.—Islamic interpretations. 2. Bible. O.T.—Criticism, interpretation, etc.—History—Middle Ages, 600–1500. 3. Islam—Relations—Judaism. 4. Judaism—Relations—Islam. 5. Islam—Relations—Christianity. 6. Christianity and other religions—Islam I. Title.
BP173.J8L39 1992 221.6'08'82971—dc20 91–29003 CIP

ISBN 0-691-07398-8

This book has been composed in Linotron Primer

Princeton University Press books are printed on acid-free paper, and meet the guidelines for permanence and durability of the Committee on Production Guidelines for Book Longevity of the Council on Library Resources

Printed in the United States of America

10 9 8 7 6 5 4 3 2 1

For Yishay, Ronit, and Orit

Contents

Abbreviations

BEO	*Bulletin d'études orientales*
BSOAS	*Bulletin of the School of Oriental and African Studies*
EI[1]	*Encyclopedia of Islam*, 1st ed.
EI[2]	*Encyclopedia of Islam*, 2nd ed.
GAL	*Geschichte der Arabischen Literatur*
GALS	*Geschichte der Arabischen Literatur* Supplement
HTR	*Harvard Theological Review*
HUCA	*Hebrew Union College Annual*
IOS	*Israel Oriental Studies*
JA	*Journal asiatique*
JAOS	*Journal of the American Oriental Society*
JQR	*Jewish Quarterly Review*
JSAI	*Jerusalem Studies in Arabic and Islam*
JSJ	*Journal for the Study of Judaism in the Persian, Hellenistic, and Roman Period*
PAAJR	*Proceedings of the American Academy of Jewish Research*
REJ	*Revue des études juives*
RSO	*Rivista degli studi orientali*
ZA	*Zeitschrift fuer Assyriology*
ZAW	*Zeitschrift fuer die Alttestamentlische Wissenschaft*
ZDMG	*Zeitschrift der Deutschen Morgenlaendischen Gesellschaft*

Preface

THIS BOOK ATTEMPTS to study medieval Muslim authors' knowledge of, and attitudes toward, the Hebrew Bible (Old Testament). The attitudes of medieval Muslims are very different from those of Christians, who concentrated mainly on the typological interpretation of the commonly shared divine text of the Bible. Muslim authors put the Biblical text itself, and its ways of transmission, to polemical scrutiny, believing that it had been falsified or tampered with. This brought about an almost scholarly Muslim critical study of the Old Testament, as well as of the New Testament, which will not be studied here in detail. It is suggested that this Muslim Bible criticism drew heavily on pre-Islamic pagan, Christian, Gnostic, and other sources, and later may have been transmitted—through both Jewish and Christian mediators—to early modern Bible criticism. Much study has still to be done to connect these different historical eras and civilizations in a field in which they are usually taken to be totally separate.

Under the influence of Christian converts to Islam, Muslim authors also took the Bible to predict the coming of Muhammad and the rise of Islam. Jewish authors often reacted, both explicitly and implicitly, to such Muslim interpretations, and sometimes Muslim authors may have recorded lost Jewish material in this context. These topics are dealt with mainly in chapter Four. An especially intriguing question is which Arabic Bible translations were available to Muslim authors. Contrary to the near-consensus among scholars, I believe that Muslim authors had to rely heavily on partial, mainly oral, Jewish and Christian translations until the fifteenth century.

This book thus touches upon many issues, but may raise

more questions than it answers. I hope, however, that it will bring its readers to look at these topics from a new point of view and show how intertwined different worlds can be.

The number of people who have helped me with this small book and to whom I am deeply grateful is so large that I cannot mention all of them here or in the footnotes (I have done so only on occasion). I am especially grateful to the Annenberg Research Institute in Philadelphia and to the Institute for Advanced Studies at the Hebrew University in Jerusalem, both of which enabled me to spend the whole 1988–89 academic year working on the final version of this book. My colleagues at both have enlightened me on many issues, and the staff of both institutes have been extremely helpful. I am also much indebted to many friends, colleagues, and students from various departments at the Hebrew University and other institutions who read parts of the manuscript and made important suggestions and corrections, especially Moshe Greenberg, Benjamin Z. Kedar, Bernard Lewis, Vera Moreen, and Sasson Somekh. Of course, I alone am responsible for the remaining faults of this book.

The verses from the Qur'an are quoted (by permission) according to M. Pickthall's translation (*The Meaning of the Glorious Koran*, published by Unwin Hyman of HarperCollins Publishers Limited) with some additions as noted, and those of the Bible mostly according to the Revised Standard Version, with some changes mainly according to modern Jewish translations. The transcription of Arabic words follows the system used by the *Encyclopedia of Islam*, except for the letter *ḳ*, for which I use *q*.

Chapter Three was published in a different version in Hebrew in *Tarbiz, A Quarterly for Jewish Studies* 55 (Jerusalem 1986): 357–79 ("Ezra-ʿUzayr: Metamorphosis of a Polemical Motif"). The Appendix was published in Hebrew in *Sephunot*, new series 5, 20 (1991), by the Ben Zvi Institute for the Study of Jewish Communities in the East, Jerusalem. My thanks to the editors of these journals for their permission to reprint them here.

The Hebrew University
Jerusalem

Intertwined Worlds

CHAPTER ONE

Introduction

THE FIRST CENTURIES of the Christian era in the Near East were marked by intensive, unique religious creativity, seldom if ever matched in the history of mankind. Christianity developed from Judaeo-Christian circles into a full-fledged system, subdividing into different denominations and giving birth to an unprecedented flourishing of theological activity, preserved, for example, in the extensive Patristic literature. At the same time, older, well-established Judaism cultivated and started to collect, at least partially, its vast body of Oral Law, the Bible having been canonized centuries before. Now the redaction of the Mishna (c. 200 C.E.) and Tosefta (c. 400 C.E.) was completed, soon to be followed by the Jerusalem (c. 400 C.E.) and Babylonian (c. 500 C.E.) Talmuds, both consisting of the elaborations and discussions of the Mishna by the later sages, called Amoraim. Several collections of Midrashic homilies were also gathered at that time, when hermeneutic literature seemed to have reached its peak. Simultaneously, a rich, variegated sectarian activity was fermenting the region and its religious traditions. Although the main Apocryphal and Pseudoepigraphic literary activity did not continue long into the Christian era, its traditions were kept alive for many generations in later Jewish and Christian literatures. In addition, Gnostic movements and ideas as well as later Neoplatonic philosophy challenged in a most serious way the established religions of the region. For hundreds of years, Judaism and Christianity, and eventually Islam, fought against the Greek, Persian, and Hellenistic pagan legacy, but were also deeply influenced by it.

Although activity in the region quieted in the last 150

years before the rise of Islam, early Islamic literature clearly echoes all the controversies. In fact, it is impossible to understand this literature properly without paying serious attention to its various predecessors, as a vast body of excellent scholarly work has shown. One should not think in terms of influences or cultural borrowing only, however. It has been said that the Near East resembles a palimpsest,[1] layer upon layer, tradition upon tradition, intertwined to the extent that one cannot really grasp one without the other, certainly not the later without the earlier, but often also not the earlier without considering the shapes it took later.

In order to find one's way through such a labyrinth of religious traditions, even in the literary corpus of a single civilization, one needs some kind of Ariadne's thread. The one I have chosen in this small book to guide us through Islamic medieval literature has two strands: the Hebrew Bible and polemical literature. Hermeneutic literature and Bible exegesis, both literal and allegorical, constituted the most fundamental part of Jewish and Christian literature up to the Middle Ages, and in the setting of polemical literature often also included some kind of Bible criticism. The deep impact of the Bible and Midrash, both on the Qur'an and its commentaries and on early Ḥadīth literature, has been studied especially thoroughly during the last 150 years. Later Muslim polemical literature, however, has received much less attention from this point of view, and it is this subject which I have taken up here: the role the Hebrew Bible played in Muslim medieval polemics.

Polemics, especially religious polemics, are an indispensable part of the continuous competition between great civilizations. They may include many different kinds of literature, from folktales and simple, sometimes only oral, folklore to the highest forms of philosophical and theologi-

[1] E. A. Speiser, according to M. Greenberg. See also S. D. Goitein, "The Intermediate Civilization/The Hellenic Heritage in Islam," in his *Studies in Islamic History and Institutions* (Leiden 1966), pp. 54–70.

cal writings, even when no explicit mention is made of any rival civilization or religion. One may even say that the crystallization of every great civilization is based to a large extent on its contacts, clashes, and competition with rival forces, for no civilization or religion can develop or prosper on its own. This seems to be true for every age, but the religious aspect of this rivalry is especially conspicuous in the Middle Ages.

In the Middle Ages, the greater bulk of interfaith polemical activity took place between Islam and Christianity, and a vast polemical literature exists, mainly in Greek, Latin, and Arabic, sometimes containing remarkable scholarly efforts to describe the other as truly and as objectively as possible.[2] This literature reflects, of course, the political and military rivalry between medieval Christianity and Islam, but it deals specifically with their different concepts of monotheism, prophecy, and Scripture.

Each of these great religions was also engaged in polemics with other religions, especially with Judaism, although their methods were diverse. This was an extremely important subject for Christianity, and therefore polemics with Judaism were integral to Christian theology from its very beginning and played a central role in its internal development. Hence the bitterness, the intensity, and the hatred that accompanied them, which often erupted into riots, pogroms, or the burning of Jewish holy books, such as the Talmud, as a consequence of some dramatic public dispu-

[2] See, e.g., M. Steinschneider, *Polemische und Apologetische Literatur in Arabischer Sprache zwischen Muslimen, Christen und Juden* (Leipzig 1877); E. Fritsch, *Islam und Christentum im Mittelalter* (Breslau 1930; reprint 1965); N. Daniel, *Islam and the West* (Edinburgh 1960); and the bibliography of M. Perlmann at the end of his article "The Medieval Polemics between Judaism and Islam," in *Religion in a Religious Age*, ed. S. D. Goitein, Association for Jewish Studies (New York 1974), pp. 103–38. I am much indebted to M. Perlmann's studies in this field.

Most of this literature, however, consists of misunderstandings and misinterpretations of the other, and often also shows lack of true interest in other religions. See, for example, B. Lewis, *The Muslim Discovery of Europe* (London 1982), p. 68.

tation between representatives of both religions. In contrast, Muslim polemics against Judaism, though present in the Qur'an and early in Ḥadīth and Sīrah literature, are much less abundant and were never really considered important by Muslim authors. This may be because there was little competition between these religions, or perhaps because of their great similarity to each other as the two strictly monotheistic religions of law. In any case, no official disputation was ever enforced upon the representatives of the Jewish (or, for that matter, Christian) community in the Islamic Empire, nor are there any records of Jewish books ever being burned as a consequence of polemical activity.

The part the Jews played in this game also varied much from the Christian West to the Muslim East. In the West, many refutations (including handy manuals of Bible exegesis) of the Christian arguments were composed, usually in Hebrew, for Jewish readers. But in the East, an almost total silence towards Muslim arguments against Judaism prevailed. We have no explicit refutations of Islamic arguments in Judaeo-Arabic literature (except for a short chapter in the tenth-century Karaite Al-Qirqisānī's great compendium of Jewish law).[3] The few other Jewish refutations of Islam are rather late and in Hebrew, such as *Ma'amar Yishmael,* ascribed to Solomon ibn Adret of thirteenth-century Barcelona, or *Keshet u-Magen* by Simeon b. Zemah Duran from fifteenth-century Algiers.[4] We should, however, consider a great part of Judaeo-Arabic medieval literature (e.g., Saadia Gaon, Jehuda Halevi, Maimonides, and

[3] See his *Kitāb al-Anwār wa-l-Marāqib* (Code of Karaite Law), ed. L. Nemoy, pt. 3 (New York 1941) ch. 15, pp. 202ff. Cf. also I. Friedlaender, "Qirqisānī's Polemik gegen den Islam," *ZA* 26 (1912): 93–100; and see the Appendix below.

[4] See *Encyclopedia Judaica* sv. "Adret, Solomon b. Abraham" and "Duran, Simeon b. Zemah"; cf. M. Schreiner, "Die Apologetische Schrift des Salomo b. Adret gegen einen Muhammedaner," *ZDMG* 48 (1894): 39–42 (reprinted in his *Gesammelte Schriften*, ed. M. Perlmann [Hildesheim 1983], pp. 271–94), where he attempts to show that Ibn Adret answered the polemics of Ibn Ḥazm. (See also M. Zucker [in Hebrew] in *Festschrift A. Kaminka* [Wien 1957] pp. 31–48.)

many others) to be both explicit and implicit attempts to refute Islam.[5] Indeed, in many cases this would be the only way to understand correctly certain passages in these writings. (The same holds true for several Bible commentaries, such as those by Ibn Ezra, or the later David Kimḥi, in which some references are totally unintelligible without taking into account their implicit reference to Christian or Muslim polemics against Judaism.)

There are at least three possible reasons for the lack of Jewish response to Islamic polemics. The first, practical reason is Jewish reluctance to offend the oppressor, especially while using his own (Arabic) language (though in Hebrew characters), as Jews usually did. The second reason is that Jews and Christians, according to several versions of the "Pact of 'Umar," were forbidden to study the Arabic language, and especially the Qur'an, considered by most Muslims to be not only the sacred book of Islam but also God's inimitable and uncreated speech. Although we know of rather late Hebrew transcriptions and translations of the Qur'an apparently meant to circumvent that prohibition, we hear of only one Jewish attempt in Arabic to refute the Qur'an directly.[6] At the same time, however, Jews used arguments taken from the Qur'an (and from later Muslim theologians and philosophers) in both their Judaeo-Arabic and, later, Hebrew writings to refute Christian tenets and point out the inner contradictions between the four Gospels.[7]

A third, less obvious reason for Jewish silence against Muslim polemics may be found in Maimonides' writings,

[5] I believe this to be true in a much more general way than it was considered by M. Schreiner, in his "Zur Geschichte der Polemik zwischen Juden und Muhammedanern," *ZDMG* 42 (1888): 597–675 (in *Gesammelte Schriften*, pp. 75–159). Cf. also S. Baron, *A Social and Religious History of the Jews*, vol. 5 (New York 1957), ch. 24.

[6] See Chapter Two, n. 26.

[7] See D. J. Lasker, *Jewish Philosophical Polemics against Christianity in the Middle Ages* (New York 1977); cf. the manuscript described in the Appendix below. In general, however, Jewish polemics against Christianity under Muslim rule were much the same as in the Christian West.

where he prohibits the Jews from teaching Muslims the tenets of Judaism, in direct contrast to Christians (*al-ʿArelim*), whom he allowed to be instructed in the commandments of the Torah. This, in spite of the fact that he explicitly acknowledged Islam as a true monotheistic religion, unlike Christianity. Maimonides explained his prohibition by pointing out that Muslims do not accept the text of the Torah as divine, whereas Christians do believe that the text of the Torah has not changed and "only" (*innamā*) misinterpret it through faulty exegesis.[8]

Indeed, Christians usually accepted the holiness of the Old Testament but accused the Jews of misunderstanding and misinterpreting it, and of reading it literally ("the letter"), whereas it should really be understood allegorically ("the spirit"). Thus exegesis became the main battlefield of Jewish–Christian polemics in the West during the Middle Ages. We have Jewish manuals of Bible exegesis containing the "wrong" Christian explanation of certain verses and the "right" explanation of the same verses with which Jews should respond. This literary activity has no parallel in Jewish–Muslim polemics, although, as we shall see in Chapter Four, some of the same controversial verses are quoted by Muslim authors who dealt with their interpretations and translations. Yet Islamic polemics were primarily directed against the Scriptures themselves (Old and New Testaments), which, in their redacted form, were never accepted as sacred by Muslims, even though their ultimate source was considered to have been a truly divine revelation. Following the Qur'an, Muslim authors tried to prove that the text of these Scriptures had been deliberately altered

[8] M. Maimonides, *Responsa*, ed. J. Blau (Jerusalem 1986), 1: 284–85 (no. 149: the Bible contradicts the "confused inventions" of the Muslims) and 2: 726; and cf. I. Twersky, *Introduction to the Code of Maimonides* (New Haven 1980), p. 452; G. F. Hourani, "Maimonides and Islam," in *Studies in Islamic and Judaic Traditions*, ed. W. M. Brinner and S. Ricks, Center for Judaic Studies, University of Denver (Atlanta 1986), pp. 153–66; and esp. J. Kraemer, "Nāmūs and Sharīʿa in Maimonides' Doctrine" (in Hebrew), *Teʿuda* 4 (1986): 185–202.

throughout the ages by both Jews and Christians. Here, then, seems to lie the most important difference between Christian–Jewish and Muslim–Jewish (and Muslim–Christian) polemics. In the first case, a commonly shared divine text is differently expounded; in the second, the text itself is put to polemical scrutiny. Therefore, as we shall see in Chapter Three, even Christian authors often explicitly defended the authenticity of the Old Testament Biblical text (which contains prophecies about Jesus) against Muslim arguments. For example, in an early document of Christian–Muslim polemics, a letter to the Caliph ʿUmar II (717–720) attributed to the Byzantine Emperor Leo III, the Christian author states that Jews and Christians share the belief in the same text, which they consider divine, but that they bitterly discuss the meaning and correct explanations of many of its verses.[9]

This is what Maimonides hinted at in his explanation to his prohibition. Theologically, Islam may be much closer to Judaism than Christianity is, but it lacks the one common ground Judaism shares with Christianity: the belief in the holiness of the same Scriptures. This may also explain why Muslim authors were usually not interested in the Talmud, knew very little about it, and rarely speculated about its mysteries[10]—because they, unlike their Christian counterparts, could attack the Biblical text directly. Even when Muslims tried to reproduce the "true and uncorrupted Bible," when they quoted, as they so often did, alleged verses from the true uncorrupted "Torah," they never attributed to the Jews any hidden daemonic doctrine or practice. Their alleged Torah verses were usually sermonic lessons, proverbial sayings, and Qur'an-like verses or stories with mor-

[9] Cf. A. Jeffery, "Ghevond's Text of the Correspondence between ʿUmar II and Leo III," *HTR* 37 (1944): 269–321. (The Armenian original version seems to be from the tenth century.)

[10] See Ch. Merhavia, *The Church versus Talmudic and Midrashic Literature (500–1284)* (in Hebrew) (Jerusalem 1970); B. Lewis, *Semites and Anti-Semites* (London 1986), pp. 104–105 and ch. 5; J. Trachtenberg, *The Devil and the Jews* (New York 1966).

als (see Chapter Two), whereas their Biblical criticism was more scientific, though often couched in harsh polemical tones. Its main purpose was to point out the many contradictions, inaccuracies, or theological impossibilities of both the Old and New Testaments, which prove that these texts had been corrupted by their respective communities and, unlike the Qur'an, had no reliable and trustworthy transmission (*Tawātur*). In their present form, therefore, these Scriptures could not be considered truly divine revelations. Thus, Muslim attitudes toward the Bible became the central issue of Muslim medieval polemics against Judaism, and developed into an almost philological scholarly study of the Biblical text.

These polemics touch on an even deeper difference between the three religions and are connected directly with the basic attitudes of Jews, Christians, and Muslims toward their own respective Scriptures. Although Jews considered the Bible, and especially the Pentateuch, to be a divine revelation, they had no doubt that Moses wrote it, and thus gave it its final stylistic shape, just as later prophets recorded other revelations in their respective books. In spite of—or perhaps because of—the great care Jewish sages (especially the Massoretes) took to establish, preserve, and hand down the original text of the Torah, a critical approach to the text developed very early in Judaism,[11] but was later suppressed. Thus, for example, the question is asked in the Talmud:

> Is it possible that Moses whilst still alive would have written "So Moses . . . died there" (Deut. 34:5)? The truth is, however, that up to this point Moses wrote, from this point Joshua, son of Nun, wrote. (*Menahoth* 30a)

[11] Cf. M. Soloveitchik and S. Rubasheff, *The History of Bible Criticism* (in Hebrew) (Berlin 1925), esp. ch. 2. See also M. Greenberg, "Jewish Conceptions of the Human Factor in Biblical Prophecy," in *Justice and the Holy, Essays in Honor of Walter Harrelson*, ed. D. A. Knight and P. J. Paris (Atlanta 1989), pp. 145–62.

Mistakes in calculations and contradictions between texts were often discussed (see, for example, *Megillah* 12a), as was the question of who composed the different books of the Bible:

> Who wrote the Scriptures: Moses wrote his own book and the portion of Balaam (Num. 23–24) and Job. Joshua wrote the book which bears his name and the last eight verses of the Pentateuch. Samuel wrote the book which bears his name and the book of Judges and Ruth. David wrote the Book of Psalms. . . . Jeremiah wrote the Book which bears his name and Lamentations. Hezekiah and his colleagues wrote Isaiah, Proverbs, Song of Songs, and Ecclesiastes. The Men of the great Assembly . . . wrote Ezekiel, the twelve minor prophets, Daniel, and the Scroll of Esther. Ezra wrote the book which bears his name and the genealogies of the Book of Chronicles up to his own time. . . . Who then finished it? Nehemiah the son of Hachaliah. (*Baba Bathra* 15a)

Although these and similar questions were usually answered traditionally and harmonized, and were only rarely asked again later (for example, by scholars like Abraham ibn Ezra), I believe that on the whole they made an impact on the rather relaxed Jewish attitude toward the external form of the Bible. This attitude may also explain the almost systematic dissection of the plain text of Scriptures by Midrashic exegesis—to an extent only rarely found even in Muslim allegorical exegesis of the Qur'an. Perhaps Jewish sages thought that the words and letters of the Bible as divine revelation could be used in any possible way to express everything considered to be related to that revelation—a way of reasoning that would be alien to Muslim medieval theologians.

Christian attitudes toward both Old and New Testaments went a step further. Early Christian theologians followed Augustine in adapting Cicero's rhetorical scheme to the doctrines of their new faith. Cicero mentioned three modes of style to address topics of different levels of importance: parva, the lower style for everyday life issues; magna, the highly decorated oratory style for the great issues of life; and temperate, for everything in between. Augustine accepted this threefold style in some way for Christian school rhetorics (Bible interpretation, moral education, and emotional excitement that leads to action), but he also advocated a totally different attitude toward the lower style, which may actually express the most sublime of ideas, in much the same way that God Incarnate chose to become humbly (*humilis*) human.[12] In this way, the simple style of the Gospels, their inner contradictions and inconsistencies, often pointed out and ridiculed by non-Christian authors, became for Christian theologians the *genus humile* or *eloquium humile* of revelation, its humble dress, parallel to the wondrous fact that the Word of God had become flesh and died on the cross. Therefore, some Christian authors did readily admit to the imperfection of their Bible, and even found virtue in it. Others tried to explain away its faults, mainly through allegorical exegesis. Only later Christian authors adhered to the belief that the Bible was also a supreme work of art.[13]

In contrast, early Muslim theologians developed a very different view of the Qur'an as the Speech of God. They may have wished to differentiate the Qur'an from earlier divine Scriptures that are, according to the Qur'an itself, taken from the same heavenly Table (*al-Lawḥ al-Maḥfūẓ*). These theologians may have unconsciously made an at-

[12] See E. Auerbach, *Literatursprache und Publikum in der lateinischen Spaetantike und im Mittelalter* (Bern 1958), ch. 1, "Sermo Humilis," pp. 25–53 (Eng. trans. by R. Manheim, *Literary Language and Its Public in Late Latin Antiquity* [London 1965]).

[13] G. von Grunebaum, *A Tenth-Century Document of Arabic Literary Theory and Criticism* (Chicago 1950), Introduction, pp. xv–xvi. Von Grunebaum mentions especially the Victorines of the twelfth century, but also the Venerable Bede (d. 735) (who knew John Cassian's [d. 435] famous definition of the four levels of interpretation of Scripture—Littera, Allegoria, Tropologia (or Moralia), and Anagogia). It would be worthwhile to find out whether this trend in later Christian theological literature developed under Muslim influence.

tempt to build an Islamic parallel to the Logos doctrine,[14] or perhaps they followed some vague notions derived from Latin rhetorics. But since the "Arabic clear book" was the basic experience of nascent Islam, it became also a central doctrine of its evolving theology. Muslims attributed to the Qur'an, as the Speech of God, unique characteristics of perfection in both content and form, and discussed them passionately for generations—so passionately that some of the disputants had to pay with their lives for their heretic views. The final consensus, which evolved before the tenth century and binds Muslims to this very day, though in a slightly mitigated form, speaks about the uncreated, inimitable miracle of the Qur'an, the transmission of which is faultless and totally reliable.

The most important question in this context was whether the Qur'an as the Speech of God was created. Originally all discussants may have been preoccupied with the rejection of anthropomorphic ideas,[15] but soon it became the privilege of the rationalist Muʿtazilites to fight for the idea of a *created* Qur'an, for some time even with the help of a state-enforced inquisition. Yet from the middle of the ninth century, the opposing Logos-like dogma that the Qur'an is the *uncreated* Speech of God (which became the perfect Book) and therefore is also eternal was accepted as a central doctrine of faith in Sunni Islam. Surprisingly, neither this dogma nor the heated discussions about it play any role in Muslim polemics against the Bible. Except for a legendary accusation that the rejected, heretic idea of a created Qur'an—like so many other unworthy issues—stems from Jewish (or Manichaean) circles,[16] Muslim au-

[14] H. A. Wolfson, *The Philosophy of the Kalam* (Cambridge, Mass. 1976), ch. 3.

[15] W. Madelung, "The Origins of the Controversy Concerning the Creation of the Koran," *Orientalia Hispanica Sive Studia F. M. Pareja Octogenario Dicata*, ed. J. M. Barral (Leiden 1974), 1: 504–25; see also J. R. Peters, *God's Created Speech* (Leiden 1976) and the Bibliography mentioned there.

[16] Madelung, "Origins," p. 505 n. 2.

thors usually did not explicitly connect this dogma with their polemics against other Scriptures. This may be connected with the fact that the first "champions of Islam in debates with non-Muslims" were mainly Muʿtazilites,[17] but it remains true for later Muslim authors as well.

Jewish authors were never attracted by the dogma of the uncreated Qur'an, although they were deeply influenced in general by Muslim theology. The pre-existence of the Torah, in which God could find a blueprint for creation,[18] was their theological limit in this case, and they did not take pains to refute this Qur'anic dogma.

From the same discussions evolved the concept of the Qur'an's miraculous inimitability (*Iʿdjāz*, the rendering of others powerless to produce such verses), either because of its unique language, style, and content, or because God obstructs any attempt to produce something similar to it (*ṣarfa*).[19] Some Qur'anic verses express the explicit challenge (*al-taḥaddī*) to imitate the Qur'an, which no one can ever successfully meet:

> And if ye are in doubt concerning that which We reveal unto Our slave (Muhammad), then produce a sūrah of the like thereof. . . . And if ye do it not—and ye can never do it—then guard yourselves against the fire prepared for disbelievers. (Sūra 2:23, 24)

When this characteristic developed into dogma in the ninth century, the emphasis was on form, on the Arabic language and style of the Qur'an rather than on its con-

[17] See S. Pines, "A Note on an Early Meaning of the Term Mutakallim," *IOS* 1 (1971): 224–35.

[18] See, for example, the Midrashim *Sifre*, Eqev, ch. 37, or *Bereshit Rabba* 1.4, 6; cf. E. E. Urbach, *The Sages, Their Concepts and Beliefs* (trans.) (Jerusalem 1975), pp. 198ff.

[19] See *EI*² sv. "Iʿdjāz" (G. von Grunebaum) where a Latin precedent of this concept is mentioned. Cf. Abdul Aleem, "Iʿjazu-l-Qur'an," *Islamic Culture* 7 (1933): 64–82, 215–33; J. Bouman, *Le Conflit autour du Coran et la solution d'al-Bāqillānī* (Amsterdam 1959). See also J. van Ess, "Sprache und Religioese Erkenntniss im Islam," *Miscellanea Mediaevalia* 13, 1 (1981): 226–35.

tents. The holy book came to be considered a matchless, unprecedented, never-to-be-repeated literary phenomenon, the greatest miracle ever (*muʿdjiza*), the final proof of Muhammad's true mission.[20] The rhetorical uniqueness of the Qur'an became the main argument for its divine character, and at the same time served as a starting point for the later, well-developed science of rhetoric in Arabic literature.

This dogma is mentioned in Muslim–Jewish (and Christian) medieval polemics, but it never became an important issue in these discussions.[21] Thus, for example, says the Ashʿarite theologian Al-Bāqillānī (d. 1013), one of the most systematic authors on the subject, in his book entitled *Iʿdjāz al-Qur'ān*:

> And if one asks: "Do you say that the Speech of God, other than the Qur'an, such as the Torah and the Gospels and the Scrolls,[22] are also inimitable (*muʿdjiz*)?" One would answer: "They are not inimitable from the point of view of style and composition (*al-naẓm wa-l-ta'līf*) at all, but they share with the Qur'an the inimitability of containing the prediction of what is hidden [e.g., the future]."[23]

Al-Bāqillānī then adds that no other Scripture was ever described in the same way that God described the Qur'an in its own verses, and that only with regard to the Qur'an

[20] On the early development of this notion and the role of prophetic miracles in interreligious polemics, cf. S. Stroumsa, "The Signs of Prophecy: The Emergence and Early Development of a Theme in Arabic Theological Literature," *HTR* 78 (1985): 101–4.

[21] This seems somewhat to contradict von Grunebaum's and Stroumsa's statements. But although the concept of *Iʿdjāz* indeed may well have evolved and developed for polemical reasons, nevertheless it was not mentioned very often in comparison with other Scriptures. Cf. P. Kraus, "Beitraege zur Islamischen Ketzergeschichte," *RSO* 14 (1935): esp. pp. 126–27, 337, 369–70.

[22] According to the Qur'an, there exist other heavenly revelations to prophets like Abraham.

[23] Abu Bakr Muḥammad ibn al-Tayyib al-Bāqillānī, *Iʿdjāz al-Qur'ān*, ed. Aḥmad Saqar (Cairo 1963), p. 31 (fol. 44). The prediction of the future and the knowledge of "hidden" things are also signs of *Iʿdjāz*.

were people challenged to bring forth anything similar to it—a challenge that could not be met. In another book, *Kitāb al-Tamhīd*, he goes into more detail about this discussion with Jews and Christians and states that if the Torah and the Gospels had passed the test of inimitability, they would have to be considered *mu'djiz*, like the Qur'an itself.[24] In general, however, there can be little doubt that the unique style and Arabic language of the Qur'an were so decisive a miracle for Al-Bāqillānī and other Muslim authors that the problematical application of theological dogmas about the Qur'an to earlier heavenly Scriptures did not really worry them.

Several Jewish authors made attempts to refute this dogma, notably the Karaites Al-Qirqisānī and Yefet b. 'Alī, as early as the tenth century, and later the poet and critic Moses b. Ezra (d. c. 1139).[25] At the same time, however, some Jewish authors were attracted by this dogma, as it so often happens in polemics. Jehuda Halevi (d. 1141), for example, after rejecting at the beginning of the *Book of Kuzari* the miracle of the Qur'an (*mu'djiza*), ascribes to the Mishna some typical *I'djāz* characteristics,[26] apparently in

[24] See Al-Bāqillānī, *Kitāb al-Tamhīd*, ed. R. J. McCarthy (Beirut 1957), pp. 153ff. Throughout the book, the subject of *I'djāz* is discussed in a polemical framework. Other Muslim authors usually deny more categorically the *I'djāz* of Scriptures other than the Qur'an. Cf. 'Alī Ibn Ḥazm, *Al-Faṣl fī-l-Milal wa-l-Ahwā wa-l-Niḥal* (n.p., 1329Hg.), 1: 106–7; 'Abd al-Djabbār b. Aḥmad, *Al-Mughnī fī Abwāb al-Tawḥīd wa-l-'Adl* (Cairo 1960), 12: 45ff.; and Samau'al al-Maghribī, *Ifḥām al-Yahūd* (Silencing the Jews), ed. and trans. M. Perlmann, *PAAJR* 32 (1964): text pp. 26, 65; trans. pp. 43, 61. See also Ibn Khaldūn, *Muqaddima*, trans. F. Rosenthal (Princeton 1958), 1: 192.

[25] See Appendix here, and cf. Moshe b. Ya'akov ben Ezra (Moses ibn Ezra), *Kitāb al-Muḥāḍara wal-Mudhākara* (Liber discussionis et commemorationis), ed. A. S. Halkin (Jerusalem 1975), pp. 36–39 (fol. 20–21), where Ibn Ezra mentions that the Muslim poet Abū-l-'Alā al-Ma'arrī (d. 1057) indeed succeeded in producing a literary rival to the Qur'an.

[26] This was already mentioned by M. Perlmann in a hidden note (B.14, p. 95) in his edition and translation of Samau'al al-Maghribī's *Ifḥām al-Yahūd*.

order to dispel any (Karaite or other) doubt with regard to it.

> Its traditions are so reliable that no suspicion of invention could be upheld. Besides this the Mishna contains a large amount of pure Hebrew which is not borrowed from the Bible. It is greatly distinguished by terseness of language, beauty of style, excellence of composition and the comprehensive employment of homonyms, applied in a lucid way, leaving neither doubt nor obscurity. This is so striking that everyone who looks at it with genuine scrutiny must be aware that a mortal man is incapable of composing such a work without divine assistance.[27]

On the whole, Muslim theological doctrines about the Qur'an played no great role in Muslim polemics against the Bible. But they laid the psychological foundations for contradictory Muslim attitudes toward the Qur'an and the Bible. Muslim authors, as sincere believers, truly considered the former to be the divine, perfect, and uncreated Word of God. They could easily explain away, therefore, any anthropomorphic expression, linguistic inaccuracies, or contradictions therein. Yet the same faults in the Bible were taken as proof that it had been falsified or as a sign that it had been composed by man.

Thus, for example, the Spanish author Ibn Ḥazm (d. 1064)[28] often compared Biblical and Qur'anic verses. He expressed his horror and disgust at the anthropomorphic

[27] *Book of Kuzari* pt. 3, 67 (Judah ha-Levi, *Kitāb al-Radd wa-l-Dalīl fī-l-Dīn al-Dhalīl*, ed. D. H. Baneth [Jerusalem 1977], pp. 141–42; Eng. trans. H. Hirschfeld, *Book of Kuzari* [New York 1946], p. 106. The revival of Hebrew in general and specific details like the attribution of the "purest Hebrew speech" to the tribes of Jehuda and Benjamin are other obvious signs of Muslim influence on Jewish thought in this respect. Cf. H. Lazarus-Yafeh, *Some Religious Aspects of Islam* (Leiden 1981), pp. 83–84, and see A. Halkin, "Medieval Attitude towards Hebrew," in *Biblical and Other Studies*, ed. A. Altmann, Brandeis University Studies and Texts 1 (Cambridge, Mass. 1963), pp. 233–48.

[28] On Ibn Ḥazm, see below, Chapter Two. The following is taken from his *Al-Faṣl*, 1: 160. See another example, ibid., 2: 75.

expressions in the Bible, such as in Deut. 4:24 ("God is a consuming fire"),[29] and added:

> One of [the Jews] asked: do you not have in the Qur'an a verse "God is the light of heaven and earth" [Sūra 24:35]?[30] I said: yes [that is true], but the Apostle of God, God's peace and blessings upon him, answered Abū Dharr's question whether he had seen God, with "Light—whence, how can I see it?" This makes it very clear that He did not mean a light which can be seen, but a light which cannot be seen, and therefore that the meaning of "light" in this verse . . . is the One who directs the people of heaven and earth, and that "light" is only one of the Names of Allah.

One is even tempted to assume that any critical approach to the Qur'an could have been easily suppressed in the Muslim world and considered heretical, precisely because Muslim rationalistic critical activity had found far less problematic territory in the critical study of the Bible. This may in fact have helped to keep the study of the Qur'an within its traditional boundaries to the present day.

In any case, Muslim critical approaches to the Bible developed along very different lines and had little to do with the theological dogmas about the Qur'an. They drew heavily on earlier pre-Islamic criticism of the Bible and constituted, in many ways, a continuation and elaboration of it, under the new guise of Islam.

[29] This verse was also used in pre-Islamic polemics against the Bible. Saadia Gaon translated it as "God's punishment is [as] a consuming fire" and took it as an example of a logically inadmissable verse that cannot be understood in its plain literal sense (see the beginning of ch. 7 of his *Book of Beliefs and Opinions*). A later Jewish convert to Islam used this verse to prove that Jews were actually "fire-worshippers." See M. Perlmann, " 'Abd al-Hakk al-Islāmī, A Jewish Convert," *JQR* 31 (1940–41): 187.

[30] This famous "Verse of Light" was interpreted in many allegorical and mystical ways in medieval Muslim literature. One of the best-known mystical books based on this verse is Abū Ḥāmid al-Ghazzālī's (d. 1111) *Mishkāt al-Anwār* (The Niche of Lights), which was translated at least twice into Hebrew in the Middle Ages. Cf. also H. Lazarus-Yafeh, *Studies in al-Ghazzali* (Jerusalem 1975), ch. 4.

CHAPTER TWO

Muslim Arguments against the Bible

MUSLIM AUTHORS used four somewhat contradictory and overlapping arguments against the Bible: *Taḥrīf* (falsification), *Naskh* (abrogation), lack of *Tawātur* (lack of reliable transmission), and Bible exegesis. Only the first two of these have been studied in some detail, though more from the theological point of view. Only three of the four arguments are based directly on Qur'anic charges, whereas the most scholarly developed argument—the lack of *Tawātur*—has no clear Qur'anic basis. Yet even the three arguments that are based on Qur'anic charges are expressed therein only generally, and became highly developed and demonstrated in detail only with later Muslim authors such as Al-Bāqillānī (d. 1013), 'Abd al-Djabbār (d. 1025), Al-Djuwaynī (d. 1085), Al-Qarāfī (d. 1285), and Ibn Qayyim al-Djawziyya (d. 1350). In the following I shall summarize briefly the main Muslim arguments against the Bible as expressed in the Qur'an and elaborated by later Muslim authors, especially the Spaniard ibn Ḥazm (d. 1064) and the Jewish convert to Islam Samau'al al-Maghribi (d. 1175).

TAḤRĪF, *TABDĪL* (FALSIFICATION, ALTERATION)

The accusation that Jews and Christians had falsified their Scriptures (*Taḥrīf*)[1] is the most basic Muslim argument against both Old and New Testaments. It was a widespread polemical motif in pre-Islamic times, often connected with the translations and quotations of Scriptures, and used by sectarian and traditional authors, including Samaritans and

[1] Cf. EI[1] s.v. "*Taḥrīf*" (F. Buhl), and see, for example, Sūra 2:75, 59.

Christians,[2] to discredit various opponents and Scriptures. In the Qur'an it is a central theme, used mainly to explain away the contradictions between the Bible and the Qur'an, and to establish that the coming of Muhammad and the rise of Islam had indeed been predicted in the uncorrupted "true" Bible (see Chapter Four). Jews and Christians were accused of having concealed or deleted verses from their Scriptures, as well as of having distorted and rewritten others. Jewish oral tradition, an unauthorized addition to Scripture that often contradicts it explicitly, is considered to be part of this falsification.[3] Later Muslim authors followed the Qur'an closely, and the motif of *Taḥrīf* also played a part in internal Shi'i–Sunni polemics regarding the Qur'an itself.[4]

"Therefore woe be unto those who write the Scripture with their hands and then say: 'This is from Allah,'—that they may purchase a small gain therewith. Woe unto them for that their hands have written . . ." says the Qur'an (Sūra 2:79) in a most general way. The great commentator Al-Ṭabarī (d. 923) explains that this verse refers to the description of Muhammad (*naʿt Muḥammad*) that was included in the original divine version of the Torah, but that Jews had "removed from its place." He also adds a Ḥadīth saying by ʿUthmān stating that Jews added to the Torah

[2] See, for example, the somewhat outdated but still valuable study by A. Bludau, *Die Schriftfaelschungen der Haeretiker; Ein Beitrag zur Textkritik der Bibel*, Neutestamentlische Abhandlungen 11, ed. M. Meinertz (Muenster 1925); cf. A. L. Williams, *Dialogue between Justin Martyr and Trypho the Jew* (London 1930), pp. 150–55. See also W. Adler, "The Jews as Falsifiers: Charges of Tendentious Emendations in Anti-Jewish Christian Polemics," in *Translations of Scripture* (proceedings of a 1989 conference at the Annenberg Research Institute), *JQR* suppl. (1990): 1–27.

[3] *Midrash Rabbah*, Numbers 14, 22, states that the Oral Law was given only to the Children of Israel, so that nobody would be able to attempt to falsify it (as the Gentiles attempted to do with the written law).

[4] See I. Goldziher, *Richtungen der Islamischen Koranauslegung*, reprint (Leiden 1952), ch. 5; J. Eliash, "The Šīʿite Qur'ān," *Arabica* 16 (1969): 15–24; E. Kohlberg, "Some Notes on the Imāmite Attitude to the Qur'ān," in *Islamic Philosophy and the Classical Tradition*, ed. S. M. Stern, A. Hourani, and V. Brown (Oxford 1972), pp. 209–24.

what they liked and deleted from it what they hated, for example, Muhammad's name. Thus, they brought God's anger upon themselves, and He recalled or took back (*rafa'a*) to heaven parts of the Torah.[5]

Another Qur'anic verse says: "And some truly are there among them who twist (*lawā*) the Scriptures with their tongues in order that you may suppose it to be from Scripture, yet it is not from the Scriptures, and they say, 'This is from God,' yet it is not from God, and they utter a lie against God and know that they do so" (Sūra 3:78). Some verses accuse the Jews of concealing much of the Book that had been revealed to Moses and showing only parts of it (Sūra 6:92)—a motif developed picturesquely in Ḥadīth and Sīrah literature and often quoted in Qur'anic commentaries. Thus, for example, with regard to Sūra 5:42–49, it was told that the Jews had asked Muhammad to judge a man and a woman of their community who had committed adultery. Muhammad asked to consult the Law of the Torah, but when the Scrolls were brought before him, one of the Jewish sages tried to cover some parts therein with his hand. He was made to withdraw his hand, and the famous "stoning verse" was uncovered, whereupon Muhammad punished the two accordingly.[6] This famous story is part of a complicated problem of Muslim law (the explicit Qur'anic punishment for adultery is flogging; see Sūra 24:2[7]), but the same motif—Jews concealing verses of the Torah, with their hands or otherwise—appears also with re-

[5] This is a typical eschatological punishment. At the end of all days, before the final redemption, the text of the Qur'an also will disappear from the book (as well as the Ka'ba from Mecca). See H. Lazarus-Yafeh, *Some Religious Aspects of Islam* (Leiden 1981), p. 30.

[6] See commentaries to the verse, and cf. J. Burton, *The Collection of the Qur'ān* (Cambridge 1977), pp. 72–104. The literature about this verse is enormous.

[7] The Biblical punishment for adultery is stoning (see Deut. 22:24 and Lev. 19:19. See also John 8:44ff.). Later, other punishments are mentioned in the Talmud (see flogging for a slave-woman designated for another man, in *Keritut* 11a following Lev. 19:20). Cf. also M. Cook, " 'Anan and Islam," *JSAI* 9 (1987): 175–76.

gard to detailed descriptions of Muhammad supposedly to be found in the Torah.[8]

Here we have again the ambivalent attitude found in the Qur'an and later Muslim theology toward earlier divine Scriptures. On the one hand, these were considered to be truly divine revelations: "He hath revealed unto thee (Muhammad) the Scripture with truth, confirming that which was (revealed) before it, even as He revealed the Torah [*Tawrāt*] and the Gospel [*Indjīl*]" (Sūra 3:3), and Jewish law was made to set precedents and thus justify even the Prophet's own practice. Jews (and Christians) were scoffed at for not adhering to their own law. On the other hand, Jews were accused of concealing, distorting, and falsifying their own Scriptures. Sometimes contradictory arguments were used simultaneously: if, for example, the Jews really worship Ezra-ʿUzayr, as an explicit verse in the Qur'an states (see Sūra 9:30; cf. Chapter Three), this is true idolatry; if, however, the present Torah does not mention this, it is an obvious sign of forgery or deletion, because the Torah then contradicts a clear statement of the Qur'an.[9]

This ambivalent attitude toward the Bible also gave rise to a widespread phenomenon in Arabic medieval and later

[8] See Muḥammad ibn Saʿd, *Kitāb al-Tabaqāt al-Kubrā*, ed. E. Sachau and E. Mittwoch (Leiden, 1917), 1, pt. 2: 89: "The descriptions of the Messenger of God, peace be upon him in the Torah and Gospel," and especially where his description cannot be found because the relevant pages of the Gospel had been pasted together with glue. Cf. also ʿAbd al-Malik b. Hishām (Ibn Hishām), *Sīrat Rasūl Allah*, ed. F. Wuestenfeld (*Das Leben Mohammed's nach Mohammed Ibn Ishaq*) (Goettingen 1859), I, 2: 382ff. (trans. A. Guillaume, *The Life of Muhammad* [Oxford 1955], pp. 239ff).

[9] This seems to be the logic of ʿAlī al-Munayyar al-Shāfiʿī (d. c. 1520) in his *Tafhīm al-Djāhilīn Dīn al-Yahūd al-Maghḍūb ʿalayhim wa-l-Naṣārā al-Ḍāllīn* (Enlightening the Ignorant about the Faith of the Jews with Whom God Is Wrathful and of the Christians Who Are Astray), ms. Arabic, Cambridge, Qq 29; see M. Perlmann, " ʿAlī al-Munayyar," in *Studies in Judaica, Karaitica and Islamica Presented to L. Nemoy*, ed. S. Brunswick (Bar Ilan 1982), pp. 181–202. Cf. also Al-Djāḥiẓ, *Al-Radd ʿalā-l-Naṣārā*, in *Three Essays of al-Jāḥiẓ*, ed. J. Finkel (Cairo 1926), pp. 27ff.; and cf. below, Chapter Three.

literature: hundreds of alleged quotations from the "true" unfalsified Bible or other heavenly books, often given on the authority of early Jewish converts to Islam.[10] Sometimes one can find even whole reconstructions of the "true" Torah or the Psalms, which are considered to be divine revelations to the prophet David.[11] Perhaps another reason for the spread of this unique literature was the fact that Arabic translations of the Bible were not easily available to Muslim authors up to the thirteenth century (see Chapter Five). Often, however, these alleged quotations contain Midrashic and other Jewish material, taken by Muslim authors to be part of the Torah itself. They may even preserve unknowingly some lost Jewish material, hard to recognize in its Arabic-Islamic disguise.[12]

Some Muslim authors went even further and stated that several Qur'anic verses could be found also in the "true" Torah or in other heavenly books of pre-Qur'anic revelations, such as the Psalms (*Zabūr*, pl. *Zubur*), the Book of

[10] See M. J. Kister, "Ḥaddithū 'an banī isrā'īla wa-lā-ḥaraja," *IOS* 2 (1972): 215–39, and cf. J. Sadan, "Some Literary Problems concerning Judaism and Jewry in Medieval Arabic Sources," in *Studies in Islamic History and Civilization in Honour of David Ayalon* (Jerusalem 1986), pp. 353–98, esp. 370ff. Contemporary Arab and Persian authors who still believe in the falsification of the Hebrew Bible use modern Bible criticism to reconstruct the "true" Torah. According to them, the "Elohist" source is the closest to the "original" Torah, whereas the "Yahvist" source shows "racist" tendencies like modern Zionism. See, for example, Muḥammad Khalīfa Ḥasan Aḥmad, *'Alāqāt al-Islām bi-l-Yahūdiyya* (The Ties between Judaism and Islam; An Islamic View of the Sources of the Present Torah) (Cairo 1986), ch. 3. Cf. M. Zand, "The Image of the Jews in Iran after the Second World War" (in Hebrew), *Pe'amim* 29 (1986): 29.

[11] See Sadan, "Some Literary Problems," pp. 396–97. Cf. P. L. Cheikho, *Quelques légendes Islamiques apocryphes*, Mélanges de la Faculté Orientale 4 (Beirut 1910), pp. 33–56. Sometimes these Psalm reconstructions begin with exact translations of the first 2 or 3 Biblical Psalms and are therefore often wrongly catalogued as Arabic translations of the Psalms. See, for example, ms. Hunt. 515 in the Bodleian Library, Oxford.

[12] See some examples in the notes to this chapter and Chapter Four below. Cf. also S. D. Goitein, "Isrā'īliyyāt" (in Hebrew), *Tarbiz* 6 (1934–35): 89–101, 510–22.

Wisdom (*Ḥikma*), and the scrolls of Abraham, Elijah, Luqmān, and others.[13] For example, a well-known Ḥadīth saying, transmitted by ʿAbdallāh b. ʿAmr b. al-ʿĀṣ, states that the description of Muhammad in Sūra 48:8 ("Lo! We have sent thee (O Muhammad) as a witness and a bearer of good tidings and a warner") is to be found in the Torah as well.[14] Legendary versions of the conversion in the year 638 of the Jewish Rabbi Kaʿb al-Aḥbār[15] to Islam state that he disclosed that the "true Torah" contained at least ten explicit verses from the Qur'an.[16] Even the famous Al-Ghazzālī (d. 1111) stated repeatedly that the well-known Qur'anic command "to enjoin right conduct and forbid indecency" (*Al-Amr bi-l-Maʿrūf wa-l-Nahy ʿan al-Munkar*) was to be found also "in the Torah" or even originated therein.[17]

The later Ibn Qayyim al-Djawziyya tells a long-famous story about Moses (on the authority of the same Kaʿb al-Aḥbār) finding in the Torah lengthy praises and descriptions of Muhammad and his people.[18] He then relates: "And [Kaʿb] the 'Ḥabr' said: Well, when Moses wondered

[13] The term *Ḥikma*, often accompanying "the Book" in the Qur'an, is also explained by some commentators as referring to the Sunna of the Prophet. For the "scrolls" (*Ṣuḥuf*), see above, Chapter One, note 22. According to Sūra 31:12ff., the pre-Islamic sage Luqmān was given wisdom and exhorted his son accordingly. See *EI*² sv. "*Luḳmān*" (B. Heller-N. A. Stillman).

[14] Muḥammad b. ʿIsmāʿīl al-Bukhārī (Al-Bukhārī), *Al-Djāmiʿ al-Ṣaḥīḥ*, ed. L. Krehl, vol. 2 (Leiden 1864), bk. 34 (Kitāb al-Buyūʿ), no. 50; cf. Chapter Four below, esp. note 8.

[15] *Aḥbār* = pl. of *Ḥabr*, from the Hebrew *Ḥaber*, "Rabbinic sage." See J. Horovitz, "Jewish Proper Names and Derivatives in the Koran," *HUCA* 2 (1925): 197–98. See also M. J. Kister and M. Kister, "Some Notes on the Jews in Arabia" (in Hebrew), *Tarbiz* 48 (1979): 233–34.

[16] See M. Perlmann, "Another Kaʿb Al-Aḥbār Story," *JQR* 45 (1955): 48–58. See also idem, "A Legendary Story of Kaʿb Al-Aḥbār's Conversion to Islam," *The Joshua Starr Memorial Volume* (New York 1953), pp. 85–99.

[17] See, for example, book 19 of Abū Ḥāmid al-Ghazzālī, *Iḥyā ʿUlūm al-Dīn* (Cairo 1356 Hg.), p. 1201 (the whole book is devoted to this precept).

[18] See Ibn Qayyim al-Djawziyya, *Hidāyat al-Ḥayārā fī-l-Radd ʿalā-l-Yahūd wa-l-Naṣārā* (Beirut, n.d.), pp. 176–77.

at all the Good which God had bestowed on Muhammad and his people he said: 'I wish I were one of his companions.' Then God revealed to him three verses of the Qur'an [all of them from Sūra 7, from verses 144, 145, and 159, about Moses himself], and Moses was truly satisfied." Ibn Qayyim then adds: "The parts [of these verses] are to be found in the Torah they [the Jews] have now, and in Isaiah's prophecy and in other prophetic books, because the word 'Torah' has a wider meaning than the specific 'Torah,'" by which (as he explains in another context) "one means the 'Book of Moses,'" namely the Pentateuch.[19] Although earlier Muslim authors also mentioned this in a very general manner, only here, in the fourteenth century, do we have an explicit acknowledgment by a Muslim author of the fact that Islamic literature used the term "Torah" in a very wide sense, as denoting Jewish and other material, different from the Biblical text itself.[20] In fact, Muslim authors did not hesitate to term the Qur'an "a new Torah" (*Tawrāt Ḥadītha*),[21] and even to suppose that the Torah was revealed to Moses at the holy sites near Mecca. The two texts were compared in other ways as well, mainly polemical, to establish repeatedly the superiority of the Qur'an to any earlier revelation. But, as we have already seen, often the same Muslim authors compared the Qur'an to the alleged as well as the authentic Torah, as far as they

[19] Ibid., pp. 113, 119, and elsewhere. Cf. also Ibn Kathīr, *Tafsīr*, to Sūra 4:110.

[20] The wide meaning of the term "Torah" is very old. Cf. W. Bacher, *Exegetische Terminologie der juedischen Traditionliteratur* (Leipzig 1899), 1: 197–231, and cf. E. E. Urbach, *The Sages, Their Concepts and Beliefs* (Jerusalem 1975), ch. 12.

[21] The Qur'an is thus termed by God Himself in a revelation to Muhammad, according to a Ḥadīth saying on the authority of Ka'b al-Aḥbār. See 'Abdallāh b. 'Abd al-Raḥmān al-Dārimī (Al-Dārimī), *Sunan* (Kitāb Faḍā'il al-Qur'ān) (Medina 1966), 2: 213, and Djalāl al-Dīn al-Suyūṭī (Al-Suyūṭī), *Al-Itqān fī 'Ulūm al-Qur'ān* (Cairo 1951), p. 51 (end of the 17th "*Naw'*"). Al-Suyūṭī adds that although these terms are interchangeable (and the Prophet Muhammad termed the Psalms of David as "Qur'an"), Muslims should no longer use the term "Torah" for the Qur'an.

knew it, treating the two as divine revelations of the same kind and pointing out the similarities or differences between them.

Let us return to the general Qur'anic accusation that Jews (and Christians) had falsified their own Scriptures. The Spanish author Ibn Ḥazm (d. 1064) was the first Muslim author to use a systematic scholarly approach to the Bible to prove in detail this Qur'anic charge, perhaps because he was one of the first Muslim authors to have real knowledge of the Biblical text, especially the Pentateuch. Ibn Ḥazm, who was a Ẓāhiri theologian, polemicist, and jurist,[22] as well as a belletrist, poet, historian, and philosopher, was a prolific and erudite writer. Much has been written about him, though most of his books have not yet been edited in a scholarly way, including his great printed compendium on "Religion and Sects" *(Al-Faṣl fi-l-Milal wa-l-Ahwā wa-l-Niḥal).*

The sources, manuscripts, chronology, and structure of this comprehensive book have yet to be studied thoroughly.[23] Apparently Ibn Ḥazm incorporated into it another lost polemical tract of his on the "exposure of the alterations introduced into the Torah and the Gospels by Jews and Christians and the demonstration of the contradictions contained in their Scriptures, which allow no metaphorical interpretation."[24] More than two hundred pages of the first

[22] See *EI*² sv. "Ibn Ḥazm" (R. Arnaldez); R. Arnaldez, *Grammaire et théologie chez Ibn Ḥazm de Cordoue* (Paris 1956); M. Asin Palacios, *Abenhazam de Cordoba*, 5 vols. (Madrid 1928–33); A. Cheijne, *Ibn Ḥazm* (Chicago 1982); I. Goldziher, *Die Ẓāhiriten, ihr Lehrsystem und ihre Geschichte* (Leipzig 1894), esp. pp. 109ff. (Eng. trans. W. Behn, *The Ẓāhiris, Their Doctrine and Their History* [Leiden 1971]).

[23] See I. Friedlaender, "Zur Komposition von Ibn Ḥazm's *Milal wa-Niḥal*," in *Orientalische Studien Th. Noeldeke gewidmet*, ed. Carl Bezold (Giessen 1906) 1: 267–281; M. Perlmann, "Andalusian Authors on the Jews of Granada," *PAAJR* 18 (1948–49): 269–89, esp. 270–72; C. Adang, "Ibn Ḥazm on Jews and Judaism," dissertation, University of Nijmegen 1985, ch. 2.

[24] *Iẓhār tabdīl al-Yahūd wa-l-Naṣārā li-l-Tawrāt wa-l-Indjīl wa-bayān tanāquḍ mā bi-aydīhim min dhālika mimmā la yaḥtamilu-l-ta'wīl.*

two books in the printed edition are devoted to this topic under an even lengthier title: "Chapter on the obvious contradictions and clear lies in the book which the Jews call 'Torah' and in others of their books, as well as in the four Gospels, which will demonstrate convincingly that they have been corrupted and are different from what Allah, praised be He, has revealed."[25] Ibn Ḥazm complements these with some more general theological arguments against both Judaism and Christianity, replete with insults and derogatory terms. At the end of his life, he wrote another venomous tractate against his Jewish rival and enemy Ibn al-Naghrīla (apparently Samuel Hanagid), who was supposed to have written a harsh pamphlet denouncing the contradictions in the Qur'an.[26] Ibn Ḥazm wards off his enemy's arguments and dwells at length, in sharp polemical language, on the contradictions and theological impossibilities he found in the Torah.

Following some scattered remarks of Muslim authors who preceded him, Ibn Ḥazm set out to enumerate the

[25] *Faṣl fī munāqaḍāt ẓāhira wa-takādhīb wāḍiḥa fī-l-Kitāb alládhī tusammīhi-l-Yahūd al-Tawrāt wa-fī sā'iri kutubihim wa-fī-l-Anādjīl al-Arbaʿa yatayaqqanu bi-dhālika taḥrīfuhā wa-tabdīluhā wa-annahā ghayru alladhī anzala Allah.* Ibn Ḥazm, *Al-Faṣl fī-l-Milal wa-l-Ahwā wa-l-Niḥal* (n. pl., 1329 Hg.), 1: 116–224, 2: 2–81. His arguments against Judaism and the Bible have been summarized by Perlmann, "Andalusian Authors," and have been translated into Spanish by M. Asin Palacios in his *Abenhazam de Cordoba*, vol. 2.

[26] Ibn al-Naghrīla is usually identified with Samuel Hanagid (see I. Goldziher, "Proben Muhammedanischer Polemik gegen den Talmud I," *Jeschurun* 8 [1872]: 76–104, reprinted in *Gesammelte Schriften*, ed. J. Desomogyi [Hildesheim 1967] 1: 136–64), or with his son Joseph. The book itself is lost, or perhaps never existed, but Ibn Ḥazm's retort has been edited by Iḥsān 'Abbās' with others of his Epistles (Cairo 1960) and was discussed (in Spanish) by E. G. Gomez, "Polémica religiosa entre Ibn Ḥazm e Ibn al-Nagrīla," *Al-Andalus* 4 (1936–39): 1–28. See also D. Powers, "Reading/Misreading One Another's Scripture," in *Studies in Islamic and Judaic Traditions*, ed. W. M. Brinner and S. Ricks (Atlanta 1986) pp. 109–21, and especially the new approach to this book by S. Stroumsa, "From Muslim Heresy to Jewish–Muslim Polemics: Ibn al-Rāwandī's *Kitāb Al-Dāmigh*," *JAOS* 107 (1987): 767–72.

cases in which the given Biblical text must necessarily have been falsified and could never be ascribed to a divinely inspired revelation. Interestingly, most of the many details he provides are already mentioned in various pre-Islamic polemical sources, such as in early Rabbinic texts or by Christian, Judaeo-Christian, anti-Christian, and Gnostic authors. Ibn Ḥazm's immediate (probably Christian) sources, however, remain unknown. His main arguments may be summarized as follows.

Chronological and Geographical Inaccuracies. Among other inaccuracies in the holy text, Ibn Ḥazm discusses at length the four streams that come out of Eden and their geographical dimensions as given in Genesis 2, and sets out to prove that not all of them could have branched off from the one river in Eden (v. 10), and that their routes and the details about the lands that they encompass are inaccurate.[27] So are the number of years allotted by the text to early Biblical personalities. They cannot be reconciled with each other and with the chronology of other Biblical events, such as the Flood. The same holds true for the chronological details of the story of Joseph, either in themselves or when they are taken together with his brother Jehuda's story.[28] According to Ibn Ḥazm, God never errs even by one minute; therefore these contradictory and inaccurate details must necessarily be considered lies and forgeries interpolated into the holy text. The same holds true for the

[27] Ibn Ḥazm, *Al-Faṣl* 1: 118–19 (the geographical terms he uses here show that he was acquainted also with Saadia's translation).

[28] Ibid., pp. 122ff., 144ff., and cf. pp. 184, 186. Problems of chronology and contradictions were raised (and harmonized) by the Rabbinic sages and by the Church Fathers. Cf. also Abū Rayḥān al-Bīrūnī, *Al-Athār al-Bāqıya 'an al-Qurūn al-Khāliya*, ed. E. Sachau (Leipzig 1878), pp. 22ff. (trans. E. Sachau, *The Chronology of Ancient Nations* [London 1879], pp. 25ff.), and 'Abd al-Malik al-Djuwaynī, *Šıfā al-Ğalīl*, in *Textes apologétiques de Ğuwainī*, ed. and trans. M. Allard (Beirut, 1968), pp. 50–55, and see P. E. Algermissen, *Die Pentateuchzitate Ibn Ḥazms* (Muenster 1933), pp. 21ff.

inaccurate and inconsistent promise attributed to God (Gen. 15:13, 16) that Abraham's children will come out of Egyptian bondage after four hundred years, and in the fourth generation, whereas it actually took them 239 years of bondage and many more generations.[29] Ibn Ḥazm also mentions several other contradictions between the "second" and "fourth" book of Moses regarding the number of the Children of Israel, the leaders and generations of each tribe, their cities, etc. He even makes a thorough attempt to prove that never could so many people have settled within the designated borders of "Palestine and the Jordan."[30]

Theological Impossibilities. The most important of the theological impossibilities are the anthropomorphic Biblical expressions that we have already mentioned. Ibn Ḥazm repeats in this context many verses well known from pre-Islamic polemics against the Bible, such as, "We shall make mankind in our own image, similar to us" (Gen. 7:26),[31] or, "Man has become like one of us—in the knowledge of good and evil" (Gen. 3:22). He expresses his horror at these terrible "Jewish lies"—as if there were many gods with God, and as if man could become one of them. He then enumerates a number of similar expressions, especially from the Pentateuch and the Psalms,[32] and repeatedly thanks God for having saved the Muslims from this error, as if he knew of no anthropomorphic Qur'anic verses.

[29] Ibn Ḥazm, *Al-Faṣl,* 1: 124–27, 158–59.

[30] Ibid., pp. 166ff. See also the comparison between the borders of the promised land and the actual borders of the land over which the Children of Israel ever ruled (ibid., pp. 127–28).

[31] Ibid., pp. 117–18, 120, 164. Cf. also E. Stein, *Alttestamentlische Bibelkritik in der Spaethellenistischen Literatur* (Lwow 1935), p. 20. Ibn Ḥazm attacks mainly the second part of this verse ("similar to us," *ka-shibhinā*). According to him, the first part ("in our image," *ka-ṣūratinā*) could be explained in an abstract way.

[32] See his quotations of Psalms 45:7, 110:1, 87:5, 78:65, 82:1, and 89:27, *Al-Faṣl,* 1: 206–7. On his different enumeration of these Psalms, see below, Chapter Five.

The anthropomorphic and anthropophatic charges were a central theme already in pre-Islamic polemics against Judaism and Christianity. Pagan authors (for example, Celsus) seem to have used them extensively to ridicule the Biblical text and the Jewish and Christian concepts of God.[33] Many verses quoted in this literature, especially from the Pentateuch, reappear not only in medieval Muslim polemics, but also with Jewish heretic authors like Ḥīwī al-Balkhī. Some of these verses became important even for the shaping of medieval Islam itself. A good example is the Islamic rejection of the anthropomorphic idea that God rested on the seventh day, which resulted in the total rejection of a weekly day of rest (see Sūra 50:38), contrary to verses like Exod. 31:17 (which Saadia translates, "And on the seventh day God left the earth uncultivated and made it rest").[34]

Later Muslim authors return frequently to the subject of anthropomorphism. Aḥmad b. Idrīs al-Ṣanhādjī al-Qarāfī (d. 1285), for example, states that because of Gen. 1:26, 27,

[33] See E. Stein (*Alttestamentlische Bibelkritik*, pp. 10ff.), who shows that Celsus must have been acquainted with Philo's allegorical interpretations of these anthropomorphic expressions in the Bible, but made use only of his Bible criticism.

[34] See Lazarus-Yafeh, *Some Religious Aspects*, p. 41, and cf. idem, "Some Halachic Differences between Judaism and Islam," *Tarbiz* 52 (1982): 207–26 (Eng. trans. in *Religion* 14 [1985]: 175–91), where other, more sociological reasons for this difference between Judaism and Islam are mentioned (agricultural versus mercantile civilization, etc.). In general, Saadia in his translation of such verses not only systematically avoids anthropomorphic and anthropophatic expressions, as some of the Targumim did earlier in a more sporadic manner, but often actually changes the meaning of such verses in far-reaching ways (as he did in the example in the text above) to ward off both Muslim and earlier polemics. See, for example, his translation of Gen. 6:6 ("And God threatened them . . . and brought pain into their hearts" instead of "God repented . . . and grieved at His heart"). See also his 20th answer to Ḥīwī on this verse (in I. Davidson, *Sa'adia's Polemic against Ḥiwi Al-Balkhi* [New York 1915]) and cf. E. Stein, *Alttestamentlische Bibelkritik*, p. 22; Samau'al al-Maghribī, *Ifḥām al-Yahūd* (Silencing the Jews), ed. and trans. M. Perlmann, *PAAJR* 32 (1964): text p. 45, trans. p. 52.

many Jews believe in a God who looks like "a white-bearded and white-haired old man sitting on a throne, while the angels stand before him and the books are read in his presence."[35]

Ibn Ḥazm also mentions later Jewish literature in this context—for example, the anthropomorphic book *Shi'ur Qomah*, which he thinks to be part of the Talmud. In a long discourse against the repulsive anthropomorphism of the Jews, full of exclamations of horror, disgust, and curses, he states that

> The Jews say that on the Night of Atonement (*Laylat 'Īd al-Kibbūr*) on the tenth of Tishrīn al-Awwal, which is Oktūbar,[36] Al-Mīṭaṭrūn,[37] by which they mean the smaller God, be God exalted above their disbelief, cries slowly while plucking his hair: "Woe unto me, I have destroyed my house and made my sons and daughters orphans, my figure is bent and I will not rise until I rebuild my house and bring my sons and daughters back to it."

From this quotation and from his discussions with Jews about the angels, Ibn Ḥazm draws the conclusion that for

[35] See the 86th question in Aḥmad b. Idrīs al-Ṣanhādjī al-Qarāfī's [Al-Qarāfī] *Al-Adjwiba al-Fākhira 'an al-As'ila al-Fādjira*, ed. Bakr Zakī 'Awād (Cairo, 1987). There can be little doubt that many Jews indeed believed in some kind of corporeal God, and were constantly reprimanded for this by their rabbis. This fact, as well as Muslim polemics against the Bible, no less than his philosophical education, compelled Maimonides to devote the first part of his *Guide* to this subject.

[36] Ibn Ḥazm, *Al-Faṣl*, 1: 223 (see also p. 224—*Eylūl wa-Tishrīn al-Awwal wahumā Satanbar wa-Uktūbar*). The use of these names of the months points, according to M. Perlmann, to a Christian source for Ibn Ḥazm; see his "Andalusian Authors," 279 n. 40. 'Alī al-Mas'ūdī, *Murūdj al-Dhahab* (Maçoudi, *Les Prairies d'or*, ed. and trans. C. Barbier de Meynard and P. de Courteille, Société asiatique [Paris 1863], 2:391) mentions only *"Tishrīn al-Awwal."*

[37] Al-Mas'ūdī (d. 956) had already mentioned Metatron, the "lesser God" of the Jews, bemoaning the destruction of the Temple in the same way; see *Les Prairies*, 2: 391, and cf. Perlmann, following Steinschneider and Schreiner, in "Andalusian Authors," p. 278.

ten days each year, the Jews worship another, smaller, God.[38]

Another theological impossibility, according to Ibn Ḥazm, is the attribution of lies and sins to the holy prophets (including Biblical personalities who are usually not taken as prophets by the Bible itself), who are considered by most (later) Muslim theologians to be infallible—at least from the time they started to proclaim their mission.[39] So how can one dare say that the prophet Lūṭ (Lot), for example,

[38] Ibn Ḥazm, *Al-Faṣl*, 1: 221–24; *Al-Radd ʿalā Ibn al-Naghrīla*, ed. I. ʿAbbās' (Cairo 1960), pp. 74–75. Cf. the Talmud, *Berakhot* 3a and 7a. Ibn Ḥazm quotes (p. 222) God moaning similarly, "like a dove," as heard by a man called Ismāʿīl (Rabbi Yishmael?), who then caught hold of God and was asked by Him to bless Him. This makes Ibn Ḥazm call the same Ismāʿīl the "stinking son of stinking parents" (Petrus Alfonsi also attacked the idea of a wailing and moaning God; see his *Dialogus*, in *Patrologia Latina*, ed. J. P. Migne, 108: 550–51). Because Ibn Ḥazm quoted the "Rabbanites" in this context and attacked the anthropomorphic book *Shiʿur Qomah* (p. 221), Perlmann thought that he might have had a Karaite (or Christian) source; but the existence of pre-Kabbalistic Jewish mystics in Spain is now well enough attested to make them a plausible source as well. In fact, in the same context, Ibn Ḥazm twice mentions Sandalphon (pp. 221, 223) as the "angel who serves the crown" (see in the Talmud, *Megillah* 13b) and tells about his discussions with Jews who maintained that Metatron for them was also only "an angel among the angels" and not "the smaller God." Nevertheless he states that Jews worship this "smaller God" for ten days each year (p. 223)—a probable reference to the ten days of Atonement that start with the beginning of the Jewish New Year (see note 36 above)—which may be connected to the Jewish mystical view that Metatron took part in the creation of the world commemorated on the Jewish Rosh Hashanah festival at the beginning of each year. See G. Shalom, *Jewish Gnosticism, Merkabah Mysticism and Talmudic Tradition* (New York 1960), esp. ch. 7, pp. 27, 28, and pp. 52–53 n. 30 (on Sandalphon). Cf. also S. Liebermann, *Shkiʿin* (in Hebrew), 2d ed. (Jerusalem 1970), pp. 11ff. A. Altmann mentions another, shorter passage of Ibn Ḥazm about the *Shiʿur Qomah*. See his article "Moses Narboni's 'Epistle on Shiʿur Qomā,' " in A. Altmann, ed., *Jewish Medieval and Renaissance Studies*, Studies and Texts 4 (Cambridge, Mass.), 1967, p. 228. The fact that Ibn Ḥazm also mentions Sandalphon seems to have gone unnoticed.

[39] See *EI*[2] s.v. " *ʿIṣma*" (W. Madelung), and cf. M. Zucker, "The Problem of ʿIṣma—Prophetic Immunity to Sin and Error in Islamic and Jewish Literatures" (in Hebrew), *Tarbiz* 35 (1965): 149–73.

slept with his daughters, who conceived two sons by their father (Gen. 19:30ff.),[40] or that Jacob, with the help of his mother, cheated his father Isaac in order to receive his blessing (Gen. 27:15ff.)? The same holds true for Abraham, who is said either to have lied (with regard to Sara—the accusation that he lied is a very old motif) or to have disbelieved God's promise to him, and for Sara, who explicitly denied God's statement that she had laughed (Gen. 12, 15, 18).[41]

Preposterous Behavior. Among these theological impossibilities, one of Ibn Ḥazm's recurring Marcionite themes is that of the stories of fornication and whoredom inserted into the most important genealogies of the Bible. Ibn Ḥazm was at a complete loss to understand how one could believe in such preposterous stories, and he saw in them the final proof of the falsification of the holy text. He seems to have been the first, at least in Muslim polemical literature, to enumerate the very large number indeed of these stories, all of which cast shadows on the moral behavior of Israelite prophets and kings and their forefathers, and show obvious disrespect toward what should have been their distinguished pedigree. We have already recounted Ibn Ḥazm's horror at the story of Lot, which he describes accurately. He also mentions Abraham's marriage to his half-sister Sara (Gen. 17:12); Jacob sleeping with Leah—taking her mistakenly for her sister Rachel (Gen. 29:15)—and thus begetting in sin their sons; the story of Reuben and Bilha (Gen. 35:22); David and the wife of Uriya the Hittite (2 Sam. 11–12); Solomon, with his many wives, who induced him to idolatry (according to 1 Kings 11); as

[40] See Ibn Ḥazm, *Al-Faṣl*, 1: 133–35, and cf. Al-Mas'ūdī, *Les Prairies*, 2: 390, and Samau'al al-Maghribī, *Ifḥām al-Yahūd*, text pp. 61–62, trans. pp. 59–60. See also *EI*[2] s.v. "*Lūṭ*" (B. Heller and G. Vajda). This Biblical story about Lot is not mentioned in the Qur'an. It was attacked already by pre-Islamic anti-Christian writers. See, for example, H. Chadwick, *Origen contra Celsum* (Cambridge, 1986), p. 220.

[41] Ibn Ḥazm, *Al-Faṣl*, 1: 131–32, 137.

well as many other examples.[42] Sometimes he also adds some Midrashic details; for example, he mentions that Joshua married Raḥav the harlot.[43] Often he also translates, almost literally, and in a most scholarly way, whole Biblical stories, for example, the story of Jehuda and his daughter-in-law Tamar (Gen. 38).[44] Usually he ends by expressing his disgust at people who, although they do believe in prophets, tell such abominable stories about them, thus befouling their own origins. He accepts, of course, Abraham, Jacob, David, Solomon, and others as prophets, following explicit verses in the Qur'an. This makes matters even worse.

"God forbid," says Ibn Ḥazm, "that Moses and Aaron, David and Solomon would come from such birth, and this is what necessarily proves that this [Bible] was invented by a heretic (*'Zindīq'*) who made fun of religion(s)." After relating the birth of Peretz (Fāris) and Zerah (Zāraḥ), illegitimate sons of Jehuda and his daughter-in-law and forefathers of David, he restates that if this and other immoral behaviors were customary among the children of Israel, their whole genealogy would be full of illegitimate children, among whom they count Moses and Aaron as well as David and Solomon.[45]

It must have been clear to Ibn Ḥazm that in these attacks on the Bible he was also refuting Christian dogma. In fact, he expressed his astonishment at the Christian accep-

[42] Ibid. pp. 134, 140, 145–49.

[43] Ibid. p. 147. Cf. in the Talmud, *Megillah* 14b. (This is not a "slip" by Ibn Ḥazm, as Perlmann suggests in "Andalusian Authors," pp. 279–80.)

[44] Ibn Ḥazm, *Al-Faṣl*, 1: 145–46, 148–49. The Levirate marriage (cf. Deut. 25:5) is a well-known polemical motif, often brought to absurdity (for example, the father having to marry his own daughter, if she was married to his brother who died—in clear contrast to the first Mishna of *Yevamoth*); see, e.g., Al-Mas'ūdī, *Les Prairies*, p. 388 (the Karaites therefore take the meaning of "brother" here to refer to more distant relatives). Ibn Ḥazm does not use Jehuda's story in this way, but he seems to imply, perhaps like Midrashic and modern critical sources, that Jehuda himself performed the "Yibbum."

[45] Ibn Ḥazm, *Al-Faṣl*, 1: 140, 146–47.

tance of the Old Testament with its corrupted text, and connected it with their acceptance of their own completely unreliable and contradictory Gospel stories.[46] In all these arguments, Ibn Ḥazm is widely followed by later Muslim authors.

Naskh (Abrogation)

The second important theme of Muslim polemics against the Bible is that of *Naskh*, or abrogation (meaning supersession), which, although primarily a theological premise, also had clear ramifications for the study of the Bible and the growth of its textual criticism among Muslim authors. This motif also stems from late Antiquity, and was used especially in Christian polemics against Judaism. In Islam it is based on several Qur'anic verses, especially on Sūra 2:106: "Such of Our revelations as We abrogate or cause to be forgotten, we bring (in place) one better or the like thereof. Knowest thou not that Allah is Able to do all things?" This verse was taken by early Muslim commentators to refer mainly to inner contradictions between different Qur'anic verses, or between the Qur'an and the Sunna tradition of the Prophet. The idea was that the *later* revelation or saying is legally the valid one, and Muslim scholars therefore invested much effort in establishing the historical chronology of Qur'anic revelations—for example, what was revealed to Muhammad early in Mecca or later in Medina (*asbāb al-nuzūl*)—and many special books were composed on these disputed verses (*al-nāsikh wa-l-mansūkh*). The verse considered to be the last revealed among others dealing with the same topic (for example, the total prohibition of drinking wine in Sūra 5:90) would then be accepted as the binding law against earlier, "abrogated" verses (prohibiting only excessive drinking or prayer while drunk, such as Sūra 4:43).[47]

[46] Ibid., 2: 2ff.

[47] Cf. on this example *EI*[2] s.v. "Khamr" (A. J. Wensinck), and see on the

The idea of Abrogation played an important role also in the highly developed science of *Uṣūl al-Fiqh*, which deals with the theory of the four (or five) "Roots (or sources) of Islamic Law," the first two of which are the Qur'an and the Sunna of the Prophet. This science, which was established first by the great Muslim Doctor of Law Muḥammad b. Idrīs al-Shāfiʿī (d. 820), is an amalgamation of linguistic, historical (and mythical), legal, theological, logical, and highly developed epistemological theories in which the transmission and inner chronology of the Qur'anic text, as well as problems connected with the authenticity and transmission of the Sunna or Ḥadīth sayings, are closely studied. (Curiously, no parallel branch of this study is to be found in either medieval Judaism or Christianity, although both civilizations were deeply influenced by other branches of Islamic law and theology.[48]) In this literature (after Al-Shāfiʿī[49]), the Sunna of Muhammad is usually considered to have the power of abrogation for explicit Qur'anic verses, because those, though divine, were supposed to have been revealed earlier.[50] In rare cases, an earlier implicit Sunna is supposed to have been abrogated by a later Qur'anic verse. One such instance occurs with regard to the direction of early Muslim prayer to Jerusalem, which

---

whole intricate issue J. Burton, *The Collection of the Qur'ān* (Cambridge 1977).

[48] See *EI*[1] s.v. "Uṣūl" (J. Schacht), and see G. Makdisi, "The Juridical Theology of Shāfiʿī: Origins and Significance of 'Uṣūl al-Fiqh,' " *Studia Islamica* 59 (1984): 5–47. Cf. H. Lazarus-Yafeh, "The Attitude to Legal Sources in Islam as Compared with Halacha" (in Hebrew), in *Proceedings of the 8th World Congress of Jewish Studies* (Jerusalem 1982), section c, pp. 47–49.

[49] Al-Shāfiʿī himself considered that abrogation could occur only in the same literary genre (among contradictory Qur'anic verses, among contradictory Ḥadīth sayings, etc.). See his *Al-Risāla* (Cairo 1904), ch. 4 (trans. M. Khadduri, *Islamic Jurisprudence* [Baltimore 1961]).

[50] See, for example, the highly sophisticated discussion of Al-Ghazzālī in his *Al-Mustaṣfā min ʿIlm al-Uṣūl* (Beirut, n.d.), 1: 107ff., esp. 117ff., where any addition to the written law (five prayers instead of the two or three mentioned in the Qur'an) is also considered to be a kind of abrogation.

was abrogated by Sūra 2:138, fixing the direction of prayer towards Mecca.[51]

In polemical theological literature against Judaism and Christianity, the idea of abrogation was used in the same manner against earlier religions and their Scriptures, without denying their heavenly source. Muslim authors argued that Christianity abrogated, by God's preordained decree, earlier Judaism, and that Islam, being the most recent of the three religions, and containing God's final and valid dispensation for mankind, abrogated the other two. According to Ibn Ḥazm, early Muslim victories over the Jewish tribes in Arabia also constitute a clear historical proof of God's wish to abrogate Judaism.

Jews, of course, did not accept this. They persistently maintained (Rabbanites and Karaites alike) that their law was eternal, never to be changed or abrogated, and they adduced many Biblical verses to this effect.[52] The fact that Saadia had already devoted a large part of the third chapter in his *Book of Beliefs and Opinions* to refute the Muslim arguments of abrogation shows that these arguments were well developed by the early tenth century.[53] The first de-

[51] See Al-Ghazzālī, *Al-Mustaṣfā*, 1: 112, 122. Cf. also Al-Shāfi'ī, *Al-Risāla*, ch. 4. (English trans. p. 133). The change of the direction of prayer is an old sectarian motif. See also Chapter Three, note 35 below.

[52] See, for example, Maimonides' "thirteen principles." The ninth principle states the eternity of Jewish law, obviously against any *Naskh*. Cf. also A. Hyman, "Maimonides' 'Thirteen Principles,'" in *Jewish Medieval and Renaissance Studies*, ed. A. Altmann, p. 128. Hyman there (in note 58) gives the Hebrew translation of the term *Naskh* as *Biṭṭul*, but does not mention the very common *Temurah* or the verb *Hemir*. Cf. also Abraham Maimonides, *Kitāb Kifāyat al-'Ābidīn*, pt. 2.2 (ed. and trans. into Hebrew by N. Dana) (Ramat-Gan 1989) pp. 149ff.

[53] One of the earliest existing epistles on *Naskh* was written by or is ascribed to the Muslim Mu'tazilite author Ibrāhīm al-Naẓẓām (d. c. 840), who supposedly discussed the problem of "*naskh al-sharā'i'*" with a Jew named Yassā b. Ṣāliḥ. The short text was published by L. Cheikho in his *Vingt traitès theologiques d'auteurs Arabes Chrètiens* (Beirut 1920), pp. 68–70. Jewish Gaonic literature also often dealt with this subject (which is mentioned already in Rabbinic literature) in polemics against both Christianity and Islam. See S. Abramson, *R. Nissim Gaon, libelli quinque*

tailed Muslim discussions of this subject in Arabic literature, however, stem from the end of the tenth or early eleventh century—for example, by the Muʿtazilite Qāḍī ʿAbd al-Djabbār (d. 1025), and especially by the Ashʿarite theologian Al-Bāqillānī (d. 1013).[54] These authors discussed the idea of abrogation, not only in the polemical context against earlier religions, but also in the more general, highly developed Muslim framework of theology discussing the attributes of God and the difficult problem of the change of what was considered to be good at one time (His commandments in Judaism) into disobedience at a later time. The dilemma of either attributing to God a change of mind (*Badā*)[55] or limiting his omnipotence in some way was one axis on which the discussions turned. The theological consensus of the Sunnis rejected *Badā*, but accused Jews and Christians of accepting it. (The early Shiʿites did, in fact, accept it.) The concept of *Naskh* was accepted by Sunni theologians, however, and was explained as part of God's preordained change in history. In polemical terms, this meant that God had preset a time limit for the validity of each of the true religions that preceded Islam. Christianity was meant to abrogate Judaism as Islam was destined to abrogate both in due course; thus there was no need to attribute a change of mind to God. According to Muslim sources,

(Jerusalem 1965), pp. 5ff. Fragments of a book on this subject by Samuel b. Ḥofni have been found in the Genizah. (See Abramson, *R. Nissim Gaon*, p. 5 n. 4.)

[54] See, for example, ʿAbd-al-Djabbār, *Al-Mughnī fī Abwāb al-Tawḥīd wa-l-ʿAdl*, vol. 12 (on "*Iʿdjāz al-Qur'ān*") (Cairo 1960), pp. 49ff., 65ff. (on the difference between *Badā* and *Naskh*), 47ff. (Jewish denial of *Naskh*); Al-Bāqillānī, *Kitāb al-Tamhīd*, ed. R. J. McCarthy (Beirut 1957) chs. 13, 14; earlier, Al-Djāḥiẓ (d. 869) had discussed some of these issues.

[55] Cf. *EI*[2] s.v. "*Badā*" (I. Goldziher and A. S. Tritton). The Biblical story quoted and often discussed in this context is Gen. 22 (see Ibn Ezra's commentary on the first verse there). See A. Rippin, "Saʿadya Gaon and Genesis 22," in *Studies in Islamic and Judaic Traditions*, ed. M. W. Brinner and S. Ricks (Atlanta 1986), esp. pp. 40ff. See also Al-Ghazzālī, *Al-Mustaṣfā*, 1: 110, 115. It was discussed also in Arabic Christian anti-Jewish treatises on *Naskh*.

some Jewish and Jewish-sectarian authors even agreed with the logical possibility of such an abrogation. They denied, however, that God would ever let this actually happen, because of his explicit promises to the contrary in the Bible.[56]

Christian theologians (like Muslim authors in some ways) found themselves in an especially complicated situation in this respect, as they had to describe their own religion as "the abrogating but never-to-be-abrogated law" (*Sharīʿa nāsikha ghayr mansūkha*). This inherent contradiction was, of course, eagerly seized upon by Jewish authors, already by the time of Saadia, who used it in polemics against both Christianity and Islam, stressing the fact that once the idea of *Naskh* is accepted, it has to be applied to every subsequent religion—each in its turn, without end.

Yet the concept of *Naskh* was also important to Muslim attitudes toward the Bible. It helped to promote the same scholarly approach described earlier. When Muslim authors realized that most Jewish theologians rejected the concept of *Naskh*, they tried to argue their case from Biblical precedents. They looked in the Bible for early examples of abrogation in order to force their Jewish counterparts into the untenable position of either admitting the doctrine of abrogation in general, and thus acknowledging Islam as the last, true religion, or admitting the existing contradictions between different Biblical statements, thus undermining the authority of their own Scriptures. Again, Ibn Ḥazm may have used and reinterpreted some material adduced by earlier Muslim authors on this as on other topics, but he was the first to scrutinize the contents of the

[56] See, for example, Ibn Ḥazm, *Al-Faṣl*, 1: 102. The Rabad I of Toledo (d. 1180) is one example of those. See Abraham ibn Dā'ūd, *Emunah Ramah* (Frankfurt 1852), pp. 75ff. (German trans., p. 94). Cf. M. Schreiner, "Zur Geschichte der Polemik zwischen Juden und Muhammedanern," *ZDMG* 42 (1888): 639ff. (also in his *Gesammelte Schriften*, ed. M. Perlmann [Hildesheim 1983], pp. 119ff.). Some Karaite authors also accepted the logical possibility of *Naskh*. See Al-Qirqisānī, *Kitāb al-Anwār wa-l-Marāqib*, ed. L. Nemoy (New York 1940), 2: 452.

Bible systematically from this point of view. He collected almost every example of possible abrogation in the Bible, thus translating another theological argument into the critical study of the Bible itself.

Ibn Ḥazm first mentions the well-known example of Jacob, who married two sisters (he even gives their names: Layyā [Leah] and Rāḥīl [Rachel]), a custom later prohibited in Lev. 18:18. In this case, he actually contrasts "Jacob's Torah" (*Sharī'at Ya'qūb*) with the later "Law of Moses" (*Sharī'at Mūsā*), thus implying that Moses abrogated a whole codex of law upheld by Jacob. He also quotes the story of the Gibeonites (Josh. 9): first God ordered the Israelites to kill all the inhabitants of the land of Canaan, then he ordered them not to harm the Gibeonites, who fooled them into thinking they had come from afar.[57] Another example he adduces is from Isa. 54:5–6, where the prophet mentions that in the future, foreign people will also serve God (apparently in his Holy Temple), in distinct contrast to Mosaic law, according to which only descendants of (the tribe of) Levi ("Lāwī" in Ibn Ḥazm's Arabic) can serve God therein. This verse, according to Ibn Ḥazm, not only is a good example of abrogation, but actually prophesies the coming of Islam, and the worship of God by Arab, Persian, and other Muslims in the mosques of Jerusalem and elsewhere.[58]

The concept of abrogation in the context of Bible criticism is also prominent in Samau'al al-Maghribī's famous tractate *Silencing the Jews* (*Ifḥām al-Yahūd*), mentioned above. Following earlier Muslim writers, Samau'al makes it clear that abrogation must include not only the prohibition of what was previously permitted, as Jews may agree—

[57] Ibn Ḥazm, *Al-Faṣl*, 1: 101 (both examples).

[58] Ibid., p. 102. Jewish commentators explain that the verse refers only to priests and Levites who were dispersed and assimilated among the Gentiles. N. Roth, "Forgery and Abrogation of the Torah," *PAAJR* 54 (1987): 215, wrongly connects this with Isa. 66:20 and with the implausible assumption that Ibn Ḥazm misunderstood "horseriders" (*fursān* for the plural of "Persians" (*furs*).

for example, with regard to various customs of their forefathers (he mentions the generally accepted example of prohibition of work previously permitted on the Sabbath); it must also include the permission of what had previously been forbidden, as Islamic law abrogated Jewish law.[59] He then adduces as an example the Jewish practice of cleansing from impurity (of the dead) by means of the ashes of a red heifer (see Num. 19), a practice that was necessarily abandoned after the destruction of the Temple. In addition, he quotes extensively, in Hebrew, from the Jewish prayer book, to show that Jewish sages practically invented most of the prayers that were unknown to Moses, just as they added many laws to the Torah, thus "increasing the burden" of law upon the Jewish people—directly contradicting Deut. 13:7, where any addition to or detraction from the Mosaic law is explicitly forbidden.[60]

After Samau'al, later Muslim authors deal mainly with the theological ramifications of the concept of *Naskh*. They seem to show little interest in its application to the study of the Biblical text, however.

Lack of *Tawātur* (Lack of Reliable Transmission)

Another Muslim concept conducive to the critical study of the Bible, elaborated upon by both Ibn Ḥazm and Samau'al and counterattacked by Jewish medieval scholars, seems to have attracted less attention from scholars. This is the accusation, not found in the Qur'an, that the transmission of the text of the Bible is unreliable and that therefore the holy text was probably tampered with.

As is well known, medieval Muslim scholars attached great importance to and discussed in detail the reliability of

[59] Samau'al al-Maghribī, *Ifḥām al-Yahūd*, text pp. 6–11, trans. pp. 34–35. Perhaps Samau'al had Saadia in mind with regard to the first category. Saadia mentioned the later prohibition of work on the Sabbath, but explicitly denied this to be abrogation (see the end of ch. 3, 7 in his *Book of Opinions and Beliefs*)—a fact that Samau'al omitted.

[60] Ibid., text pp. 16–17, 20–21, trans. pp. 38–39, 40–41.

any piece of information (*khabar*), especially of religious data. Usually this was done by supplying several unbroken chains of reliable transmitters for the Qur'an, and especially for every Ḥadīth saying of the Prophet Muhammad. At a very early stage in Islamic literature, the 'Ulamā worked out a complicated system for studying the reliability of the individual transmitters and of the chains as a whole. They saw this as their only means of separating the inauthentic sayings of the Prophet from the authentic ones. Their scientific technique was highly developed,[61] although we may disagree with their suppositions and conclusions. Yet when Muslim authors looked closely at the Biblical text of both the Old and New Testaments, they found to their astonishment that these texts had no reliable chains of transmission and that neither Jews nor Christians seemed very anxious to establish them.[62] The Muslim authors, therefore, stressed the miraculous character of the unbroken, reliable, and public transmission (*Tawātur*) of the Qur'an, so different from earlier Scriptures.[63] Some even claimed that any belief in either the Torah or the Gospel relied upon the Qur'an, which confirmed their heavenly source and corroborated much of their material. Jews and Christians should therefore draw the unavoidable conclusion that they must believe in the Qur'an and the Prophet Muhammad as well, whereas Muslims should know that

[61] See, for example, J. van Ess, "Ein unbekanntes Fragment des Naẓẓām," *Der Orient in der Forschung*, Festchrift Otto Spies, ed. W. Hoenerbach (Wiesbaden 1967), pp. 170–207; cf. more generally I. Goldziher. *Vorlesungen ueber den Islam*, 2d ed. (Heidelberg 1925), ch. 2 (Eng. trans. A. and R. Hamori, *Introduction to Islam, Theology and Law* [Princeton 1981]); H.A.R. Gibb, *Mohammedanism* (London 1953), ch. 5; and esp. I. Goldziher, *Mohammedanische Studien* 2 (Halle 1890), chs. 1–8 (Eng. trans. S. M. Stern, *Muslim Studies* [London 1971]).

[62] In a way, pagan authors, like Celsus, had already accused Christians of having corrupted the reliable transmission of tradition.

[63] See 'Abd Al-Djabbār, *Al-Mughnī*, 12: 143ff., and Al-Bāqillānī, *Kitāb al-Tamhīd*, ch. 12. See also Al-Ghazzālī, *Al-Mustaṣfā*, 1: 132ff. Ibn Ḥazm (*Al-Faṣl*, 2: 83) also stressed that less time had passed since the appearance of Muhammad than since Moses. Usually *Khabar al-Āḥād* (information passed through one chain only) is contrasted with *Tawātur*. Only some Mu'tazilites and heretics raised the possibility of *Tawātur* for a lie.

they are permitted to believe only in those prophets and parts of earlier Scriptures confirmed by the Qur'an.[64]

Jewish authors argued that the public revelation of the Torah at Mt. Sinai had provided ample *Tawātur* for it, and that the very fact that Jews in different parts of the world as well as Christians had shared and used the same text of Scriptures for hundreds of years guaranteed its authenticity.[65]

Ibn Ḥazm took another step into this kind of Bible criticism by skillfully using a rather obscure ancient Jewish tradition. He explained that only one copy of the Pentateuch was usually kept by the High Aaronid priests in the Temple in Jerusalem, where the people would go only three times a year, most of them never entering it. This went on for four hundred years, during which time the corrupted Levite priests (he mentions the sons of Eli) might have easily altered the text of the holy Scriptures. (It is fascinating to notice in this context the change that the status of priests had undergone: whereas in ancient times they were considered the guardians and keepers of the holy tradition and Scripture, after the prophets and the advent of Christianity and the Gospels, they may even be charged with the falsification of Scripture!) The priests were the only ones, according to Ibn Ḥazm, to whom Moses delivered the whole written Torah, according to God's command. Only one chapter ("Sūra") was written down by Moses for all of Israel, as Ibn Ḥazm learns from Deut. 31:22: "And Moses wrote this song [Ha'azinu] . . . and taught it to the Children of Israel."[66]

[64] See Ibn Ḥazm, for example, *Al-Faṣl* 1: 104 and 203. Cf. also Ibn Qayyim al-Djawziyya, *Hidāyat al-Ḥayārā*, ch. 13. This is also the view of contemporary authors. See Muḥammad Khalīfa Ḥasan Aḥmad, *'Alāqāt al-Islām bi-l-Yahūdiyya*, ch. 1.

[65] See, for example, *Ibn Kammūna's Examination of the Three Faiths*, ed. and trans. M. Perlmann (Berkeley 1967) [text], 1971 [trans.], ch. 2. In Jehuda Halevi's *Book of Kuzari*, the reliability of Jewish Oral Tradition, as against Karaite objections, is discussed in the same terms.

[66] Ibn Ḥazm, *Al-Faṣl*, 1: 199ff. (Ibn Ḥazm conveniently ignores the end of the verse). See also below, Chapters Three and Five. Ibn Ḥazm quotes a literal translation of the song into Arabic (pp. 200–201). Such prophetic

The first part of Ibn Ḥazm's argument here must be a negative version of the Rabbinic tradition that one authoritative copy of the Pentateuch was always deposited in the archives of the Temple as a standard copy to prove the authentic reading against any forgeries. According to some Midrashic sources, however, Moses wrote on the last day of his life not one but "thirteen scrolls of the Torah, twelve for the twelve tribes and one which he deposited in the ark so that if one wished to forge something they would produce the Scroll deposited in the ark" and thus prove (like Greek authors in Alexandria, according to S. Liebermann) the authentic reading.[67] Although these Midrashic sources are rather late, it is difficult to decide whether they already constitute a polemical response to Muslim arguments, or whether they should be seen in the context of similar pre-Islamic—mainly Christian anti-Jewish—charges.[68] These Midrashic sources were later used also by Maimonides, for example, in his Introduction to the *Mishneh Torah* and elsewhere, no doubt to refute the same charges raised by Ibn Ḥazm and other Muslim authors.[69] The same polemical arguments of falsification of the Hebrew Bible lived well into nineteenth-century Christian Bible criticism, which found it could not rely on the given text of the Old Testament.[70]

words rebuking the Children of Israel were sometimes used in Muslim literature as they were in Christian literature.

[67] See Deut. 31:26; and see the story with the (late) sources in L. Ginzberg, *Legends of the Jews* 3: 439, 4: n. 900; cf. S. Lieberman, *Hellenism in Jewish Palestine* (New York 1950), pp. 86, 200. Cf. also M. A. Friedman on the Hebrew term *Katuv uMunah*, in *Leshonenu* (in Hebrew) 48–49 (1985): 49–52.

[68] Jews were accused of having deleted explicit verses predicting the coming of Jesus, of confusing the various chronologies in order to change the fixed date for the coming of the Messiah, etc. See Williams, *Dialogue between Justin Martyr and Trypho the Jew*, pp. 150–55.

[69] See my forthcoming article, "Taḥrīf and Thirteen Scrolls of Torah," *JSAI* 18 (1992).

[70] Cf. for example, Paul de Lagarde, *Materialien zur Kritik und Geschichte des Pentateuch* (1987; reprinted Wiesbaden 1967), p. xii. Cf. also

This holds true to some extent also for the most interesting detail of Ibn Ḥazm's Bible criticism: following earlier pre-Islamic sources, he accused Ezra the Scribe of having purposely corrupted the Biblical text. As we shall see in more detail in Chapter Three, Samau'al al-Maghribī, the Jewish convert to Islam, claimed to supply, a hundred years later, the missing motive for this mischievous deed of Ezra, namely, his priestly hatred for the Royal House of David. According to Samau'al, Ezra wanted to discredit the Davidic royal dynasty with which the priestly families competed for power. Therefore, he added the many stories of fornication and whoredom into Biblical genealogies. "I swear to God," says Samau'al, "that Ezra achieved his purpose, for in the Second Commonwealth which they (the Jews) had in Jerusalem, it was not the Davidists who reigned, but the Aaronides."[71] Ezra, as the forger of the Bible, reappears in various forms in later European writings, but with Spinoza he became again the canonizer of the Bible, as he apparently was already thought of by some pre-Islamic authors like Porphyrius (see Chap. Three and Six).

Samau'al, however, has further historical explanations for the Bible's lack of a reliable tradition of transmission. According to him, the history of the Jews is full of recorded invasions and assaults that devastated their country, and under such conditions the transmission of their holy text must have suffered. As a result, some traces of their antiquities may even have been blotted out completely:

> When the political independence of a nation is coming to an end through foreign domination and occupation of its land, the true record of its past is obliterated. . . . The succession of such

---

R. H. Popkin, *Isaac La Peyrere (1596–1676)* (Leiden, 1987), ch. 4, esp. pp. 44, 46, 48ff.

[71] *Ifḥām al-Yahūd*, text pp. 62–63, trans. p. 60. In modern Bible criticism as well, the suggestion was made that these stories were inserted into the Bible by Israelite authors who wished to discredit the Davidic dynasty. See J. Milgrom, "Religious Conversion and the Revolt Model for the Formation of Israel," *Journal of Biblical Literature* 101–2 (1982): 173–74.

events continues until at last the learning of a nation is displaced by ignorance. The more ancient a nation is and the more the various empires expose it to humiliation and grief—the more it is fated to suffer the obliteration of its records. This is what has happened to the Jews.[72]

In addition, Samau'al claims, the Jews themselves were responsible for losing, even burning or destroying, their own Scriptures, through their recurring idolatry and the killing of their own prophets.[73] "And which book or religion can be preserved under these circumstances?" asked Ibn Hazm earlier, while reciting (with some mixed-up additions, based perhaps on Talmudic sources) the general Biblical motif of the books of Judges or Kings, of Israel's constant return to idolatry, and mentioning several judges and kings by still-recognizable names.[74] Later Muslim authors follow in the same vein.

The motif of unreliable transmission can be traced back from Bible criticism proper into scholastic medieval theology with Al-Qarāfī, who followed both Ibn Ḥazm and Samau'al closely in his polemics against Christianity. In the 81st question of his *Al-Adjwiba al-Fākhira ʿan al-As'ila al-Fādjira*, he says that the Jews must necessarily be in error since they rely on the Torah, which is a "nondiscriminating" book (*ghayr mutamayyiza*); that is, it contains all sorts of history: that which predated Moses, happened at his time, or came after him, as well as many things that Moses himself did not say:

And if the Torah [of Moses] was mixed up with other [books]—one cannot adduce from it arguments, because proof can be based only on the words of the Lawgiver (*Ṣāḥib-al-Sharʿ*) but nobody else, and if his words were mixed up with those of others the proof of everything becomes worthless, because the

[72] *Ifḥām al-Yahūd*, text pp. 54–55, trans. p. 56.

[73] Ibid., text pp. 55–56, trans. p. 57; and see more details in Chapter Three below, and note 55 there (on the motif of killing prophets).

[74] See Ibn Ḥazm, *Al-Faṣl*, 1: 193–96; cf. below, Chapter Three, and notes 51–52 there (some Talmudic parallels).

words are not clearly his own and thus no argument can be built up.

Muslim Bible Exegesis

Several verses in the Qur'an call for a Muslim quasitypological or teleological reading of the Bible and the New Testament—for example, Sūra 7:157: "Those who follow the Messenger, the Ummī[75] Prophet, whom they will find described in the Torah and Gospel which they have," or Sūra 61:6: "And when Jesus son of Mary said: O Children of Israel! Lo, I am the Messenger of Allah unto you, confirming that which was (revealed) before me in the Torah, and bringing good tidings of a messenger who cometh after me, whose name is [Aḥmad].[76]. . ."

Therefore the fourth argument of Muslim polemicists against the Bible makes use of the interpretation of the Biblical text as a prophecy predicting the coming of Muhammad and the rise of Islam. As we shall see in more detail in Chapter Four, this kind of Muslim Bible interpretation started rather early in Islam, apparently under the influence of Christian converts, but it never developed into a full-fledged literary genre of Arabic literature, and never became as important for Islam as the typological and allegorical interpretation of the Hebrew Bible was for Christianity. As mentioned above, Muslim authors could adduce many alleged descriptions of Muhammad from the "true" unfalsified Torah, and full or exact translations of the Bible into Arabic were apparently not as easily available to them as scholars used to think (see Chapter Five), two factors that may help explain why this kind of interpretation failed to develop. Nevertheless, Muslim authors managed to col-

[75] See Chapter Four, pp. 108–9.

[76] Pickthall here gives "the Praised One." The two words meaning "whose name is Aḥmad" were taken by some scholars to be an interpolation. See A. Guthrie and E.F.F. Bishop, "The Paraclete, Al-Munhamanna and Aḥmad," *The Muslim Word* 41 (1951): 251–56, and W. M. Watt's answer, *The Muslim World* 43 (1953): 110–17. Cf. Chapter Four below.

lect Biblical verses, which they quoted in almost literal translations, and they took these verses to foretell the rise of Muhammad and the coming of Islam.

These verses were supposed either to stem from the authentic holy Scripture before it was falsified, or to have escaped alteration because of their vague, implicit message, which did not catch the attention of the forgers. In this way, the inherent contradiction of relying on a corrupt text was solved, and detailed proof could be found in the existing Biblical text for the general Qur'an and Ḥadīth claims that Muhammad and his exact description were foretold in the Torah. Some Muslim authors even seem to have accepted this kind of interpretation *instead* of the doctrine of falsification of the Scriptures, notably Ibn Khaldūn (d. 1406). In two of the manuscripts of his *Prolegomena* (*Muqaddima*) (but not in most printed editions), Ibn Khaldūn says "that the statement concerning the alteration [of the Torah by the Jews] is unacceptable to thorough scholars and cannot be understood in its plain meaning, since custom prevents people who have a [revealed] religion from dealing with their divine Scriptures in such a manner."[77]

As we shall see in Chapter Five, Muslim commentators often quoted different versions of Arabic translations of the relevant Biblical verses, and sometimes even accompanied them with corrupted phonetic transcriptions of the Hebrew original. This is unique in Arabic medieval literature, wherein even those genres which rely most heavily on Biblical and Midrashic material, such as the *Tales of Prophets* literature (*Qiṣaṣ al-Anbiyā*) or historiography, usually do

[77] See the text in E. M. Quatremère's edition (Paris, 1858), 1: 12–13, and cf. F. Rosenthal, trans., *Ibn Khaldūn, The Muqaddimah* (Princeton 1958), pp. 20–21. Ibn Khaldūn connects this with the problem of impossible (or miraculous) numbers of the Children of Israel in the Torah and quotes vaguely Al-Bukhārī in this context (Rosenthal, *Muqaddimah*, p. 20 n. 52). Some earlier Muslim authors shared Ibn Khaldūn's view, but did not express themselves so clearly. Cf., for example, Fakhr al-Dīn al-Rāzī (d. 1210), *Kitāb al-Muḥaṣṣal fī Afkār al-Mutaqaddimīn wa-l-Muta-'akhirīn* (Cairo, 1323 Hg.), p. 154.

not contain exact, literal quotations from the Biblical text. Therefore, this fourth argument of Muslim polemics against the Bible is perhaps of more importance for the study of medieval Arabic translations of the Bible than for the study of Islamic thought and literature itself.

CHAPTER THREE

Ezra-ʿUzayr: The Metamorphosis of a Polemical Motif

As WE HAVE SEEN, Ezra the Scribe plays an important role both in Muslim medieval polemics against the Bible and in pre-Islamic and modern Bible criticism. In the first context, his role is usually negative; he is the deliberate falsifier of the text. In the second context, especially among modern European Bible critics, he came to be regarded positively as the canonizer and conservator of the Biblical text. Ezra's different roles often interchange, however; Islamic literature has also preserved the positive image of Ezra as the loyal restorer of the lost Biblical text, whereas modern European Bible criticism has also kept alive the traditional charges of the falsification.[1]

In this chapter, I shall try to show that Islam received both images of Ezra from earlier Jewish, Samaritan, Christian, and anti-Christian sources, but that it was only his negative image that became clearly associated with medieval Muslim Bible criticism through the writings of Ibn Ḥazm (d. 1064), who was apparently the first to have connected both. Despite the thorough documentation of Ezra's many-faceted figure in post-Biblical Jewish and Christian literature,[2] however, he remains somewhat enigmatic as ʿUzayr in the context of Islamic literature.[3]

[1] See Chapter Two above, esp. note 70.

[2] See M. E. Stone, "The Metamorphosis of Ezra: Jewish Apocalypse and Medieval Vision," *Journal of Theological Studies* 33 (1982): 1–18; R. A. Kraft, "Ezra Materials in Judaism and Christianity," in *Aufstieg und Niedergang der Roemischen Welt* 2, ch. 19.2 (Berlin and New York 1979), pp. 119–36.

[3] See the attempts to explain the name ʿUzayr and its origins in *EI*[1] s.v.

Only a single verse of the Qur'an (Sūra 9:30) mentions Ezra explicitly, by his Arabic name " 'Uzayr." The identification of 'Uzayr with Ezra is generally accepted in Arabic literature, although some Muslim authors disagree.[4] The verse itself has raised many questions for both Muslim commentators and modern scholars: "And the Jews say: Ezra ['Uzayr] is the Son of Allah, and the Christians say: The Messiah is the son of Allah. That is their saying with their mouths. They imitate the saying of those who disbelieved of old. Allah (Himself) fighteth against them! How perverse are they!"

The entire Sūra apparently belongs to the later Medinese period of the Prophet and comprises numerous Jewish and anti-Jewish motifs. In the verses immediately preceding the one quoted here, an attempt is made to distinguish between the unclean idol worshippers (9:28) and the Jewish and Christian "People of the Book," who were supposedly at a higher level of belief. But they, too, have strayed from monotheism: the Jews worship their sages (*Aḥbār*); the Christians worship their monks and Jesus, son of Mary (9:31). This accusation, with its early Samaritan and later Karaite overtones, is no doubt intended to cast on both Jews and Christians the slur of idol worship—the chief point of contention between strictly monotheistic Islam and

" 'Uzayr" (B. Heller); cf. R. Blachere, *Le Koran, traduction nouvelle*, vol. 3 (Paris, 1950), p. 1083 n. 3; and B. Heller, "Éléments parallèles et origine de la légende des sept dormands," *REJ* 49 (1904): 190–280.

[4] Ibn Ḥazm, for example, does not mention 'Uzayr in his great compendium on religions and sects, though he fiercely attacks " *'Azrā al-Warrāq*" (Ezra the Scribe) and charges him with forging the Bible. See *Al-Faṣl fī-l-Milal wa-l-Ahwā wa-l-Niḥal* (n. pl., 1329 Hg.), e.g., 1: 117, 187, 210ff. But in his epistle against Ibn al-Naghrīla, he explicitly identifies the same with the 'Uzayr mentioned in the Qur'anic verse. See Iḥsān 'Abbās', ed., *Al-Radd 'ālā Ibn al-Naghrīla wa-Rasā'il Ukhrā l'ibn Ḥazm al-Andalusī* (Cairo 1960), p. 72, and cf. below. Samau'al al-Maghribī (d. 1175), who often follows Ibn Ḥazm, explicitly rejects the identification of Ezra with 'Uzayr, basing his unintelligible rejection on linguistic arguments. See *Ifḥām al-Yahūd* (Silencing the Jews), ed. and trans. M. Perlmann, *PAAJR* 32 (1964): text p. 63, trans. p. 60.

the Arab tribes.[5] The accusation itself is saliently polemic, as evidenced in other verses of the Qur'an; for example: "It is not (possible) for any human being unto whom Allah had given the Scripture and wisdom and the Prophethood that he should afterwards have said unto mankind: 'Be slaves of me instead of Allah' " (Sūra 3:79). The name 'Uzayr does not usually appear in these contexts, however, whereas Jesus, son of Mary, or *Al-Masīḥ*, is mentioned in many of these polemic verses. It is therefore of particular interest that the well-known essayist Al-Djāḥiẓ (d. 869) mentions among the Christian arguments against the Qur'an (to which he responds at length) the verse on 'Uzayr as evidence that the Qur'an contains explicit inaccuracies, as it is well known that the Jews do not worship 'Uzayr.[6]

In later Islamic literature as well, usually only the Christians are accused of worshipping a human being. As the Islamic scholars learned more of Judaism, they increasingly avoided levelling this charge against the Jews, and even tried to minimize the importance of the verse that explicitly mentions Ezra-'Uzayr. Thus they declared, for example, that only a small group of Jews (*baʿḍuhum*) had worshipped 'Uzayr and that this group had long since disappeared.[7] Others asserted that the verse was not to be un-

[5] For that reason, some Islamic commentators also associated Sūra 9:30 with the idolatrous Arab belief in the three daughters of Allah. See, for example, Al-Ṭabarī and Al-Zamakhsharī on the verse, and cf. J. Wansbrough, *Quranic Studies* (Oxford 1977), pp. 122–23. See also Al-Djāḥiẓ, *Al-Radd 'alā-l-Naṣārā*, in *Three Essays of al-Jāḥiẓ*, ed. J. Finkel (Cairo 1926), pp. 27ff. Of course, Jesus is considered to be merely a prophet in Islam, not God incarnate; see *EI*[2] s.v. " 'Īsā" (G. C. Anawati), and see H. Lazarus-Yafeh, *Some Religious Aspects of Islam* (Leiden 1981), pp. 51, 57.

[6] See Al-Djāḥiẓ, *Al-Radd*, esp. pp. 27, 33. Cf. also Al-Qāsim ibn Ibrāhīm's (d. 860) interesting statement that he had never met a Jew who worshipped 'Uzayr! See W. Madelung, *Der Imām al-Qāsim ibn Ibrāhīm* (Berlin 1965), p. 90.

[7] Muslim Qur'an commentators and other authors have different thoughts about who the members of this group might have been: some Medinese Jews (the name Finḥāṣ occurs in this context often; see also note 33 below), Yemenite Zaddokites (Ibn Ḥazm), or others. A late Jewish

derstood literally, and some associated it with the accusation in the succeeding verses by explaining that the Jews "worship" their sages in the sense of unquestioningly accepting their halakhic stringencies, which were never mentioned explicitly in the Torah.[8] (This, too, is a frequent motif in Samaritan, Christian, Islamic, and Karaite anti-Jewish polemical literature.) Only the famous eleventh-century jurist Al-Māwardī listed the prohibition against Christians mentioning Jesus (*Al-Masīḥ*) or Jews mentioning ʻUzayr among the restrictions of the "Pact of ʻUmar" on both, as if the Jews actually mentioned ʻUzayr in their daily prayers.[9] The parallel between ʻUzayr and Jesus in the Qur'anic verse also generated the early Islamic discussion of whether Ezra-ʻUzayr was a prophet, as Jesus is perceived in Islam. Echoes of this discussion are evident in later commentaries on Sūra 4:135, and the answer is usually positive, although some Muslim authors believe that Ezra-ʻUzayr was removed from the "list of Prophets" because he "questioned predestination" (*al-Qadar*).[10]

The name ʻUzayr itself is perceived as derogatory in Arabic, because of both its diminutive form (usually belittling in Arabic) and its negative implication in the verse in ques-

convert claimed that the Karaites of Al-Ḥidjāz worshipped ʻUzayr. See Saʻīd b. Ḥasan (converted in 1298), *Masālik al-Naẓar*, ed. and trans. S. A. Weston, *JAOS* 24 [1904]: 349 [trans. p. 376]).

[8] See ʻAbd-al-Djabbār, *Tanzīh al-Qur'ān ʻan al-Maṭāʻin* (Beirut, n.d.), pp. 164–65, and Al-Qurṭubī, *Aḥkām al-Qur'ān*, on the verse. Cf. Samauʻal al-Maghribī, *Ifḥām al-Yahūd*, text pp. 71, 82ff., trans. pp. 64, 69 ff. (This was later copied literally by Ibn Qayyim al-Djawziyya [d. 1350], in his *Hidāyat al-Ḥayārā fī-l-Radd ʻalā-l-Yahūd wa-l-Naṣārā* [Beirut, n.d.], pp. 183ff.)

[9] See ʻAlī al-Māwardī, *Al-Aḥkām al-Sulṭāniyya* (Cairo 1909), p. 129 (trans. E. Fagnan, *Mawerdi, les statuts gouvernementaux* [Alger 1915], p. 306).

[10] Ibn Qutayba (d. 889) already mentions this topic in his *Kitāb al-Maʻārif*, ed. ʻAlī ʻAbd al-Laṭif (Cairo 1934), p. 23. See also Al-Zamakhsharī and Al-Bayḍāwī on the verse, and Ismāʻīl b. ʻUmar ibn Kathīr, *Al-Bidāya wa-l-Nihāya* fī-l-Ta'rīkh (Cairo 1932), 1: 41, 46. This problem may be connected with ʻUzayr's infallibility as a prophet.

tion.[11] Nevertheless, a number of figures in early Arabic literature bore this name or the name ʿAzrā.[12] Some Jews also seemed to avoid the name Ezra, perhaps because of its negative connotations in the Islamic world.[13] In general, Ezra and his work received little attention in medieval Jewish thought, in contrast to the central place he was to occupy in the beginnings of modern Biblical criticism.

From Al-Ṭabarī (d. 923) on, however, we find much Islamic exegesis that views Ezra-ʿUzayr, regarded as the same person, in a very positive light. The following example is taken from Al-Ṭabarī's comprehensive history book, from the story about the Jews' return to Zion.[14]

> When the [Israelites] returned to Palestine, they did not have God's covenant with them, for the Torah was captured from them and burned and lost. And ʿUzayr was among the captives [exiles] in Babylon and returned [with them] to the Land. He would cry over [the loss of] the Torah day and night, going off and wandering sorrowfully through the deserts and wadis. [Once], when he was sitting mourning and crying over the To-

[11] Most of the Muslim commentators dealt with the verse only from the linguistic point of view.

[12] See, for example, Abu Djafar Mohammed ibn Djarir al-Ṭabarī (Al-Ṭabarī), *Taʾrīkh al-Rusul wa-l-Mulūk* (*Annales*), ed. M. J. de Goeje (Leiden 1964), 2d ser., 3: 1915; Muḥammad ibn Saʿd, *Kitāb al-Tabaqāt al-Kubrā*, ed. E. Sachau and K. V. Zetterstein (Leiden 1909), 4: 147; and cf. Aḥmad b. ʿAlī ibn Ḥadjar al-ʿAsqalānī, *Tahdhīb al-Tahdhīb* (Beirut 1968), 7: 191ff.

[13] See J. Horovitz, *Koranische Untersuchungen* (Berlin 1926), pp. 127–28; and H. Z. Hirschberg, "Maqron Baʿal Qarnayyim and Ezra-ʿUzayr, Son of God" (in Hebrew), *Leshonenu* 15 (1947): 125–33. Recent Geniza studies do not seem to confirm this assumption, and Jews carrying the name Ezra (and even ʿUzayr) occur there quite often. See M. Gil, *Palestine during the First Muslim Period* (in Hebrew), vol. 3 (Tel Aviv 1983), index. See M. A. Friedman, *Jewish Marriage in Palestine*, a Cairo Genizah study (Tel Aviv and New York 1980), 2: 410.

[14] Al-Ṭabarī, *Taʾrīkh al-Rusul wa-l-Mulūk* (*Annales*), ed. M. J. de Goeje and I. J. Barth, 1st ser., repr. (Leiden 1964), 1: 669–670. ʿIzz al-Dīn ibn al-Athīr (d. 1233) repeats this story verbatim in his *Al-Kāmil fī-l-Taʾrīkh, Chronicon quod perfectissimum*, ed. C. J. Tornberg (Leiden 1851), 1: 270–71). See also al-Ṭabarī's commentary on Sūra 9:30.

rah, a man approached him and said "O 'Uzayr, what has brought you to tears?" And he answered: "I am crying for the Book of Allah[15] and His covenant, which were in our hands. And because of our sins and the Lord's anger against us, Allah has caused our enemy to rule over us, and they have killed our young men, destroyed our land, and burned our Book of Allah, and [that book] alone can successfully guide us in this world and the next." And he added: "Why should I cry if not for that?" Said [the man]: "Would you like that [book] to return to you?" Asked [Ezra]: "Is there a way?" Answered [the man]: "Of course. Go back, fast, purify yourself and your clothing and [return] tomorrow to meet [me] in this place." 'Uzayr went back and fasted and purified himself and his clothing and returned to the place where they had met and sat there. Then the same man came to him with a vessel of water, and he was an angel Allah had sent to him, and he let him drink from the vessel. And the Torah returned to [his consciousness] and ['Uzayr] returned to the children of Israel and he placed the Torah before them and they recognized it—what it allowed and what it forbade, its commandments and desirable acts and its punishments.[16] And they loved him greatly, as they had never loved him before, and the Torah remained in their possession and they fared well with it. 'Uzayr, too, stayed with them, acting righteously until Allah took him to Himself. . . .[17] After that, events resumed, until they called 'Uzayr son of Allah, and Allah once again sent them a prophet, as was His way, in order to mend their ways and command them to observe the Torah and what is in it.[18]

[15] *Kitāb Allah*, usually designating the Qur'an.

[16] The text uses common Muslim terminology: *Ḥalāl wa-Ḥarām*, *Sunan wa-Farā'iḍ*, *Ḥudūd*, etc.

[17] This motif seems to echo Gen. 5:24 on Henoch, and Sūra 4:150 on Jesus. Because of this, 'Uzayr has been identified with Henoch and even Osiris. Cf. Paul Casanova, "Idris et 'Ouzair," *JA* 205 (1924): 356–60 (p. 359, Mohammad Magdi Bey).

[18] The expression *Iqāmat al-Tawrāt* used here seems to be the translation of the Hebrew term *yissud ha-Torah* used in the Talmud with regard to Ezra and other personalities. Cf. *Sukka* 20a, and see H. Lazarus-Yafeh, "Tadjdīd al-Dīn: A Reconsideration of Its Meaning, Roots and Influence

Al-Tha'labī, the eleventh-century author of *Tales of the Prophets* (*Qiṣaṣ al-Anbiyā*, entitled *'Arā'is al-Madjālis*),[19] recounts this tale in even greater detail, as do later historiographers and Qur'an commentators. Although the story's details occasionally vary, its structure is the same in all versions, as are its basic elements: the loss of the Torah scroll through (the Jews') sins and troubled times, its miraculous return by Ezra-'Uzayr, complete and precise conformity between the lost version (also miraculously returned) and the one supplied by Ezra, the joy of the children of Israel, and their admiration of Ezra, exaggerated to the point of worship.[20]

Several scholars[21] have already discussed the similarity between this story and the Jewish apocalyptic book *The Vision of Ezra* (or the *Apocalypse of Ezra*, usually referred to as the "Fourth Ezra"), which was widely disseminated during the Middle Ages in Arabic translations that were apparently based on the Christian Greek translation from the Hebrew and on Syriac and Coptic versions of the book.[22] Muslim authors were undoubtedly familiar with many motifs from this book, such as the miraculous return of the

in Islam," in *Studies in Islamic and Judaic Traditions*, ed. W. M. Brinner and S. Ricks (Atlanta 1986), pp. 99–108.

[19] Abū Isḥāq Aḥmad al-Tha'labī al-Nīsābūrī (Al-Tha'labī) *Qiṣaṣ al-Anbiyā al-musammā 'Arā'is al-Madjālis* (Cairo, n.d.), pp. 309–10.

[20] Some of these motifs are known from Talmudic literature; see C. D. Ginsberg, *The Massorah* (London 1883), p. 680. See also Ibn Ḥazm, *Al-Faṣl*, 1: 192 (Jeremiah buries "*al-Surādiq wa-l-Tābūt wa-l-Nār*" in order to save them).

[21] See, for example, B. Heller, "Éléments parallèles," and H. Z. Hirschberg, "Maqron and Ezra-'Uzayr" (in Hebrew), *Leshonenu* 15 (1947): 130ff.

[22] See G. Graf, *Geschichte der Christlichen—Arabischen Literatur*, vol. 1 (Vatican City 1944), pp. 219–21, and the Arabic editions of Ewald (1893), Gildemeister (1877), and Violet (1910). On a Syrian-Arabic version, cf. also P.S.J. van Koningsveld, "An Arabic Ms. of the Apocalypse of Baruch," *JSJ* 6 (1975): 205–7, and M. Stone, "A New Manuscript of the Syro-Arabic Version of the Fourth Book of Ezra," *JSJ* 8 (1977): 183–84. Although these manuscripts are rather late, one can safely assume that the book was known in an Arabic translation long before.

Torah scroll through the angel's drink. Thus, for example, Al-Ṭabarī, Al-Thaʿlabī, Ibn al-Athīr (d. 1233), and Ibn Kathīr (d. 1373) all present different versions of the image of the mourning woman (originally identified with Jerusalem) that recurs in Fourth Ezra.[23] Also, in Al-Thaʿlabī's *Tales of the Prophets*, the story of Ezra follows that of Daniel, as in the Hebrew Bible, although the author does not explicitly state that Ezra was Daniel's disciple. Daniel's Apocalypse was well known in Arabic translations, however, and Daniel was prominent in Islamic borrowings from Jewish and Christian literature as a whole.[24] The motif of the hundred-year sleep, associated in Islam with Sūra 2:259 and with 'Uzayr, may also have its source in Daniel and his dream.[25]

Of particular interest is the theme of total conformity be-

[23] See Al-Ṭabarī and Ibn Kathīr on Sūra 9:30, and Al-Tha'labī, *Qiṣaṣ*, p. 311. The mourning woman (a motif known also in Rabbinic literature) is taken by them to represent the earthly world.

[24] See F. Macler, "L'Apocalypse arabe de Daniel," *Revue d'histoire des religions* 49 (1904): 265–305; and K. Berger, *The Apocalypse of Daniel* (Greek text and trans.) (Leiden 1976). Ibn Ḥazm (*Al-Faṣl*, 1: 210) considers Daniel to be the last Old Testament prophet, as in Christianity. It is possible that the name of one of Daniel's companions, 'Azariah, was confused by Arab authors with El'azar and 'Uzayr (see in the Talmud, *Berakhot* 27b). In fact, Samau'al al-Maghribī claims that Al-'Uzayr is the Arabic form of El'azar and not of Ezra (*Ifḥām al-Yahūd*, text p. 63, trans. p. 60).

[25] Some scholars connect it with the Talmudic story about Ḥoni (*Ta'anit* 23a). The Qur'anic verse tells about a man, whose name is not mentioned, who passed near a decaying city (identified by some commentators with Jerusalem) and refused to believe that its inhabitants may be resurrected. God made him fall asleep for one hundred years; when he woke up, he was the eyewitness to his own ass's resurrection. Early Muslim traditionalists, like 'Iqrima and Qatāda, stated that this man was Ezra-'Uzayr. Others, like the convert Wahb b. Munabbih, thought it was Jeremiah (Irmiyā b. Ḥalqiyā) or Ezekiel or Elijah (Al-Khiḍr). Thus the connection between Ezra and Jeremiah (and Baruch) in Apocalyptic literature was kept alive in Muslim tradition. See B. Heller, "Éléments parallèles"; and cf. M. Schreiner, "Bemerkungen zu Koran 2, 259," *ZDMG* 42 (1888): 436–38 (reprinted in *Gesammelte Schriften*, ed. M. Perlmann, [Hildesheim 1983], pp. 72–74). See also Yāqūt, *Mu'djam al-Buldān*, s.v. "*Al-Maqdis*" (*Jacut's Geographisches Woerterbuch*, ed. F. Wuestenfeld [Leipzig 1869], 4:593).

tween the lost version of the Torah and the one Ezra dictated. This motif already appears in Al-Ṭabarī, and Al-Tha'labī expands upon it:

> Then ['Uzayr] said: "O Children of Israel! Behold, I have brought you the Torah." And they answered: "O 'Uzayr, do not deceive us!" And he tied a pen to each finger and wrote with all his fingers until he finished writing the whole Torah from the tablet of his heart, and he revived the Torah and the Sunna for them. And when the sages returned [from exile], they took out the book they had buried and compared it with the Torah of 'Uzayr and found it identical and said: "Allah has given him this only because he is His son."

In another variation in the same source, Ezra learns the Torah by heart before the destruction of the Temple, remembers it one hundred years later, and dictates it anew. When the sages take the (original) Torah out of its hiding place and the two are compared, "they did not find a missing verse or a [missing] letter, and they were greatly amazed and said: 'Allah did not give the Torah to the heart of any one of us after it was lost, but only to him [to 'Uzayr], for he is His son. Therefore the Jews say "Uzayr son of Allah.' "[26]

This repeated emphasis on the authenticity of Ezra's version of the Torah, like Rabbinic descriptions of the Septuagint,[27]—seems comprehensible only as a polemic counterreaction to those who accused Ezra of falsifying the Torah. Although there is no explicit evidence in Arabic literature prior to Ibn Ḥazm, we may assume that Al-Tha'labī was familiar with such arguments, either directly from the Jewish–Christian material he studied in composing his book, or from other sectarian sources of information. It is quite possible that Al-Tha'labī, through his tale of Ezra, not

[26] Al-Tha'labī, *Qiṣaṣ*, p. 310. The simultaneous writing with all his fingers seems to echo and outdo the dictation to five men simultaneously in Fourth Ezra.

[27] Muslims knew the story of the Septuagint and used it in polemical contexts; see Chapter Five.

only explicated the strange Qur'anic verse, but also tried to defend Ezra and the authenticity of his version of the Torah against early arguments of falsification.

Al-Thaʿlabī, like Al-Ṭabarī before him, sees Ezra as a positive figure, as did most Jewish and Christian writers. Indeed, the extravagant expressions of admiration for Ezra in Rabbinic literature, and the frequent comparisons between Ezra and Moses ("Ezra would have been found worthy to bring the Torah—to the Children of Israel—had Moses not preceded him . . . and even though [the Torah] was not given [by him]—the alphabet was changed by him" [*Sanhedrin* 21b]) may already represent a polemic reaction to arguments against Ezra. But Muslim authors like Al-Ṭabarī and Al-Thaʿlabī did not yet consider associating Ezra with the Qur'anic polemic against Judaism and the authenticity of the Torah, as did Al-Thaʿlabī's contemporary in the West, Ibn Ḥazm.

Some criticism of Ezra and his redaction of the holy Scriptures appears already in late Rabbinic literature, and in more detail in Samaritan, Christian, and anti-Christian Hellenistic literature, as well as in later Karaite literature. This material could have reached Muslim authors from any one of these and other plausible sources.

The Rabbinic apprehension about the possible inaccuracy of Ezra's redaction of the holy Scriptures was associated with the Masoretic system as a whole, as in the following quotation from *Aboth d'Rabbi Nathan*: "Thus said Ezra: If Elijah should come and say to me: why did you write in this manner (doubtful words)? I will answer him: I have already dotted them; but if he should say: You have written them correctly—I shall remove the dots from them." According to Lieberman, grammarians in Alexandria marked doubtful passages with points.[28]

[28] See *Aboth d'Rabbi Nathan*, ed. S. Schechter (Vienna 1887), version A, p. 51; and S. Lieberman, *Hellenism in Jewish Palestine* (New York 1950), p. 44, where the passage is quoted. Cf. *Aboth* version B, ch. 37, p. 98.; and see A. J. Saldarini, *The Fathers According to Rabbi Nathan* (translation and commentary) (Leiden 1975), p. 224 n. 56. See also A. E.

Certain books of the Apocrypha also seem to critize Ezra implicitly in their silence about him and their attribution of his enterprise to Nehemiah.[29] This negative attitude toward Ezra the Scribe could also have entered Islam through Samaritan sources (which, by contrast, adulate Moses).[30] These very sources themselves make little mention of Ezra, however, even though the Samaritans undoubtedly saw him as a negative figure who, by changing the alphabet of the sacred texts and adding to them, brought about the falsification of the Torah. Nevertheless, Samaritan writings contain few explicit condemnations of Ezra, and the curses against him were apparently transmitted chiefly by allusion, and were handed down orally from generation to generation.[31] At least one of the later Samaritan chronicles in Arabic does state explicitly that Ezra and Zerubavel (who is also mentioned in Islamic polemics against Judaism, for example by Ibn Ḥazm) "added to and subtracted from, changed and falsified" (*zādū wa-naqqaṣū wa-baddalū wa-ḥarrafū*) the Torah text. It is hard to determine, however, whether this is an early Samaritan motif expressed here in Arabic, in a language influenced by that of Islamic polemics against Judaism, or whether the motif itself should be considered another example of the general impact Islam had on Samaritan literature.[32]

Urbach, "The Derasha as a Basis of the Halakha and the Problem of the Soferim" (in Hebrew), *Tarbiz* 27 (1948): 166–82 and n. 179.

[29] For example, *Ben Sira* and the author of 2 Macc. See P. Hoeffken, "Warum schwieg Jesus Sirach ueber Ezra?" *ZAW* 87 (1975): 184–202.

[30] On the Samaritan influence on early Islam in general, see J. Finkel, "Jewish, Christian and Samaritan Influence on Arabia," *Macdonald Presentation Volume* (Princeton 1933), pp. 147–66; and P. Crone and M. Cook, *Hagarism: The Making of the Islamic World* (Cambridge 1977), ch. 4.

[31] I am very grateful to Prof. Z. Ben-Hayyim for these remarks and some of the following references. See A. E. Cowley, *Samaritan Liturgy* (Oxford 1959), p. 514b.

[32] See Abū-l-Fatḥ al-Sāmirī, *Kitāb al-Ayyām*, ed. E. Vilmar (n.p., 1865), pp. 74–75. Cf. also *Chronicum Samaritanum*, ed. T.W.J. Juynboll (Leiden 1848), ch. 45. Elsewhere in Samaritan polemics, Ezra does not

The possibility that the negative image of Ezra-ʿUzayr in Islam has a Samaritan source is strengthened by the mention in early Islamic exegesis of Pinhas ben ʿAzaryah (Finḥāṣ ibn ʿAzūrā) as the one who argued with his Jewish contemporaries that ʿUzayr was the son of God.[33] Elʿazar and Pinhas are among the forebears of Ezra the Priest (Ezra 7:5), but it may well be that they became known in the Islamic world only through Samaritan sources, although only the late Samaritan Chronicles in Arabic testify clearly to this.[34] Both Ezra and Pinhas are negatively associated in early Muslim Qur'an exegesis with Muhammad's change of the direction of prayer (*qiblah*) from Jerusalem to Mecca, and this may be a faint echo of the Samaritan arguments against replacing the sanctity of Mt. Gerizim with that of Jerusalem.[35] A later Samaritan reference to this issue and to the confusion of names can perhaps be found also in the *Sharḥ al-Asāṭīr* manuscript, a commentary of unknown authorship on the Samaritan Midrashic chronol-

---

seem to be mentioned at all. See also A. S. Halkin, "Samaritan Polemics against the Jews," *PAAJR* 7 (1935–36): 13ff.

[33] See Al-Ṭabarī's commentary to Sūra 9:30, and cf. above, note 7. Cf. also A. Geiger, *Was hat Mohammed aus dem Judenthume aufgenommen?* 2d ed. (Leipzig 1902), p. 191, and see Ibn Ḥazm, *Al-Faṣl*, 1: 187. Geiger already remarked (*Was hat Mohammed*, p. 15) that Pinhas was also the one who ridiculed God "as being poor" in the context of Sūra 3:181 (see Al-Ṭabarī on the verse). The same verse is connected also by Al-Djāḥiẓ with ʿUzayr, but without mention of Pinhas; see his *Al-Radd*, pp. 33–34.

[34] See Abū-l-Fatḥ al-Sāmirī, *Kitāb al-Ayyām*, passim; cf. an earlier Samaritan chronicle published by M.A.D. Neubauer, "Chronique Samaritaine," *JA* 6th ser., 13 (1869): 390–470.

[35] Al-Ṭabarī relates in his commentary, on the authority of Ibn ʿAbbās, ʿIqrima, and Saʿīd b. Djubayr, that some Jews (among them Salām b. Mushkam and Nuʿmān b. Awfā) came to the Prophet complaining that they could not follow him because he had changed the direction of prayer and did not believe that ʿUzayr was the son of God. Therefore Sūra 9:30 was revealed. Most commentators follow Al-Ṭabarī in this. Cf. also Ibn Hishām, *Sīrat Rasūl Allāh*, ed. F. Wuestenfeld (*Das Leben Mohammed's nach Mohammed Ibn Ishaq*) (Goettingen 1858), I, 1: 388–89, 398–99. There (p. 352) one ʿUzayr b. ʿUzayr is mentioned also as having asked the Prophet some provocative questions. Cf. A. Guillaume's translation, *The Life of Muhammad* (Oxford 1955), pp. 263ff.

ogy *Asāṭīr*, republished by Z. Ben-Hayyim in *Tarbiz.*[36] The Midrash mentions "a Levite named ʿAzraz ben Pani" accused of starting idolatry and establishing "a shrine of idol worship" that would create a rift within the community.[37] In the manuscript commentary (p. 17a), ʿAzraz is identified with Ezra (and, accordingly, Pani is a corruption of the name Pinhas, as Ben-Hayyim notes, differing with Gaster).

Yet, despite the reasonable possibility that Samaritan arguments against Ezra found their way into Islam, and perhaps even into the Qur'anic verse about ʿUzayr, Samaritan literature apparently contains no explicit references to falsification of the Torah by Ezra the Scribe. Only the "Dustān," a small group that split away from the other Samaritans, mentions Ezra and especially his new Torah—but in a positive way.[38]

Ezra has many aspects in early Christian literature, and Islam could have drawn from it both his positive (Al-Thaʿlabī) and his negative image (Ibn Ḥazm). This literature already echoes some early Bible criticism by Jewish-Christian or Gnostic groups, and various arguments against Ezra and his redaction of the Scriptures are voiced both here and even more in Hellenistic anti-Christian literature. These arguments appear mostly as a secondary motif, along with other anti-Jewish and anti-Christian motifs. Ezra appears in various roles (priest, king, prophet, miracle-worker, father of faith, etc.). As a positive figure, he is usually identified with Shealtiel, son of Zerubavel;[39] in

[36] See Z. Ben-Hayyim, "The Book of Asāṭīr (with Translation and Commentary)," *Tarbiz* 14 (1943): 104–25, 174–90; 15 (1944): 71–87.

[37] Ben-Hayyim, "Book of Asāṭīr," *Tarbiz* 15, p. 82, ll. 18–20.

[38] Cf. *Encyclopedia Judaica* s.v. "Dustān" (A. Loewenstamm) and the bibliography mentioned there. See also Abū-l-Fatḥ, *Kitāb al-Ayyām*, pp. 82–83, 151–57, 159–64. Al-Shahrastānī, in his *Milal wa-Niḥal* (ed. W. Cureton [London 1846]), 1: 170 (German trans. T. Haarbruecker [Halle 1850–51], p. 258) mentions this group among the Samaritans, but without any connection to Ezra.

[39] This identification is to be found also in Muslim literature, but not with Ibn Ḥazm (see his *Al-Faṣl*, 1: 152, 210).

his negative role, he is associated with the rejection or even the deception of the Samaritans.[40]

As early as the second century, Justin Martyr, in his (imaginary?) debate with Trypho, mentions Ezra in connection with the omission of Biblical verses alluding to the coming of Jesus and other corruptions of the sacred Scripture. He does not accuse Ezra of falsifying the texts, however.[41] That was done in the third century by the Hellenistic writer Porphyrius in his anti-Christian work *Adversus Christianos*. Porphyrius argues against the Christian thesis based on Moses and the Torah:

> Nothing was preserved from the Torah of Moses, and it is said that all its texts were burnt together with the Temple. The writings later composed in his name were written in an imprecise manner 1,180 years after the death of Moses by Ezra and his disciples.[42]

Porphyrius's approach here is indeed scholarly and scientific, like that of modern Bible critics. It seems very plau-

[40] See R. Kraft, "Ezra Materials," p. 127; and M. Stone, "Metamorphosis," p. 2.

[41] A. L. Williams, ed., *Dialogue between Justin Martyr and Trypho the Jew* (London 1930), pp. 150–55. Justin connects the falsification of the Scriptures with the sin of worshipping the calf. According to the Qur'an (Sūra 20:87–96) and later commentators, this worship was introduced to Israel by a Samaritan (Al-Sāmirī), whose name, according to the commentators, also happened to be Aaron. (Aaron himself is considered in Islam to be a prophet and, as such, infallible). As in Jewish tradition, the calf actually made some sounds (Sūra 20:88), because (according to Muslim commentators) the ingredients of which it was made included a pinch of soil upon which Gabriel's horse had trodden. It is curious that one of the surnames of 'Alī is Abū-l-Turāb, meaning "The Father of Soil," or "One Who Possesses Soil." Cf. Crone and Cook, *Hagarism*, p. 177, and Ibn Kathīr on the verse, as well as Ghevond's text (see below, note 43), p. 292. See also 'Alī al-Mas'ūdī, *Murūdj al-Dhahab wa-Ma'ādin al-Djawāhir* (*Les Prairies d'or*, ed. and trans. C. Barbier de Meynard and P. de Courtillee [Paris 1861–77], 2: 390); Ibn Ḥazm, *Al-Faṣl*, 1: 162–63; and Ibn Qayyim al-Djawziyya, *Hidāyat al-Ḥayārā*, p. 149.

[42] See M. Stern, *Greek and Latin Authors on Jews and Judaism*, vol. 2 (Jerusalem 1980), p. 480 (frag. 465E); E. Stein, *Alttestamentlische Bibelkritik in der Spaethellenistischen Literatur* (Lwow 1935), pp. 28, 43.

sible that medieval Islamic polemics against Judaism and the Torah, particularly the writings of Ibn Ḥazm, may have been intermediaries that transmitted such ideas to modern authors. As mentioned in Chapter Two, one of the most basic Qur'anic accusations against the Jews and the Christians is that of having falsified their own sacred Scriptures (*Taḥrīf, Tabdīl*), apparently in order to deny that Muhammad was foretold therein. Ezra appears in this context already in one of the earliest documents of Christian-Islamic polemics, preserved only in Armenian and Latin and never mentioned in Arabic literature: the "debate" supposedly conducted by correspondence between the Caliph ʿUmar II and Leo III the Isaurian.[43] Leo responds to ʿUmar's accusations that the (Christian) holy Scriptures were written by man (as opposed to the Qur'an, which is the Word of God), that they were lost several times, and that Ezra was the one who redacted their "second version." Leo defends Ezra, arguing that the divine spirit was upon him and that he was infallible, and that the Torah he restored to the Children of Israel was therefore identical to the one the exiles brought with them when they returned to the Land of Israel.[44] How strange that in this debate between a Christian and a Muslim (whether it contains a kernel of historical truth or is merely a later literary device), the Christian has to defend the authenticity of the Hebrew Bible (because it contains the prophecies of the coming of Jesus) against the Islamic prosecutor. Indeed, the Christian does so while stressing the bitter argument between Jews and Christians over the correct interpretation of those verses. When it came to the authenticity of the text itself, however, Jews

[43] A. Jeffery, "Ghevond's Text of the Correspondence between ʿUmar II and Leo III," *Harvard Theological Review* 37 (1944): 269–331; Crone and Cook, *Hagarism*, pp. 163 n. 26, 165 n. 52. Jeffery accepts the possibility that such a correspondence might have actually taken place, and in any case considers the text to be an early document of the eighth century. See also Chapter One, esp. note 9.

[44] A. Jeffery, "Ghevond's Text," pp. 277, 288–90.

and most Christians stood together against Muslim accusations that they had tempered with it.[45]

The Karaites also criticized Ezra, although they accepted the authenticity of the Biblical text, which is the cornerstone of Karaite thought. Yet Ezra figures in the polemic between the Rabbanites and the Karaites in another way: the tenth-century author Al-Qirqisānī accused the rabbis of attributing the Torah not to Moses himself but rather to Ezra. Had the Muslims known this, he adds, they would have argued even more strongly that the original Torah of Moses was lost (in the days of Nebuchadnezzar).[46]

It should be added here that often it is very difficult to identify the sources of certain polemic arguments, or even the later context in which they appear. For example, S. Abramson cites as a Karaite argument (countered by the North African Gaon Rav Nissim [d. 1062] in a Genizah fragment) the accusation of the loss of the Torah scroll (referring to 2 Kings 22, the story of the discovery of the Torah scroll during the reign of Josiah) and the assumption that only some of the Song of Ha'azinu portion of the Torah has a reliable tradition of authentic transmission. Ezra the Scribe is also mentioned in this context. As we shall see, the same arguments were voiced by Rav Nissim's Muslim contemporary, Ibn Ḥazm, who is supposed to have debated the issue with Rav Nissim's father-in-law, Samuel Hanagid! These arguments may in fact derive from Christian (or anti-Christian) sources (which Abramson mentions in an earlier context)[47] from which Ibn Ḥazm drew his arguments, and may have nothing to do with the Karaites.

[45] With regard to other polemical topics, however (for example, the importance of religious law), Jews were often in alliance with Muslims against Christian concepts. See, for example, Al-Djāḥiẓ, *Al-Radd*, pp. 21ff., and Ibn Qayyim al-Djawziyya, *Hidāyat al-Ḥayārā*, ch. 11.

[46] Al-Qirqisānī, *Kitāb al-Anwār wa-l-Marāqib*, ed. L. Nemoy, pt. 1 (New York 1939), p. 15; pt. 2 (New York 1940), p. 295; or the English translation by L. Nemoy, in *HUCA* 7 (1930): 331. Cf. also L. Nemoy, "Ibn Kammūnah's Treatise on the Differences between Rabbanites and Karaites," *JQR* 63 (1972–73): 97–135, esp. 105, 114.

[47] Cf. S. Abramson, *Rav Nissim Ga'on* (in Hebrew) (Jerusalem 1965),

As noted, Ibn Ḥazm was the first, the most systematic, and the most original author among Muslim polemicists against Judaism and Christianity. While his arguments against the Torah (and the New Testament) are expressed in polemical, almost anti-Semitic terms, replete with ridicule of and revulsion for the Jews, his level of argumentation and systematic critical approach to the text often equals the standard of modern Bible criticism. As has been mentioned, Ibn Ḥazm probably drew from earlier pre-Islamic polemic sources, both anti-Christian and anti-Jewish; his criticism of Christian theology and literature is no less severe than his denunciations of Judaism. It appears, however, that he had a particularly thorough knowledge of and easy access to anti-Christian (and Jewish-Christian) sources.[48]

We may reasonably assume, therefore, that the negative image of Ezra appearing first in Arabic literature in Ibn Ḥazm's writings also has Jewish-Christian or anti-Christian roots. Ibn Ḥazm's younger contemporary in the east, ʿAbd al-Malik al-Djuwaynī (d. 1085), may have come across the same sources, or taken ideas from Ibn Ḥazm himself, although he presented them in an extremely abridged way.[49] Ibn Ḥazm, however, developed this theme into an all-comprising theory, the essence of which is that the Torah, as known to the Jews (and Christians), was intentionally falsified and corrupted by "Ezra the Scribe." As we have seen in Chapter Two, Ibn Ḥazm, as a devout Ẓāhiri, could not accept the existence of any contradiction or imprecision in a divine text considered to be God's word.

---

pp. 348–60 (this fragment was first published by B. M. Lewin [*Sinai* 6 (1942): 149–51], who thought the author was Saadia Gaon) and pp. 552–53. See also S. Abramson, *Problems in Gaonic Literature* (in Hebrew) (Jerusalem 1974), p. 274. On the role the "Ha'azinu" portion played in Muslim polemic, see below. On possible Christian sources of Ibn Ḥazm, see also Chapter Five.

[48] On Ibn Ḥazm, see Chapter Two above.

[49] See *Textes apologétiques de Ĝuwainī*, ed. M. Allard (Beirut 1968), pp. 44ff. and 47, where he mentioned " ʿAzrā's passion for the continuation of his leadership." He may constitute a literary link between Ibn Ḥazm and Samau'al.

He stated repeatedly that an error in the calculation of even one single minute (not to mention years, as in the Bible) cannot be attributed to God. Nor can we ascribe to Him tales of promiscuity, lies, and abomination about His prophets and chosen ones. Ibn Ḥazm had no doubt, therefore, that the Bible was indeed falsified and that fictitious stories were interpolated into it, and he holds Ezra the Scribe and Priest (*Hārūnī*) responsible. He heaps abuse upon Ezra, for the most part without mentioning his name, calling him a heretic (*Zindīq*), a liar, a crook, stupid as an ass, arithmetically deficient and wrong-headed, one who seeks to ridicule faith and religion and make a mockery of God and His prophets.[50]

Ibn Ḥazm also tried to prove that only the priests of the tribe of Levi (in the Temple) possessed a complete text of the Torah, while the rest of the Israelites apparently knew only the text of the Song of Ha'azinu, as indicated in Deut. 31:22. Ibn Ḥazm quotes a complete literal translation of this song (very different from Saadia's translation)[51] and adds that wars, fires and exile had also played their part in damaging the Jewish Torah text, as did the Jews' own burning of the Torah scroll[52] and the erasing of the names of God from it by kings of Israel and Judah.[53]

In the book written against his archenemy (Ibn al-Nagrīlah), Ibn Ḥazm recapitulated his polemics on this issue:[54]

> They acknowledge that throughout the entire period of their rule, the Torah was in the sole possession of the priests. Thus, for a period of almost 1,200 years, the Torah was handed down from one single person to another—a situation that (almost)

[50] Ibn Ḥazm, *Al-Faṣl*, 1: 119, 127, 129, 150, 155, 198, etc.

[51] Ibid., pp. 200–201; cf. Chapter Five below.

[52] The burning of the Torah (here by Jews) is mentioned also by Porphyrius, or may be based on the Mishna, *Taʿanit* 4, 6 or on a literal (mis)understanding of Talmudic sayings, such as, "This verse aught to have been burned were it not for . . ." (*Ḥulin* 60a).

[53] Ibn Ḥazm, *Al-Faṣl*, 1: 193–96. Cf. Chapter Two. In the Talmud, similar stories are told about other Israelite kings (cf. *Sanhedrin* 102b–103a).

[54] See Iḥsān ʿAbbās', ed., *Al-Radd ʿalā Ibn al-Naghrīla*, p. 77.

guarantees alterations, substitutions, distortions, interpolations and omissions, all the more so since most of their kings and all of the masses throughout most of the period were idol-worshippers who had turned their backs on their faith and even killed their own prophets.[55] It must therefore be assumed that the true Torah was undoubtedly lost and changed under those conditions. And they admit that Yehoahaz ben Yoshiah [Yehū'āhāz b. Yūshiyā],[56] the Davidic king who ruled over the entire people of Israel, after the kingship came to an end in the other tribes, erased from the Torah the names of God praised be He and inserted the names of idols. And they also admit that his brother who ruled after him, Eliakim ben Yoshiah [Elyāqīm b. Yūshiyā], burned the entire Torah and wiped out its remnants during his reign—before Nebuchadnezzar [Bukht-Naṣr] overcame them. They admit also that Ezra, who wrote (the Torah) for them from his memory after it was lost, was only a scribe (*Warrāq*) and not a prophet. But a certain group among them says that he was the son of God, and that group has disappeared.[57] And what could be (worse) than those (additions) which were (interpolated) into their Torah?

Ibn Ḥazm then goes on to contrast the Qur'an and its trustworthy transmission, accepted by everyone, with the defects of the Torah. At the same time, Ibn Ḥazm also believed that some Biblical verses allude to the coming of Muhammad; but this kind of exegesis is not very frequent in his writings.

Despite this lack of consistency, Ibn Ḥazm was undoubtedly the one who, by being the first to make Ezra into a wicked scoundrel who had intentionally corrupted the Scriptures, raised the general Islamic arguments against the Bible to an essentially higher level of systematic textual

[55] This is a Qur'anic motif, the origins of which may be found in early Christian or Midrashic literature. See B. Halpern-Amaru, "The Killing of the Prophets," *HUCA* 54 (1983): 153–80. See also Jer. 2:30.

[56] In *Al-Faṣl*, 7:193: Ibn Ḥazm mentions a more corrupted form of this and other names.

[57] See above, note 7.

criticism. Other Muslim authors simply follow him, notably the above-mentioned Jewish apostate Samau'al al-Maghribī, who added many details to support Ibn Ḥazm's theories.[58] In his vitriolic *Ifḥām al-Yahūd (Silencing the Jews)*, which he wrote in Baghdad in 1163, after his conversion to Islam, Samau'al supplied the "motive" for Ezra the Scribe's falsification of the Torah. He rejected the identification of Ezra with ʿUzayr and translated the word "scribe" (after mentioning also the Hebrew *Hasofer* in Arabic transcription) with *al-Nāsikh*, a word that the Islamic reader could not fail to associate with the theory of abrogation (*Naskh*). According to Samau'al, Ezra, being of a priestly family (*Hārūnī*), sought to prevent the rule of the Davidic dynasty during the days of the Second Temple as it had in the times of the First. For that reason, says Samau'al, Ezra invented tales of incest (Lot and his daughters, Jehuda and Tamar, etc.) to sully David's origins; and in fact, he achieved his goal: during the Second Temple period, the regime was in the hands of the priests of the house of Aaron, not the Davidic dynasty.[59]

Samau'al al-Maghribī accepted Ibn Ḥazm's hypothesis that only the Song of Ha'azinu was entrusted to the entire people of Israel and that therefore it was the only part of the Torah to be considered reliably transmitted.[60] His description of the oral transmission of the Torah by the priests and its loss during the wars is closely modelled after the Islamic tradition (which he does not explicitly mention) for collecting and redacting the Qur'an,[61] yet with special em-

[58] It seems likely that Samau'al followed Ibn Ḥazm directly, but there may exist some literary links in between. See above, note 49.

[59] Samau'al al-Maghribī, *Ifḥām al-Yahūd*, text pp. 62–63, trans. p. 60. (Cf. above, Chapter Two, and note 71 there.)

[60] Samau'al al-Maghribī, *Ifḥām al-Yahūd*, text pp. 49–50, trans. p. 54.

[61] Ibid., text pp. 50–51 (54–56), trans. pp. 54–55 (56–57). This story is accepted as historical by Muslim authors, but not by scholars. See, for example, T. Noeldeke and F. Schwally, *Geschichte des Qur'āns*, vol. 2 (Leipzig 1919), and R. Burton, *The Collection of the Qur'ān* (Cambridge 1977), pp. 117ff. Cf. also the introduction by thirteenth-century Jewish

phasis on the difference regarding the authenticity of the respective texts. The Jewish priests knew only a small part of the Torah by heart (Samau'al intentionally uses the Islamic term *Ḥafẓ* denoting memorization of the Qur'an), and many of those who knew the Torah by heart were lost in Nebuchadnezzar's decimation. In the early years of Islam, the same fate befell many of those who knew the Qur'an by heart, in the famous Battle of Al-Yamāma in 633. But the immediate concern of the first Caliphs to recollect and put the Qur'an into writing saved it in its authentic version. Yet Ezra gathered the Torah only after a long time, from his own and other priests' memories, and he rewrote it himself (the verb *laffaqa* used in this context by Samau'al carries connotations of patching and falsification). He was greatly admired for this by the people of Israel (who believe that light emanates from his grave in southern Iraq "to this very day"),[62] but the Torah in the Jews' possession is in fact *Kitāb ʿAzrā*, the Book of Ezra, and not *Kitāb Allāh*, the divine book of God.[63]

Later Islamic polemic literature largely followed Ibn Ḥazm and Samau'al al-Maghribī,[64] including popular[65] and

---

commentator David Kimḥi (Radak) to the Book of Joshua, and his commentary on 2 Kings 17:14.

[62] Samau'al al-Maghribī, *Ifḥām al-Yahūd*, text p. 51, trans. p. 55. There exist various traditions as to where Ezra was buried. Josephus thinks in Jerusalem (*Antiquitates Judaicae* 11.5); Benjamin of Tudela mentions southern Iraq (Basra); others suggest the vicinity of Nablus (Yāqūt, *Muʿdjam al-Buldān*, ed. F. Wuestenfeld [Leipzig 1868], 3: 745) or Damascus (Ibn Kathīr, *Al-Bidāya wa-l-Nihāya*, 1: 41). See also L. Ginzberg, *Legends of the Jews*, vol. 4 (Philadelphia 1947), p. 335.

[63] Samau'al al-Maghribī, *Ifḥām al-Yahūd*, text p. 51, trans. p. 55. *Kitāb Allah* is a common epithet for the Qur'an. Could it be that this erudite zealot convert, who became Muslim for chiefly utilitarian reasons, was actually an atheist or agnostic who had his doubts about Islam as well? Or did he just interchange the terms, as was common (see above)?

[64] See, for example, Ibn Qayyim al-Djawziyya, *Hidāyat al-Ḥayārā*, ch. 7, and Mudjīr al-Dīn al-Ḥanbalī, *Al-Uns al-Djalīl fī Ta'rīkh al-Quds wa-l-Khalīl* (Jerusalem 1973), pp. 152–53.

[65] For example, see Ms. Cambridge, Qq 29, mentioned above in Chapter Two, note 9, and described by M. Perlmann in his " ʿAlī al-Munayyar," in

Shi'ite polemics[66] as well as Modernist literature.[67] The negative image of Ezra and his falsification of the Torah were generally accepted, and Ezra was once again identified with the Qur'anic 'Uzayr. Although this identification seems self-evident, it may have been fostered also by Ibn Ḥazm's implications in his polemic against Samuel Hanagid and by Samau'al's remarks about the Jews' excessive admiration of Ezra and his tomb in Iraq, which contradicted his request to refrain from identifying Ezra with 'Uzayr.

The Rabad I (Rabbi Abraham ben David [Ibn Dā'ūd] Halevi) of Toledo (d. 1180) is one of the few Jewish writers who explicitly mentions Ezra. He does so in his response to the claim that the Torah was falsified: "Let us assume that Ezra came from Babylonia and wrote an altered Torah—then why did the people thank him for it? And why was it obeyed near and far? . . . And we have never heard of anyone who blamed Ezra in any way. . . ."[68] Similar arguments were presented during the same period by his Christian contemporary Peter the Venerable (d. 1156), who re-

---

Studies in Judaica, Karaitica and Islamica presented to L. Nemoy, ed. S. Brunswick (Bar Ilan 1982), pp. 181–202. Ezra-'Uzayr is mentioned often therein.

[66] For example, the twelfth-century Shi'ite Qur'an commentator Al-Ṭabarsī in his polemical *Kitāb al-Iḥtidjādj* (n.d.), pp. 7ff., denounced the Jewish appellation of 'Uzayr as "son of God," even as an expression of respect only. He added that as Moses was found by God more worthy of prophethood than 'Uzayr, the Jews could then call him God's brother, father, or Shaykh!

[67] See, for example, the Modernist journal *Al-Manār* (ed. M. 'Abduh), vol. 3 (May 3, 1903), as well as the *Manār* Qur'an Commentary (index). Cf. the contemporary author Muḥammad Khalīfa and a contemporary Persian parallel in M. Zand's survey, "The Image of Jews in Iran after the Second World War" (in Hebrew) *Pe'amim* 29 (1986): 117.

[68] See Abraham ibn Dā'ūd, *Emunah Ramah* (in Hebrew trans.) (Frankfurt 1852), pp. 75ff., esp. pp. 79–80 (German trans. pp. 99–101), and M. Schreiner, "Zur Geschichte der Polemik zwischen Juden und Muhammedanern," *ZDMG* 42 (1888): 628–30 (reprinted in *Gesammelte Schriften*, pp. 112–15).

sponded comprehensively to the claim that the sacred Scriptures had been falsified, and especially to the accusation against Ezra in this context.[69]

The noted Jewish philosopher from Baghdad, Ibn Kammūna (d. 1285), also tried to promote a positive view of Ezra the Scribe as the redactor of the holy Scriptures, though he identified Ezra with 'Uzayr. In his scholarly response to the accusation that the Jewish scriptures are not authentic, Ibn Kammūna says:

> Ezra, to whom the opponents ascribe the reintroduction of the Torah after its alleged disappearance, is famous for reverence, great righteousness, and piety. It is he whom the Muslims called 'Uzayr; they and some of the Jews claim he was a prophet, but even those who question his prophethood do not question his great righteousness and piety. Therefore it cannot be imagined that he would have permitted himself to tamper with and distort the divine scripture.[70]

Later in the same work, Ibn Kammūna attempts to demonstrate that the Biblical text, universally accepted by Christians as well as Jews, could not have been corrupted, that the lost Torah scroll found in the Temple does not prove that the entire Torah was lost, and so on. 'Abd al-Ḥaqq al-Islāmī,[71] a fourteenth-century Jewish convert to Islam, also mentions 'Uzayr as the redactor of the holy scriptures (*"khātama-l-kutub-allatī bi-l-Tawrāt"*) in a polemical anti-Jewish treatise, and he even attributes to 'Uzayr the first verse of the third chapter of the Book of Malachi (the Rabbinic sages identified Ezra with Malachi).

It is clear that Jews were aware of Islamic polemics against Judaism, and we know that Jews responded to Muslim theological theories such as abrogation, and to

[69] J. Kritzeck, *Peter the Venerable* (Princeton 1964), pp. 178ff.

[70] *Ibn Kammūna's Examination of the Three Faiths*, trans. M. Perlmann (Berkeley 1971), pp. 53ff.; Arabic text, ed. M. Perlmann (Berkeley 1967), p. 90.

[71] See M. Perlmann, " 'Abd al-Hakk al-Islāmī, A Jewish Convert," *JQR* 31 (1940–41): 189.

Muslim typological interpretation of Biblical verses (see Chapter Four). But the authenticity of the text of the Torah was too sensitive a subject for public discussion, as Maimonides implied in his Responsum (see Chapter One). This may be why Ezra received so little attention in this context in medieval Jewish literature.[72] It is quite possible, however, that the Muslim systematic, critical approach to the Biblical text and to Ezra the Scribe reached Europe through Jewish or Christian links, one of which could have been Abraham ibn Ezra.

Ibn Ezra (d. 1164) was one of the first Jewish medieval scholars to deal with problems of Bible criticism. He is frequently mentioned as the first "scholarly" interpreter of the Torah.[73] As mentioned above, he could have found rudiments of this approach already in the writings of Rabbinic sages. But it was perhaps his ties with the Islamic world and its polemic against the Torah that gave particular impetus to Ibn Ezra's approach. He travelled extensively in the Islamic East, as well as in the West, knew Arabic very well, and could easily have read some of Ibn Ḥazm's or Samau'al's writings. He must have heard about the noted Jewish philosopher of Baghdad, Abū-l-Barakāt Hibbat Allāh (Nethanel b. Eli [d. 1164–65])[74] and his so-called "circle" of disciples, which included Abraham's own son Yizhak ibn Ezra—although it is doubtful whether at that time he still had direct contacts with his son. It certainly is noteworthy that Abū-l-Barakāt converted to Islam at the end of his life. Apparently Yizhak ibn Ezra also converted for a short time. The most famous convert of this "circle" is, of course, Samau'al al-Maghribī. The idea that holy Scriptures were re-

[72] Ezra is often mentioned in Rabbinic Responsa, as a survey kindly made for me by the Computerized Informations Service of Bar Ilan University in Israel has shown. But he is never mentioned in the context discussed here.

[73] See also a more reserved approach on this issue in *Encyclopedia Miqra'it* (in Hebrew) s.v. "Parshanut," 8: 680 (U. Simon).

[74] See S. D. Goitein, *A Mediterranean Society*, vol. 2 (Berkeley and Los Angeles 1971), ch. 7a; *EI*[2] s.v. "Abū-l-Barakāt" (S. Pines).

corded by later redactors, as well as other problems of "high" textual criticism, were certainly raised among these intellectuals and could have easily reached Ibn Ezra. Perlmann's contradictory suggestion, that it was Samau'al who drew his ideas from Ibn Ezra by way of his son,[75] seems much less plausible to me, as Samau'al perpetuated and developed many aspects of Ibn Ḥazm's polemical approach to the Bible and to Judaism.

In any case, Ibn Ezra seems to have been among those who transmitted these ideas to the West and tried to associate them with earlier Rabbinic critical remarks on the Biblical text. Spinoza therefore mentioned Ibn Ezra explicitly in his writings as a critical-scholarly interpreter of the Bible and as the one who first doubted Moses' authorship of the text. Spinoza is also the first modern Bible critic to see Ezra, like earlier Greek and Hellenist authors, as the central figure in the history of the redaction of the Bible and the canonization of the twenty-four books.[76]

Thus were both positive and negative images of Ezra transmitted through Islamic polemics to the incipient Bible research in premodern Europe, helping this science to formulate new approaches to the Bible.

[75] See M. Perlmann, "The Medieval Polemics between Judaism and Islam," in *Religion in a Religious Age*, ed. S. D. Goitein, Association for Jewish Studies (New York 1974), pp. 133–34.

[76] See Spinoza, *Tractatus ideologice-politicus*, ch. 8. (Spinoza ascribes to Ibn Ezra his own ideas about Ezra.)

CHAPTER FOUR

Muslim Bible Exegesis: The Prediction of Muhammad and Islam

MUSLIM BIBLE EXEGESIS has been mentioned above as one of the Muslim arguments against the Bible. According to Muslim authors, several verses in the Bible, if rightly understood, predict the coming of Muhammad and the rise of Islam as God's true and last revelation to mankind (see Chapter Two). The assumption underlying this argument was that the verses thus expounded stem from the original true Scriptures, having miraculously escaped falsification. A possible reason for this escape was their vague and implicit message, which (according to Muslim authors) had to be rediscovered through special hermeneutical efforts.

Several scholars have mentioned this hermeneutic literature or studied some of the best-known examples of it.[1] But its full extent has remained largely unknown, even though this literature is closely connected with the intricate issue of the history of Arabic Bible translations and is indispensable for the understanding of medieval Jewish hermeneutics, which often reacted to it both explicitly and implicitly. Moreover, the study of this Muslim exegetical literature—which is much easier today than it was a century

[1] E. Ashtor (Straus) published a list of Biblical verses used in Muslim polemics in the *Memorial Volume for the Vienna Rabbinical Seminary* (in Hebrew) (Jerusalem 1946). See also W. M. Watt, "The Early Development of the Muslim Attitude to the Bible," *Transactions, Glasgow University Oriental Society* 16 (1955–56): 50–62. On the other hand, two studies devoted to the veneration of Muhammad in Islam never mention this aspect; see Tor Andrae, *Die Person Muhammeds in Lehre und Leben seiner Gemeinde* (Stockholm 1918), and A. Schimmel, *Und Muhammad ist Sein Prophet* (Diederich Verlag 1981).

ago—may also prove to be important for the evaluation of current scholarly efforts to reassess early Muslim history.

The quotations of Biblical verses and their interpretations in Muslim Arabic literature do not sustain the new approach suggested recently in Islamic studies that assumes an old forgotten proto-Jewish phase of early Islam.[2] Quite to the contrary, this Islamic literature shows clear signs of Biblical knowledge that increased over the years, as well as many indications that this knowledge was imparted in the beginning through both Christian and Jewish converts to Islam. Muslim authors' acquaintance with Biblical and later Jewish material did *not* become dim and vague with time, but rather increased and slowly became more exact and extensive. Without denying in any way the deep influence Judaism (and Christianity) exerted on early Islam, one must accept that only a few rather late Muslim authors show an extensive knowledge or true understanding of Jewish Scriptures and hermeneutic literature.

Muslim authors up to the thirteenth century seem to have used only specific lists of Biblical verses to be expounded as alluding to the Prophet and Islam (like the Christian "Testimonia"). They never tried a comprehensive typological prefigurative approach to a whole Biblical text, which apparently was not available to them (see Chapter Five). In fact, their Biblical interpretation never developed into a literary genre of its own, and early examples of it are often more sophisticated than the later ones. (None can in any way be compared to the highly developed literature of Qur'anic commentaries.) Because of the basic Muslim attitude toward the Biblical text (see Chapter Two), as well as toward Judaism and Christianity in general, Biblical interpretation never became as important for Islam as it was for Christianity, although it was integral to Muslim authors'

[2] See, for example, P. Crone and M. Cook, *Hagarism: The Making of the Islamic World* (Cambridge 1977); J. Wansbrough, *Quranic Studies: Sources and Methods of Scriptural Interpretation* (Oxford 1977); idem, *The Sectarian Milieu* (Oxford 1978); P. Crone, "Jāhilī and Jewish Law: The Qasāma," *JSAI* 4 (1984): 153–201.

polemical attempts to prove Muhammad's prophethood and the authenticity of his divine message to all mankind.

The only explicit Biblical quotation in the Qur'an (Sūra 21:105, Psalm 37:29)[3] is already explained in this way, and the "righteous slaves who shall inherit the earth" are taken by Muslim commentators to be the Muslim believers who will inherit paradise, or the world or even the Holy Land.[4] The famous Muʿtazilite author ʿAbd al-Djabbār (d. 1025) found in this verse not only an explicit confirmation of the true prophethood of Muhammad and the rise of Islam, but also a clear allusion to the great conquests of the first four caliphs. He polemicized at length with those who tried to invalidate his interpretation by pointing out that other, less righteous conquerors, like the Qarmatians or the Byzantines, also had inherited the land.[5] In this context, ʿAbd al-Djabbār mentions that earlier Scriptures contain many references to Muhammad, as generations of converts have shown (he gives the name of only one Jewish convert to Islam, ʿAbdallāh b. Salām), and speaks of four Muslim authors who composed specific books (apparently lost) about these prophecies, among them Ibn Qutayba (see below).

In the *Sīra* of the prophet by Ibn-Isḥāq–Ibn-Hishām, a large section is devoted to how "The Arab Soothsayers (Kuhhān), Jewish Rabbis (Aḥbār), and Christian Monks foretell his coming." Here, following Qur'anic accusations, the Jews especially are blamed for withholding intentionally from the Muslims detailed Biblical information about the coming of the Prophet. This section includes the famous New Testament verse (John 15:26) about the Para-

[3] See M. J. de Goeje, "Quotations from the Bible in the Qoran and the Tradition," in *Semitic Studies in Memory of A. Kohut*, ed. G. A. Kohut (Berlin 1897), pp. 179–85, and A. Baumstark, "ArabischeUebersetzungen eines Altsyrischen Evangelientextes und die Sure 21, 105 zitierte Psalmenuebersetzung," *Oriens Christianus*, 3d. series, 9 (1934): 165–88.

[4] See the commentaries to the verse, esp. Al-Zamakhsharī.

[5] See ʿAbd al-Djabbār, *Tathbīt Dalāʾil al-Nubuwwa*, ed. ʿAbd al-Karīm ʿUthmān, vol. 2 (Beirut 1966), pp. 252–53; G. Graf, *Geschichte der Christlichen Arabischen Literatur*, vol. 1 (Vatican City 1944), p. 43.

clete, apparently translated into Arabic from the Syriac (hence *Munaḥamnā*) and taken as alluding to Muhammad.[6]

Ḥadīth literature contains more detailed descriptions of Muhammad, based on alleged Biblical verses (*fī-l-Tawrāt*). Some parts, in fact, faintly echo Isaiah (for example, 42:2–3), perhaps in a Christological interpretation (cf. also below), but most have no scriptural basis. The following is a recurrent example:[7]

> It is told on the authority of ʿAmr b. al-ʿĀṣ that the Prophet is described in the Bible exactly in the same way as he is in Sūra 48:8ff. [see Chapter Two] and adding: "and his name will be Al-Mutawwakil—the one who trusts God—he will be neither harsh nor coarse nor will he raise his voice in the market streets. He will return good for evil and be forgiving. . . ."

The rest of the passage varies in different Ḥadīth sayings and in later biographical and hagiographical writings, but all are alleged quotations from the *Tawrāt*.

This combination of purported Biblical quotations and almost literal translations of Biblical verses is a striking feature of medieval Arabic literature that should always be kept in mind.[8] As has been mentioned, sometimes parts of

[6] See R. Sellheim, "Prophet, Caliph und Geschichte: Die Muhammed—Biographie des Ibn Isḥāq," *Oriens* 18–19 (1965–66): 57; and cf. J. Wansbrough, *Quranic Studies*, pp. 65ff.; S. H. Griffith, "The Gospel in Arabic: An Inquiry into Its Appearance in the First ʿAbbasid Century," *Oriens Christianus* 69 (1985): 137ff. See also above, Chapter Two, note 8.

[7] See, e.g., Al-Bukhārī, *Al-Djāmiʿ al-Ṣaḥīḥ*, ed. L. Krehl, vol. 2 (Leiden 1864), bk. 34 (Kitāb al-Buyūʿ), no. 50; bk. 65 (Tafsīr), Sūra 48, Bāb 3; Ibn Ḥanbal, *Musnad* (Beirut, n.d.), 2: 174; Al-Dārimī, *Sunan* (Medina 1966), 1:2.

[8] Even exact, almost literal, translations of Biblical verses into Arabic may contain specific additions (or changes) by Muslim authors, especially regarding the root Ḥmd, which is taken to allude to the Prophet's name and to Muslim forms of prayer. See G. Graf, *Geschichte*, 1: 45–46, 50, etc.; and cf. ʿAli b. Rabban, *Kitāb al-Dīn wa-l-Dawla*, ed. A. Mingana (Manchester 1923), and trans. A. Mingana (*The Book of Religion and Empire by ʿAlī Ṭabarī*) (Manchester 1922), esp. chs. 18, 19, and 26. Cf. note 99 below. See also R. G. Khoury, "Quelques réflexions sur les citations de

these quotations are based on Midrashic and later Jewish sources, taken by Muslims to be an integral part of Scripture itself.

Early Arabic literature developed a specific literary genre called *Dalā'il* or *A'lām al-Nubuwwa* ("Proofs" or "Signs of Prophethood"). The authors of books in this genre tried to show that Muhammad's unique personality, the miracles he performed, and the worldly success of his message prove the authenticity of his prophethood. Most of these books include also a section dealing with Biblical (Old and New Testament) verses foretelling the coming of Muhammad and rise of Islam. Books of this genre have been preserved only from the ninth century on, yet it seems plausible that some books written much earlier may have been lost. It has been suggested that with the rise of Islam the "traits that distinguish a true prophet from a false one . . . became a key issue" and that it must have been "Islam which had to come with 'proofs of prophecy' in response to Christian and Jewish incredulity."[9]

Three of the earliest existing, or partly existing, books of this kind were composed in the ninth century: *Ḥudjadj al-Nubuwwa* (Decisive Arguments for Prophethood), by Al-Djāḥiz (d. 869);[10] *Dalā'il al-Nubuwwa* (Proofs for Prophethood), by Ibn Qutayba (d. 889); and *Kitāb al-Dīn wa-*

la Bible dans les premieres générations islamiques," *BEO* 29 (1977): 269ff., and Griffith, "The Gospel in Arabic," pp. 138ff.

[9] See S. Stroumsa, "The Signs of Prophecy: The Emergence of an Early Development of a Theme in Arabic Theological Literature," *HTR* 78 (1985): pp. 101–14, esp. p. 105; cf. D. Sahas, *John of Damascus on Islam* (Leiden 1972), pp. 80–81, where he speaks of direct "Christian provocation" in this context. All the books we know of that were written about this topic, however, stem from the ninth century. See M. J. Kister, "The Sīrah Literature," in *Arabic Literature to the End of the Umayyad Period*, ed. A. F. Beeston, T. M. Johnstone, R. B. Serjeant, and G. R. Smith (Cambridge 1983), p. 355.

[10] Printed in *Rasā'il al-Djāḥiẓ*, ed. Ḥasan al-Ṣandūbī (Cairo 1933). Cf. Stroumsa, "Signs of Prophecy," pp. 106ff. This book contains no Biblical verses, although Al-Djāḥiẓ quoted the Bible in his other writings, for example in his *Al-Radd 'alā-l-Naṣārā*, in *Three Essays of Al-Jahiz*, ed. J. Finkel (Cairo 1926).

l-Dawla (*Book of Religion and Empire*), by ʿAlī b. Rabban (written about 855).[11] The authenticity of the latter two books, which contain many Biblical verses typologically explained, has been contested. Ibn Qutayba's book has been contested because it has been lost, except for lengthy quotations several hundred years later by Ibn al-Djawzī (d. 1201) in his *Al-Wafā bi-Aḥwāl al-Muṣṭafā*.[12] Yet, as we have seen above, ʿAbd al-Djabbār also mentioned Ibn Qutayba in this context almost two hundred years earlier, so the book must have existed. As for Ibn Qutayba's Biblical references therein, we know from his other existing writings that he had some knowledge of the Bible, and he quotes what seems to be an early Bible translation into Arabic.[13] ʿAlī b. Rabban's book raised even more doubts and was condemned by M. Bouyges as a modern literary forgery, but nevertheless it has been accepted as authentic by most scholars.[14] The author, a Christian convert to Islam,

[11] ʿAlī b. Rabban, *Kitāb al-Dīn* ed. A. Mingana and trans. A. Mingana (as *Book of Religion and Empire*).

[12] Ibn al-Djawzī, *Al-Wafā bi-Aḥwāl al-Muṣṭafā*, ed. Muṣṭafā ʿAbd-al-Waḥīd, 2 vols. (Cairo 1966). Ibn Qutayba is quoted mainly in the fourth chapter dealing with Biblical references to Muhammad and his community (see 1: 62–72 and index). C. Brockelmann was the first to draw attention to Ibn Qutayba's book and to Ibn al-Djawzī's quotation from it. See his "Ibn Ğauzī's Kitāb al-Wafā bi-Faḍā'il al-Muṣṭafā," in *Beitraege zur Assyriologie und Semitischer Sprachkunde* 3 (1898): 1–59, and cf. his "Muhammedanische Weissagungen im Alten Testament," *ZAW* 15 (1895): 135–42. Ibn Qutayba is quoted apparently also by Ibn Ḥazm (d. 1064) in his *Al-Uṣūl wa-l-Furūʿ* (Cairo 1978), 1: 193, and later by Ibn Taymiyya (d. 1328) in his *Al-Djawāb al-Ṣaḥīḥ li-man baddala Dīn al-Masīḥ* (Cairo 1905), 3: 282. Cf. also I. Goldziher, "Ueber Bibelzitate in Muhammedanischen Schriften," *ZAW* 13 (1893): 315–24, esp. pp. 318ff. (reprinted in *Gesammelte Schriften*, ed. J. Desomogyi [Hildesheim 1967], 3: 312ff.).

[13] See G. Vajda, "Judaeo-Arabica 1, Observations sur quelques citations bibliques chez Ibn Qotayba," *REJ* 99 (1935): 68–80, and G. Lecomte, "Les Citations de l'Ancien et du Nouveau Testament dans l'oeuvre d'Ibn Qutayba," *Arabica* 5 (1958): 34–46 (Lecomte did not mention Brockelman at all, and did not use Vajda's article). Cf. Graf, *Geschichte*, 1: 48ff.

[14] See the discussion and bibliography in E. Fritsch, *Islam und Christenthum im Mittelalter* (Breslau 1930), pp. 6–12; D. S. Margoliouth, "On the *Book of Religion and Empire* by ʿAlī b. Rabban al-Ṭabarī," *Proceedings*

was certainly instrumental in introducing Biblical typology to Islam. He quotes a long list of Biblical verses in Arabic, apparently translated from the Syriac (and following the Nestorian or East Syrian version), a small part of which later became the stock list of Biblical verses among Muslim authors.

From the tenth century on, Muslim authors of other disciplines, such as historiography, geography, Qur'an commentaries, and *Milal wa-Niḥal* books,[15] join the authors of *Dalā'il* literature in quoting and expounding Biblical verses as referring to the Prophet Muhammad, the rise and conquests of Islam, Mecca, the Muslim prayer, pilgrimage, etc. This Muslim hermeneutic approach to the Bible was known to Jews[16] as well as to Christians even in Europe.[17] There it was easily understood (though rejected), since the Muslims used not only some Christian typological methods but very often also the same Biblical verses. Sometimes the Christological meaning of a verse was simply transferred from Jesus to Muhammad. In other cases, the verse was taken to allude to both Jesus and Muhammad.[18]

The Biblical material is quoted in various translations, sometimes accompanied by corrupted phonetic transcrip-

---

of the British Academy 16 (1930): 165–82; F. Taeschner, "Die Alttestamentlischen Bibelzitate vor allem aus dem Pentateuch im Al-Ṭabarī's *Kitāb ad-Dīn wad-Dawla*, und ihre Bedeutung fuer die Frage nach der Echtheit dieser Schrift," *Oriens Christianus*, 3d ser., 9 (1934): 23–39; cf. Graf, *Geschichte*, 1: 44ff., and Mingana's introduction to his translation of 'Alī b. Rabban's *Kitāb al-Dīn wa-l-Dawla* (Book of Religion and Empire), and his remarks, e.g., on pp. 88, 92, 98, 99, etc.

[15] Books on other religions and Muslim sects constituted an important part of Muslim medieval religious literature.

[16] See Al-Qirqisānī, *Kitāb al-Anwār wa-l-Marāqib* (*Code of Karaite Law*), ed. L. Nemoy, pt. 3 (New York 1941), p. 296 (Muslims believe that Muhammad is mentioned in the Bible through hints and allusions).

[17] See for example, B. Z. Kedar, *Crusade and Mission, European Attitudes toward the Muslim* (Princeton 1984), p. 85.

[18] In Muslim polemics, the Jewish rejections of Jesus and Muhammad are often lumped together. See, for example, Samau'al al-Maghribī, *Ifḥām al-Yahūd* (Silencing the Jews), ed. and trans. M. Perlmann, *PAAJR* 32 (1964): text pp. 24–27, trans. pp. 42–44.

tions of the Hebrew original.[19] Although most Muslim authors copy from each other, and use the same Biblical verses, it is difficult to point to one common source of translation or interpretation. Some Muslim authors quote different (oral?) translations of the same verse (see Chapter Five) and mention the Hebrew original or Syriac (for example, ʿAlī b. Rabban), or the story of the translation of the Septuagint and even a Coptic translation of the Bible.[20] Others mention oral (imaginary?) discussions with Jews or Christians about the correct interpretation of a Biblical verse (see below), and in some cases may even have preserved lost authentic Jewish translations and interpretations in their reports of these discussions.

There are great differences between the authors. Some quote only a few Biblical verses, others adduce lengthy lists of up to fifty verses with different possible interpretations of the same verse.[21] Jewish and Christian converts to Islam play an important role in this literature, but they often seem to be less reliable than other authors, not only because imaginary Biblical verses are quoted on their authority in early Islamic literature (Kaʿb al-Aḥbār, Wahb b. Munabbih, and others; see Chapter Two), but also because

[19] Transcriptions of Biblical verses in Hebrew in Arabic letters can be found in most of the authors quoted below and many others, such as Al-Bīrūnī, Ibn Ẓafar, Al-Muṭahhar al-Maqdisī, Pseudo-Ghazzālī, Samau'al al-Maghribī, Al-Qarāfī, Ibn Qayyim al-Djawziyya, Ibn Khaldūn, and Abū-l-Fidā. Cf. P. Kraus, "Hebraeische und Syrische Zitate in Ismāʿīlītischen Schriften," *Der Islam* 19 (1931): 243–63, and Baumstark's "Zu den Schriften al-Kirmānī's," *Der Islam* 20 (1932): 308–13.

[20] See Pseudo-Ghazzālī, *Al-Radd al-Djamīl li-Ilāhiyyat ʿĪsā bi-Ṣarīḥ al-Indjīl*, ed. and trans. R. Chidiac (Paris 1939), p. 47, and H. Lazarus-Yafeh, *Studies in Al-Ghazzālī* (Jerusalem 1975), pp. 470ff. On Arabic Bible translations made from Coptic, cf. also below, Chapter Five. On the Septuagint, see Chapter Six, p. 137.

[21] Compare, for example, Abū Nuʿaym al-Iṣfahānī, *Kitāb Dalā'il al-Nubuwwa*, 2d ed. (Haiderabad 1950), Al-Faṣl al-Khāmis, pp. 32ff., with the long lists of Muḥammad ibn Ẓafar al-Makkī al-Ṣiqillī (Ibn Ẓafar), *Khayr al-Bishar bi-Khayr al-Bashar* (Cairo 1863), Al-Ṣinf al-Awwal, pp. 4ff., or with Al-Qarāfī, *Al-Adjwiba al-Fākhira ʿan al-As'ila al-Fādjira* ed. Bakr Zakī ʿAwād (Cairo 1987), Al-Bāb al-Rābiʿ.

some later converts do not hesitate intentionally to misquote authentic Biblical verses or to invent nonexistent interpretations of others.[22] In any case, the most innovative typological interpretations of Biblical material do not stem from convert authors, although very few Muslims had a truly extensive knowledge or deep understanding of the whole Bible. The books most frequently quoted in a typological context are Genesis, Deutero-Isaiah (who is explicitly said to have prophesied the coming of both Jesus and Muhammad),[23] and the Psalms; but the number of verses used is limited and the same verses are repeated over and over again. In the remainder of this chapter, I will present examples of Muslim Bible exegesis in five areas: the desert motif and comfort verses; the conquering army; Muslim prayer and pilgrimage; messianic verses; and epithets and descriptions of Muhammad.

The Desert Motif and Comfort Verses in Deutero-Isaiah

Biblical references to the desert[24] were usually taken by Muslim exegetes to refer to Al-Ḥidjāz and Mecca, especially when accompanied by "Arab" names such as Hagar and Ishmael in Genesis, or Midyan, Kedar, Nevajoth, and

[22] Cf. below and see, for example, Sa'īd b. Ḥasan, *Masālik al-Naẓar*, ed. and trans. S. A. Weston, *JAOS* 24 (1904): esp. text pp. 326–29, trans. pp. 362–65. Cf. also the British Library, ms. Add. 9660 of 'Abd al-Ḥaqq al-Islāmī, described by M. Perlmann in " 'Abd al-Hakk al-Islāmī, A Jewish Convert," *JQR* 31 (1940–41): 171–91.

[23] See, for example, Al-Ṭabarī, *Ta'rīkh al-Rusul wa-l-Mulūk (Annales)*, ed. M. J. de Goeje and I. J. Barth, (1st ser., repr. Leiden 1964), 2: 638.

[24] See *Theologisches Woerterbuch zum A.T.*, ed. G. J. Botterweck, H. Ringgren, and H. J. Fabry, vol. 4 (1983), s.v. "Midbar" (S. Talmon). The Muslim approach to the desert is very pragmatic and contains no parallel to the Jewish idealization of it in Biblical prophecies or to the negative Christian attitudes. Cf. Sarah Kamin's comparison between Rashi and Origines on the Song of Songs, in *Annual of Bible and Ancient Near East Studies* (in Hebrew) 7–8 (1983–84): 238.

others in Deutero-Isaiah.[25] In this way, many prophetic comfort verses could easily be viewed as references to the coming of Muhammad and the rise of Islam. ʿAlī b. Rabban was probably the first to introduce this approach to Islam, following Christological interpretations. Thus, for example, he explains Isa. 40:3–5:

> Do you know—may God guide you—a nation which God has called from the desert and wilderness and to which He has made the rough places straight, the sterile lands fertile and the dry land rich with pasture; to which he has made the valleys overflow with water for their thirsty ones and to which he has subjugated the giants and the kings whom He has represented by the above hills and mountains—except this Arab nation for which the Tigris became like a beaten track?[26]

In the same vein he explains other verses, such as Isa. 42:11–13:

> To whom does the wilderness belong, o my cousins, except to His nation? And who is Kedar, except the descendants of Ishmael, peace be with him, who inhabit caves and give *Ḥamd* [praise] to the Lord and declare his praises at daybreak and at midday? And who is he, who rebuked, became mighty and killed his enemies except Muhammad, may God bless him and save him, and his nation? As to the meaning of David's saying: "The Lord shall come forth," we have demonstrated above that the name "Lord" refers to men of high standing and noble.[27]

[25] In Midrashic and medieval Jewish literature, these names were taken to designate Arabs and Muslims. Cf. M. Steinschneider, *Polemische und Apologetische Literatur in Arabischer Sprache* (Leipzig 1877), pp. 254ff.; but it is unlikely that these genealogical connections are of any historical value. See I. Eph'al, " 'Ishmael' and the 'Arab(s)': A Transformation of Ethnological Terms," *Journal of Near Eastern Studies* 35 (1976): 225–35.

[26] ʿAlī b. Rabban, *Kitāb al-Dīn* (ed. A. Mingana), p. 85 (enumerated as chap. 19), and Mingana's trans., pp. 99–100, which is quoted here and in the following examples.

[27] ʿAlī b. Rabban, *Kitāb al-Dīn*, Arabic text p. 79, trans. p. 92. The text is quoted as "Psalm 152, attributed to Isaiah"; cf. Mingana's note on trans. p. 92. The words *bi-Ḥamd al-Rabb* are the translation of "give glory to the

Al-Djāḥiẓ quotes the same verses from Isaiah 42,[28] whereas Al-Māwardī (d. 1058) in his *A'lām al-Nubuwwa* quotes both examples from Isaiah (as chapters 19 and 20—the last one, according to him, mentioned also by David in his Psalm 153) and adds: "And the land of Kedar is the land of the Arabs because they are the children of the Arabs, and the meadows (refer to) the palms and trees and springs in the surroundings of Mecca."[29]

Some Muslim commentators combine a literal understanding of the desert with a more symbolic one, following Isaiah himself. Thus the message of Islam is depicted sometimes as water breaking forth in the desert and causing it to blossom (in this context Isa. 35:1ff. is often quoted) or as light shining in the darkness. Ibn Ẓafar (d. 1169), for example, quotes at length, though somewhat inaccurately, Isa. 60:1–7 ("Arise and shine for thy light is come. . .") and adds:

> These verses are addressed to the noble city of Mecca, to which good tidings of the [future] pilgrimage of Muhammad's community [to it—see below] are brought. The darkness which engulfed the earth before [Muhammad] is the darkness of polytheism (*Shirk*) and the one who dispelled it with the Book of God is Muhammad, peace be upon him. And Kedar is the father of the Arabs.[30]

Lord." The last verse quoted (v. 13) is understood by 'Alī b. Rabban as referring to Muhammad, not to God.

[28] See Al-Djāḥiẓ, *Al-Radd*, p. 28.

[29] Al-Māwardī, *A'lām al-Nubuwwa* (Cairo 1935), pp. 103–4.

[30] Ibn Ẓafar, *Khayr al-Bishar*, p. 16. See also M. Schreiner, "Zur Geschichte der Polemik zwischen Juden und Muhammedanern," *ZDMG* 42 (1888): 625ff., esp. p. 627 (reprinted in *Gesammelte Schriften*, ed. M. Perlmann [Hildesheim 1988] p. 111). Some of these verses are quoted also by other Muslim authors as referring to Mecca. See, for example, Ibn Qutayba-Ibn al-Djawzī, *Al-Wafā bi-Faḍā'il al-Muṣṭafā* (henceforth cited as Ibn Qutayba/Ibn al-Djawzī), pp. 70–71; Fakhr al-Dīn al-Rāzī, *Mafātīḥ al-Ghayb* (Cairo, n.d.), 1: 321; Al-Qarāfī, *Al-Adjwiba al-Fākhira*, Bishāra 26; Ibn Taymiyya, *Al-Djawāb al-Ṣaḥīḥ*, 3: 307; Ibn Qayyim al-Djawziyya, *Hidāyat al-Ḥayārā fi-l-Radd 'alā-l-Yahūd wa-l-Naṣārā* (Beirut, n.d.), p. 105 and others. Perhaps the addition of the vocative *Yā dār al-Salām* ("Oh,

Other comfort verses are explained more allegorically. The best example is Isa. 54:1ff., where the barren and desolate woman is taken to be Mecca, because no prophet ever appeared there before Muhammad, whereas Jerusalem always had many children, that is, prophets. Ibn Qutayba quotes the end of the first verse as saying, "because your people will be more than Mine," and explains:

> His people are the inhabitants of Jerusalem [Bayt al-Maqdis] from among the Banū Isrā'īl and He means that the people of Mecca—with all those who will come there on pilgrimage [Ḥadjdj and 'Umra; see below]—will be more [in number] than the people of Jerusalem. [God] compared Mecca to a barren woman with no children because before the Prophet there was only Ismā'īl there and no book was revealed there.[31] He certainly could not have meant Jerusalem to be barren, because a home of prophets and a place of divine revelation cannot be likened to a barren woman.[32]

Ibn Ẓafar follows the same translation and explication, but explains also that Mecca is considered barren because it is situated in "an uncultivated valley" (Sūra 14:37), then adds:

> And the verse "your people will be more than Mine"—if it escaped falsification and wrong expression, because [the preposition] *min* is superfluous—should be read: "Your people will be the most of Mine"—meaning that the Muslims will be the most God-fearing people [literally, keeping His commandments] and those who assert most deeply His unity.[33]

Al-Qarāfī (d. 1285) follows the same translation and explanations and adds that in fact, the Muslims outnumber any

Jerusalem") in Saadia's translation of Isa. 60:1 (following the Targum) was meant also to refute such Muslim interpretations.

[31] Interestingly, Abraham and his "Scroll" (see, for example, Sūra 87:19) are never mentioned in this context. See also below.

[32] See Ibn Qutayba/Ibn al-Djawzī, pp. 69–70 (starting with a printing error—"*Sirī*" [Surrī?], which does not appear in later quotations of the same verse; see below).

[33] Ibn Ẓafar, *Khayr al-Bishar*, p. 20.

other truly believing community, because the Christians are in clear error and the number of Jews who believe in the *Tawrāt* is exceedingly small.[34]

In the same way, the parable of the vineyard in Ezek. 19:10–14 is understood to refer to Mecca, especially verse 13 ("a plant planted in the wilderness, a neglected, dry and thirsty land").[35] ʿAlī b. Rabban explains:

> He who has questioned the preceding prophecy and quibbled over it, will be silenced and convinced by this one. God—may His name be blessed—has told us that He will extirpate the root of the Jews, destroy the mass of them, and annihilate their might and their beauty, which He has compared with the vine, together with its rods and branches. Then He added an illuminating and clear saying, when He—may He be blessed and exalted—declared that He will plant a new plant in the wilderness, and in the neglected and dry land, the branches of which shall bring forth a fire which will devour the branches of the first vine in order that no strong rod and no branch should be found in it to rise up to power and authority. The meaning of 'rod' and 'branch' is power. And the power of the Jews and their might have disappeared from the surface of the earth, and another strong rod, yea, many other strong rods and branches rose up to a mighty power and a firm and civilized administration. In that the above prophecy has been realized.

He then adds:

> And Ezekiel—peace be with him—said at the end of his book that God showed him a house, the plan and the bounds of which an angel was directing. He described its pillars, its halls, its court-yards, and its doors; and the angel told him to remember all these and to ponder over them. But since the description

[34] Al-Qarāfī, *Al-Adjwiba al-Fākhira*, Bishāra 34. Cf. also Ibn Qayyim al-Djawziyya, *Hidāyat al-Ḥayārā*, pp. 105–6.

[35] Muslims exegetes apparently were not acquainted with the well-known vineyard parable in Isa. 5. They did use New Testament vineyard parables, however. See some (modern) examples in H. Stieglecker, *Die Glaubenslehren des Islam* (Paderborn 1962), pp. 551ff. On the problematics of this verse in Ezekiel, cf. *The Anchor Bible*, vol. 22, M. Greenberg, *Ezekiel, 1–20* (New York 1983), pp. 353–55, 358–59.

> of this house was too long, I noticed that people either deliberately or carelessly have believed it to be unintelligible and ambiguous; therefore I did not mention it; but on the evidence of numerous and obvious prophecies and testimonies, it is clear that the description of the house that God planned and sketched through the prophet Ezekiel—peace be with him—applies to Maccah, because it contains features which do not fit the temple of Jerusalem, built after the return from the deportation to Babylon. If somebody rejects this, let him put the description in harmony with the temple built in Jerusalem in order that we may believe him; if he fails, let him then believe what we have told him and declared to him.[36]

Ibn Qutayba gives a shorter but very similar translation of Ezek. 19:13, whereas Al-Māwardī adds: "The one who will appear from the desert—in him the Jews will find death."[37] Ibn Ẓafar also explains: "There is no doubt that the neglected and thirsty desert is the land of the Arabs and the plant which God planted there is Muhammad, peace be upon him, and He thus disgraced the Jews through him."[38]

Muslim authors also took the name Zion (Ṣahyūn) as referring to Mecca (see also below), but it is not clear whether they were aware that Jewish commentators derived this name from the root *Ziyya*, meaning "desert."[39]

The Conquering Army

Prophetic descriptions of the mighty army (such as in Isaiah or Jeremiah) upon which God will call to punish Israel

[36] See 'Alī b. Rabban, *Kitāb al-Dīn* text pp. 109–10, trans. pp. 128–29. Ezekiel's vision of the future Temple (and law) was indeed considered to be of an eschatological nature; according to Origines, the Rabbis forbade the study of the relevant chapters (as they did with other esoteric chapters). See G. Shalom, *Jewish Gnosticism, Merkabah Mysticism and Talmudic Tradition* (New York 1960), p. 38.

[37] See Ibn Qutayba/Ibn al-Djawzī, p. 71, and Al-Māwardī, *A'lām al-Nubuwwa*, p. 105.

[38] Ibn Ẓafar, *Khayr al-Bishar*, p. 18; cf. Ibn Qayyim al-Djawziyya, *Hidāyat al-Ḥayāra*, p. 122.

[39] See, for example, Rashi to Isa. 35:1, and cf. below, note 62.

are often interpreted by Muslim commentators to allude to the Muslim army that conquered the world.

ʿAlī b. Rabban, for example, quotes Isa. 5:26–30 (he mentions the "third Faṣl" of Isaiah) and adds:

> This is the saying of the Most High God. And the children of Ishmael, peace be with him, the nation of the Prophet—may God save and bless him—are those for whom God hissed. And they came from their country with haste, without weariness and sloth; their arrows were sharp and their bows bent; the hooves of their horses were like rock and flint and their roaring was like the roaring of lions; it is they who had prey from east and west and no one could escape them. The Giants became like lambs with them and dust was stirred by their onslaught, while paths and defiles were too narrow for them.[40]

In the same way, Jer. 5:15–16 is quoted by Abū-l-Faḍl al-Saʿūdī, who composed in 1535 a summary or selection of excerpts (*Muntakhab*) from Ṣāliḥ al-Gaʿfarī's *Takhdjīl man ḥarrafa-l-Indjīl (The Putting to Shame of Those Who Falsified the Gospel)*, written around 1200.[41] Al-Saʿūdī says that in these verses, Jeremiah points to the Arab victory over Jews, Christian and others, because God empowered the Arab monotheists over those who denied God, worshipped the calf and idols, and added other gods to God.

Psalm 149 is a favorite of Muslim exegetes in this context. ʿAlī b. Rabban and Ibn Qutayba give two almost exact but very different translations of most verses of this Psalm. Ibn Qutayba then adds: "Which nation except the Arabs has two-edged swords (*dhawāt shufratayn*) and who except God will punish those who do not worship Him? And who of the prophets is the messenger with the sword except our Prophet, peace be upon him?" ʿAlī b. Rabban explains in the same vein:

[40] See ʿAlī b. Rabban, *Kitāb al-Dīn*, text p. 80, trans. p. 94.

[41] See E. Fritsch, *Islam und Christenthum*, p. 17, and F. J. van den Ham, ed., *Disputatio pro religione Muhammedanorum adversus Christianos*, 2 vols. (Leiden 1877, 1890). See the Cairo print (1322 Hg.) of Al-Saʿūdī's *Muntakhab*, p. 145 (Bushrā 25).

> Do you not see . . . that these peculiarities refer exclusively to the Prophet . . . and to his nation? It is he who has the two-edged sword with him, it is he who with his nation executed vengeance upon the giants of Persia and the tyrants of the Greek and others, and it is he whose followers have bound the kings with chains and conducted their nobles and their children in chains and fetters and who sing to God in their beds and glorify Him morning and evening and continually in saying: God is supremely great (*Takbīr*) and much praise (*Ḥamd*) be to God.[42]

Al-Māwardī and Ibn Ẓafar follow Ibn Qutayba's translation and explanation,[43] and Ibn Ẓafar adds:

> These, may God strengthen you, are extremely convincing and important verses, among those predicting the coming of Muhammad, peace be upon him, which are to be found in the holy Scriptures, and *Ahl al-Kitāb* cannot discard them. We have quoted them according to translations which they themselves use and write in their books and therefore they cannot refute us by claiming that they have been falsified. . . .[44]

Al-Qarāfī and later authors also quote this Psalm, apparently in the same translation, and take it to refer to the Arabs, their conquests, and their worship (*bi-l-Adhānāt*; see below).[45] Al-Qarāfī stresses that the text mentions "ven-

[42] See verses 4–9 in 'Alī b. Rabban, *Kitāb al-Dīn*, text p. 78, trans. p. 91, and verses 1–9 in Ibn Qutayba/Ibn al-Djawzī, p. 65. Cf. C. Peters, "Psalm 149 in Zitaten islamischer Autoren" (which could be supplemented by additional examples), *Biblica* 21 (1940): 138–51.

[43] See Al-Māwardī, *A'lām al-Nubuwwa*, p. 108 and Ibn Ẓafar, *Khayr al-Bishar*, pp. 20–21.

[44] These remarks are very interesting indeed, especially as no similarity can be found between Saadia's translation of this Psalm and the one used by Ibn Qutayba and Ibn Ẓafar. In addition, according to Ibn Ẓafar here, the Jews themselves seem to have sometimes used the charge of falsification of their Scriptures to defend themselves against Muslim typological exegesis.

[45] See Al-Qarāfī, *Al-Adjwiba al-Fākhira*, Bishāra 19, and Ibn Taymiyya, *Al-Djawāb al-Ṣaḥīḥ*, 3: 296.

geance upon the nations," not upon one nation only, and Moses fought only the inhabitants of one nation, Al-Shām.

Ibn Qayyim al-Djawziyya adduces Qur'anic verses and Ḥadīth sayings in order to prove that only Muslims fit the description of this Psalm. Only they praise God incessantly, call people to prayer by human voice five times a day, continuously recite the *Takbīr* in everyday life as well as during the Ḥadjdj. Only the Muslims "sing aloud His praise upon their beds" because "they remember Allah standing, sitting, and reclining" (Sūra 3:191), and only they use the two-edged swords, which are therefore called "Arab swords." He adds that the Christians denounce those who fight the unbelievers with the sword like the Muslims do, but they should remember that Moses, Joshua, David, Solomon, and other prophets fought the unbelievers in the same way.[46]

A unique allegorical interpretation connects Gen. 15:9–10 (combined with the Qur'anic version of this covenant in Sūra 2:260) with the worldwide Muslim conquests. The Jewish convert Sa'īd b. Ḥasan says in his *Masālik al-Naẓar*, written in 1320, that "the wise men among the Children of Israel" explain that in these verses from the "Scrolls of Abraham" (*Ṣuḥuf Ibrāhīm*), the divided beasts represent the nations that preceded Abraham and perished. But the birds, which were not divided, allude to Ismā'īl and his offspring, who will never perish.[47] This notion may be based

[46] See Ibn Qayyim al-Djawziyya, *Hidāyat al-Ḥayārā*, pp. 101–2. This was a recurring theme in Christian-Muslim polemics from the start. Cf. *The Apology of Al-Kindī* (London 1911), pp. 179–82. (According to Al-Kindī, Christian compassion abrogated the earlier Old Testament divine command to fight.)

[47] See Sa'īd b. Ḥasan, *Masālik al-Naẓar*, text pp. 345–46, trans. pp. 374–75. Cf. the rather late Midrashic sources, which interpret the turtledove in Gen. 15:11 to refer to the Muslims, or Gentiles in general, and the vulture to symbolize the King-Messiah (see, for example, *Pirkei de-Rabbi Eliezer*, ch. 28, and esp. Margaliot's edition of Yemenite mss. of *Midrash Hagadol* to Genesis). See also Saadia's commentary to this verse (in M. Zucker's edition, *Sa'adya's Commentary on Genesis*, The Jewish Theological Seminary of America [New York 1984], p. 359), and cf. M. Soko-

on some (lost?) Jewish Midrashic material, although, as has been mentioned, Saʿīd is hardly a reliable source and often intentionally misquotes Biblical verses and their interpretations. Yet this explanation may also be based on earlier Muslim(?) interpretation of Isa. 46:11, where the "sweeping bird from the east," translated into Arabic as the "bird from the remote desert," is taken to symbolize the Prophet Muhammad and the quick spread of his message and kingdom.[48]

Sometimes even a specific victory or battle of the Prophet Muhammad is thought to have been foretold in the Bible. For example, the famous battle of Badr is alluded to, according to Ibn Qutayba, by Isaiah in a verse that seems to be a combination of prophetic phrases with Muslim additions: "And they will thresh the nations as [on] a threshing floor [see Isa. 41:15] and misfortune will befall the Arab unbelievers until they flee."[49] According to Ibn Taymiyya and Ibn Qayyim al-Djawziyya, the later battle of Ḥunayn and other victories of the Prophet are also alluded to in this and the following verses.[50]

Finally, mention must be made of Gen. 16:12 ("And he will be a wild man, his hand will be against every man . . ."), which, like other blessings to Ishmael, is taken by Muslim authors to refer also to Muhammad and the early

lov, "The Attitude of Karaite Commentators to Islam" (in Hebrew), *Shalem* 3 (1981): 311 n. 11. Some late commentaries to *Bereshit Rabba* 88, 5 also take the bird(s) that ate from the baskets of Pharaoh's chief baker (Gen. 40:17) to allude to the Messiah. (Saʿīd b. Ḥasan often used Midrashic material in his polemical quotations of Biblical verses. Compare, for example, his quotation of Gen. 49:1–2 in *Masālik al-Naẓar*, text p. 326, trans. p. 362 with *Bereshit Rabba* 98, 3–4).

[48] Al-Qarāfī, *Al-Adjwiba al-Fākhira*, Bishāra 51. He adds that if the bird were to be understood literally the verse would have no meaning at all.

[49] See Ibn Qutayba/Ibn al-Djawzī, p. 72, and cf. Ibn Ẓafar, *Khayr al-Bishar*, p. 21. In the following, the victorious swords and bows of the (Arab) army are mentioned. Brockelman did not recognize the part from Isaiah (see above, note 12).

[50] See Ibn Taymiyya, *Al-Djawāb al-Ṣaḥīḥ*, 4:5, and Ibn Qayyim al-Djawziyya, *Hidāyat al-Ḥayārā*, p. 120.

conquests of Islam.[51] Ibn Qayyim al-Djawziyya even adds that the Jews agree to this interpretation[52] but deny any Biblical reference to Muhammad's prophetic message. The end of the verse is usually translated into Arabic in the following way: "And every [nation] will stretch out their hands in obedience [to Ishmael, not against him]." The Hebrew term *pere' adam* ("as a wild ass") in this verse is translated as either *waḥsh* or *'īr*, which was later (already with Al-Māwardī) corrupted or changed by the copyist into *'ayn* ("the best of").[53]

Muslim Prayer and Pilgrimage

As we have seen, Muslim exegetes claim that several Biblical verses contain references to Muslim ways of worship. Verbs of calling, praying, singing, or praising God and proclamations of His uniqueness are usually taken to be equivalents of the Muslim terminology of prayer, such as *Tasbīḥ*, *Tahlīl*, *Takbīr*, *Adhān*, *Ḥamd*, and so on. This is the case

[51] See, for example, Ibn Qutayba/Ibn al-Djawzī, pp. 61–62; 'Alī b. Rabban, *Kitāb al-Dīn*, text pp. 67–72, trans. pp. 78–79, 83ff.; Ibn Ẓafar, *Khayr al-Bishar*, p. 5 (quoting different translations of the verse, as he often does); Al-Māwardī, *A'lām al-Nubuwwa*, p. 102; Fakhr al-Dīn al-Rāzī, *Mafātīḥ al-Ghayb*, 1: 319; Al-Qarāfī, *Al-Adjwiba al-Fākhira*, Bishāra 5; Ibn Taymiyya, *Al-Djawāb al-Ṣaḥīḥ*, 3: 219; Ibn Qayyim al-Djawziyya, *Hidāyat al-Ḥayārā*, pp. 81, 100–101.

[52] See, in fact, Saadia's and Abraham Maimuni's commentaries on the verse, and compare Ibn Ezra's commentary on the verse. Karaite polemicists, however, used the verse to state that Ishmael as a dweller of the desert had no share in the land of Israel. See Sokolov, "The Attitude of Karaite Authors," p. 311.

[53] This is the explanation of J. Sadan. See Steinschneider, *Polemische und Apologetische Literatur*, p. 326 (300); and Schreiner, "Zur Geschichte der Polemik," pp. 627, 643–44 (neither Steinschneider nor Schreiner understood where " 'ayn" came from). Cf. F. Taeschner, "Die Alttestamentlischen Bibelzitate," pp. 29, 33. See also C. Peters, "Grundsaetzlische Bemerkungen zur Frage der Arabischen Bibeltexte" *RSO* 20 (1942–43): 129–43, esp. 134ff.; Margoliouth, "On the Book of Religion and Empire," pp. 177–78; and S. Baron, *A Social and Religious History of the Jews*, vol. 5 (New York 1957), p. 89 and vol. 6 (New York 1958), pp. 263ff.; N. Daniel, *Islam and the West* (Edinburgh 1966), p. 128.

also with the Hebrew root *zvḥ* in Isa. 42:11 (meaning "cry out aloud" or "shout"), following perhaps the Jewish traditional use of the verb in Aramaic.[54] The Jewish convert to Islam Saʿīd b. Ḥasan even quotes Isa. 42:12 in Hebrew in Arabic characters, from an imaginary *Scroll of Elijah* (*Ṣuḥuf Ilyās*), and translates: "They shall assert their belief in the unity of God from every high pulpit (*minbar*)."[55] Curiously, the Jewish poet Moses ibn Ezra (d. 1139) also takes Isa. 42:11 to refer to the Arabs, but in a different context. According to him, "let them shout from the top of the mountains" refers to the famous (linguistic) creativity of the Arabs.[56]

Indeed, Muslim pride in the Arab language is also mentioned in their Bible exegesis, mainly with regard to Zeph. 3:8–10. ʿAlī b. Rabban, for example, explains that "the chosen language is the perspicuous Arabic, which is neither unintelligible nor barbarous nor sophistical. It is this language which became common to the Gentiles who spoke it and were rejuvenated by the new dispensation that it brought to them." He then mentions Hebrew as the old language of prophets, as well as Syriac, Greek, and Persian which never spread so far as did Arabic.[57] Al-Māwardī explains the same verse thus: "It is well known that Arabic is the chosen language, because it engulfed the world and most of the languages shifted to it so that every [language] except it became rare."[58]

[54] See, for example, ʿAlī b. Rabban, *Kitāb al-Dīn*, text p. 78, trans. p. 92 (he quotes Psalm 152, "attributed to Isaiah"); Ibn-Qutayba/Ibn al-Djawzī, p. 68; Al-Māwardī, *Aʿlām al-Nubuwwa*, p. 104; Ibn Ẓafar, *Khayr al-Bishar*, p. 21; Al-Qarāfī, *Al-Adjwiba al-Fākhira*, p. 247; Ibn Taymiyya, *Al-Djawāb al-Ṣaḥīḥ*, 3: 303–9; Ibn Qayyim al-Djawziyya, *Hidāyat al-Ḥayārā*, p. 104; cf. J. Levy, *Woerterbuch ueber die Talmudim und Midrashim* (Berlin 1924), 3: 177.

[55] See Saʿīd b. Ḥasan, *Masālik al-Naẓar*, text p. 331, trans. p. 365.

[56] See Moshe ben Yaʿakov ibn Ezra (Moses ibn Ezra), *Kitāb al-Muḥāḍara wal-Mudhākara* (Liber discussionis et commemorationis), ed. A. S. Halkin (Jerusalem 1975), pp. 38–39.

[57] ʿAlī b. Rabban, *Kitāb al-Dīn*, text p. 105, trans. pp. 121–22.

[58] See Al-Māwardī, *Aʿlām al-Nubuwwa*, p. 106; cf. Wansbrough, *Quranic Studies*, pp. 80–85.

Other Biblical verses are taken to refer to the Ḥadjdj. Ibn Qutayba, for example, also takes Isa. 5:26ff. to refer to the Muslims. But unlike ʿAlī b. Rabban, he explains that the "lifted sign" refers to prophecy, and the whistle to the call to perform the pilgrimage to Mecca. He finds an exact correspondence between the Biblical and the Qur'anic verses (Sūra 22:27): "And proclaim unto mankind the pilgrimage. They will come unto thee on foot and on every lean camel." Other authors follow him.[59] Ibn Ẓafar omits the comparison between the Biblical and Qur'anic verses, but explains that the Biblical verse must necessarily refer to Mecca and the Ḥadjdj, because Jerusalem was already at that time a well-visited center of pilgrimage. Also, Isaiah often mentions Mecca and the desert and predicts the rise of Muhammad from Quraysh.[60]

Similarly, the "precious cornerstone" in Isa. 28:16 is understood as referring to the Black Stone at the Kaʿba.[61] Ibn Qutayba seems to be the first to interpret this verse in this manner, interpolating in his translation the Muslim explanation of the name Zion (*Ṣahyūn wa-hiya Bayt Allāh*)[62] and changing slightly the end of the verse into "a stone in a precious corner" (*zāwiyya mukarrama*). Few Muslim authors take up this subject, but Ibn Qayyim al-Djawziyya does so using an even clearer Islamic term in this context (*zāwiyyat Rukn*). He adds "that Zion according to Ahl-al-Kitāb is Mecca, and the Black Stone which kings and lesser

[59] See Ibn Qutayba/Ibn al-Djawzī, pp. 68–69. Cf. also Ibn Qayyim al-Djawzīyya, *Hidāyat al-Ḥayārā*, p. 107. (Ibn Qayyim al-Djawziyya often compares and connects Biblical and Qur'anic verses.) See also Ibn Taymiyya, *Al-Djawāb al-Ṣaḥīḥ*, 3: 303–9.

[60] See Ibn Ẓafar, *Khayr al-Bishar*, p. 21.

[61] See Ibn Qutayba/Ibn al-Djawzī, p. 69.

[62] See the same explanation of *Ṣahyūn* (Zion) in Ibn Ẓafar, *Khayr al-Bishar*, p. 19, in another context. The early Church already considered itself to be Zion, as opposed to "Sinai in Arabia" (Hagar); see Gal. 4:24–25. Jewish commentators sometimes connected the term with *Ziyya* ("desert"; see above, note 39) or understood it to refer to the Messiah or to the Jewish exile of Babylon. For an Ismāʿīlī interpretation of the term Zion (the *Imām*), cf. S. Stern, *Studies in Early Ismāʿīlism* (Jerusalem 1983), p. 93, following Kraus, "Hebraeische und Syrische Zitate."

people kiss was assigned exclusively to the Prophet Muhammad and his Umma."[63]

Isa. 54:11–12 is also quoted by Muslim exegetes in this context, apparently because of the precious stones mentioned therein. Ibn Qutayba and Ibn Ẓafar quote the verses and connect them with the "new name" (Isa. 62:2), which according to Ibn Qutayba will be *Al-Masdjid al-Ḥarām* instead of the Kaʿba.[64] Al-Qarāfī apparently quotes a different translation and connects the verses with the rebuilding of the Kaʿba by the ʿAbbasid Caliph Al-Mahdī and others.[65] He adds that it is impossible to think that this verse refers to Jerusalem, because Jerusalem never became a center of idol worship and corruption, as was Mecca during the *Djāhiliyya*, and it never became a peaceful shelter for pilgrims, as Mecca has become since the rise of Islam. But the same verses may have been taken by Muslim authors to refer to the Dome of the Rock in Jerusalem.[66]

Even eschatological prophetic visions of the beasts living peacefully together are taken by Muslim commentators to refer to the existing circumstances at the *Ḥaram* of Mecca. Ibn Qutayba, for example, thinks that Isa. 65:25 describes the actual behavior of animals inside the *Ḥaram* (where they do not hurt nor destroy), whereas upon leaving it they return to their natural habits of hunting and killing their prey.[67] Ibn Qayyim al-Djawziyya connects the same verse directly with the Qur'anic epithet for Mecca, "the safe land" (*al-balad al-amīn*, Sūra 45:3) and with other verses

[63] See Ibn Qayyim al-Djawziyya, *Hidāyat al-Ḥayārā*, pp. 106–7. Cf. Stieglecker, *Die Glaubenslehren des Islam*, p. 555.

[64] See Ibn Qutayba/Ibn al-Djawzī, p. 70, and Ibn Ẓafar, *Khayr al-Bishar*, p. 14 (with several variations, some due to copyists' or printing errors). Cf. Ibn Qayyim al-Djawziyya, *Hidāyat al-Ḥayārā*, p. 105.

[65] Al-Qarāfī, *Al-Adjwiba al-Fākhira*, Bishāra 27.

[66] See S. D. Goitein, "Jerusalem during the Arab Period," in his *Palestinian Jewry in Early Islamic and Crusader Times* (in Hebrew) (Jerusalem 1980), p. 13; cf., for example (only implicitly), Aḥmad b. Muḥammad ibn al-Faqīh, *Mukhtaṣar Kitāb al-Boldān*, ed. M. J. de Goeje (Leiden 1885), pp. 97, 99–101, or Ibn Kathīr, *Al-Bidāya wa-l-Nihāya* (Cairo 1932), 8: 280–81.

[67] See Ibn Qutayba/Ibn al-Djawzī, p. 70.

in the Qur'an, such as Sūra 28:57 and Sūra 106:5, where Mecca is mentioned as the "safe sanctuary" and its inhabitants as safe from fear.[68]

Very popular with Muslim exegetes in this context is most of Isa. 60, which is taken by many to refer to Mecca, the Ḥadjdj, the (pre-Islamic) keepers of the Ka'ba (*sadanat al-Ka'ba*), the gifts brought to the ever-opened gates of the *Ḥaram*, and so forth, mainly due to the mention of Kedar, Midyan, Nevajoth (copyists' or printing error in Arabic: Bena'oth), and other "Arab" names therein.[69] Ibn Qutayba adds in his translation of verse 11: "And you will be taken as *Qibla* [direction of prayer] and be called after that 'God's city' [*Madīnat al-Rabb*, referring apparently to the end of verse 14]."

Finally, mention should be made of the fourteenth-century Moroccan Jewish convert to Islam whom we know only as 'Abd al-Ḥaqq. In his anti-Jewish pamphlet,[70] he uses mainly Gemmatria—combining the numerical value of letters, a technique well known also to Muslim authors (see below)—in order to find many Biblical allusions to Muhammad, Mecca, Muslim prayer, and worship. Samples of his interpretations are quoted by Perlmann. 'Abd al-Ḥaqq states, for example, that the Hebrew word *yeyaḥelu* ("they shall have hope for") in Isa. 42:4 equals 64, which is the sum of *Aḥmad* (53) plus *five* daily prayers, plus Friday (six).[71] In the full text of 'Abd al-Ḥaqq's book, he also explains that the word *we-hinneh* ("and behold") in Gen. 1:31 adds up to 66: *Aḥmad* (53), plus the *five* daily prayers, plus Friday (the *sixth* day), plus the *two* additional prayers on

[68] Ibn Qayyim al-Dawziyya, *Hidāyat al-Ḥayārā*, p. 106.

[69] See Ibn Qutayba/Ibn al-Djawzī, p. 70. See also another translation in Al-Māwardī, *A'lām al-Nubuwwa*, p. 103; cf., e.g., Ibn Ẓafar, *Khayr al-Bishar*, pp. 15–16; Al-Qarāfī, *Al-Adjwiba al-Fākhira*, Bishāra 39; Ibn Qayyim al-Djawziyya, *Hidāyat al-Ḥayārā*, p. 105. Cf. also Ibn Taymiyya, *Al-Djawāb al-Ṣaḥīḥ*, 3: 307; Fakhr al-Dīn al-Rāzī, *Mafātīḥ al-Ghayb*, 1:321.

[70] See Perlmann, " 'Abd al-Haḳḳ al-Islāmī," pp. 171–91.

[71] Perlmann, " 'Abd al-Haḳḳ al-Islāmī," p. 182, and see other examples there, and cf. below, Chapter Five, p. 125.

the festivals. (His translation there of "and behold it was very good" is: "and the best-of creation—is *Aḥmad!*")[72]

Messianic Verses

We have already mentioned several messianic verses, which Muslim commentators took to refer to Muhammad and the rise of Islam. Since Islam places much less emphasis on eschatology than either Judaism or Christianity,[73] Muslims usually did not understand such verses in a messianic context. They did understand them to refer historically to either Jesus or Muhammad (or both), however, and used in their interpretation of these verses well-known motifs from Jewish-Christian and Greek anti-Christian polemics.

Gen. 49:10 is a good example. This famous verse, which held a place of pride in Jewish-Christian polemics, was also incorporated into the stock list of Muslim polemics, though in a different way and at a rather late stage, perhaps first introduced by the Spanish author Ibn Ḥazm (d. 1064).[74] The mere fact that he adduces this verse and that in his translation of it he seems to follow the Vulgate may be considered additional proof of the assumption that he used mainly Christian (and anti-Christian) material.

Ibn Ḥazm's understanding of the verse as an historical prophecy that has not come true also shows traces of Jewish-Christian polemics, although he does not follow the typical messianic Christian interpretation:

> This verse is untrue because the sceptre departed from Yahūdhā and leaders from his offspring, but the One sent (*mabʿūth*),[75] whom they await, did not come. The kingdom of Yahūdhā found its end in the time of Bukht-Naṣr [Nebuchad-

[72] Brit. Lib. Ms. Add. 9660, pp. 13–19 (by my numeration).

[73] See H. Lazarus-Yafeh, *Some Religious Aspects of Islam* (Leiden 1981), ch. 4.

[74] On Ibn Ḥazm, see above, Chapter Two, esp. note 22.

[75] This is the Vulgate version.

nezzar] more than one thousand and five hundred years ago, except for a short time only under Zurbā'īl b. Ṣalthā'īl [Zerubavel b. She'altiel]. I have repeated this passage to one of their [the Jews'] most learned polemicists, namely Ishmū'āl b. Yūsuf al-Lāwī, the famous author known as Ibn al-Naghrāl,[76] in the year 404 Hg. [C.E. 1013], and he said to me: "The Exilarchs (*Ru'ūs al-Djawālīt*) are the offspring of Dā'ūd and from the sons of Yahūdhā and they [have] leadership and kingdom and authority unto our days."[77] But I told him: "This is a mistake, because the *Ra's al-Djālūt* cannot exert power on the Jews or on anybody else and this is therefore a title only, but no reality."

Ibn Ḥazm then discusses Jewish history since the destruction of the first temple in more detail, to prove that this verse is untrue (and therefore a forgery) because "God forbid that one of the prophets may be given the lie."[78]

The Jewish convert to Islam Samau'al al-Maghribī (d. 1175) does not follow Ibn Ḥazm's translation or interpretation in this case, as he so often does. Instead, he goes for a typically Christological interpretation of the same verses:

We say to them: Is it not in the Torah that you have [here follows the verse in Hebrew, in some of the mss. in Arabic transcription], which means: "Kingship shall not depart from the people of Judah nor the staff from amongst them until the Messiah has come." They cannot deny that. We then say to them: Do you not know that you once had a state and kingdom up to the advent of Jesus, and that then your kingdom came to an end? If you do not have a kingdom today, it follows from the Torah that the Messiah has already been sent.

We also say to them: Was it not since the mission of Jesus—

[76] Apparently Samuel Hanagid, against whom Ibn Ḥazm later wrote his *Al-Radd 'alā ibn al-Naghrīla* (ed. Iḥsān 'Abbās' [Cairo 1960]).

[77] This interpretation is Talmudic (see *Sanhedrin* 5a) and is therefore of little historical importance for later times.

[78] Ibn Ḥazm, *Al-Faṣl fī-l-Milal wa-l-Ahwā wa-l-Niḥal* (n.p., 1329 Hg.), 1: 152–53. E. Ashtor (Straus) in his list of Biblical verses in the *Memorial Volume for the Vienna Rabbinical Seminary* does not mention this verse at all.

> upon whom be peace—that the kings of Rome ruled over the Jews and Jerusalem, and that the state of the Jews came to an end and the Jews were dispersed? They cannot deny this without becoming absurd. So it follows from their own source, from the Torah, that Jesus the son of Mary is the Messiah they were expecting.[79]

Samau'al here gives expression to (and later elaborates on) the common Muslim view, based on the Qur'an, that Jesus as a prophet was rejected by Jews in the same way they later rejected Muhammad.

Later Muslim authors simply take the verse to allude to Muhammad. Thus Al-Qarāfī, quoting a third translation based perhaps on a Jewish Messianic interpretation of the verse ("until comes the One to whom everything—or everybody—will belong") says: "And nobody came afterwards to everybody except the Messenger of God, peace be upon him, and therefore he is meant, in order to keep Jacob's words free from defect."[80]

Let us return to Samau'al al-Maghribī and his Christian-like anti-Jewish explanation of some other well-known messianic verses (Isa. 11:6–7). After quoting the verses inaccurately ("The wolf and the lamb shall all pasture and lie down together, and the cow and the bear shall pasture together, and the lion shall eat straw like the ox"), he adds some most unusual "information":

> They also believed that when this expected Messiah has come he will gather them all in Jerusalem, the sovereignty will be theirs, the world will be emptied of all others, and death will be kept from them for a long time. It is still their custom to follow the lions into their thickets and to throw straw in front of the lions to see just when they eat it.[81]

[79] See Samau'al al-Maghribī, *Ifḥām al-Yahūd*, text p. 23, trans. pp. 41–42.

[80] See Al-Qarāfī, *Al-Adjwiba al-Fākhira*, Bishāra 2. Printing errors must be taken into account here. Cf. also Ṣāliḥ al-Dja'farī, in Al-Sa'ūdī, *Muntakhab*, p. 141.

[81] Samau'al al-Maghribī, *Ifḥām al-Yahūd*, text pp. 41–42, trans. p. 50.

It is hard to know whether this is sheer malignant fantasy on Samau'al's part, or is copied from a Christian author, or—although it seems far-fetched—perhaps reflects some Jewish folkloristic customs totally unknown to us. There was also a general Muslim tendency to read the Bible literally. Goldziher remarks with regard to Gen. 4:7 ("sin lies at the door") that Muslim commentators misunderstood the verse in a very literal manner (Jews write their sins on their doors in order to be forgiven).[82]

Isaiah 21:6, well known for its messianic connotation in Jewish literature, was also taken by Muslim exegetes to refer to Muhammad (the rider of the camel).[83] Ibn Qutayba and 'Alī b. Rabban translate the verse differently but explain it similarly. The passage as Ibn Qutayba quotes it is shortened and slightly different. It mentions a rider of an ass and a rider of a camel (*djamal*), whom the watchman overhead talking to each other and saying, "Babylon (*Bā-*

Cf. Maimonides' explanation that these verses refer to the future peaceful existence of Israel among the nations. (*Mishneh Torah*, Shoftim, Hilkhot Melakhim. 12, 1.)

[82] I. Goldziher, "Ueber Bibelzitate," p. 318 (a Ḥadīth saying of 'Abd-Allāh b. Mas'ūd). This may be a reference to the Jewish "Mezuzah."

[83] See Steinschneider, *Polemische und Apologetische Literatur*, p. 329 (he quotes only Al-Bīrūnī), who stressed that Jewish authors (like Maimonides in his *Epistle to Yemen*) accepted this Muslim interpretation. On the Jewish Apocalyptic writings (the *Secrets*, and especially the *Prayer* attributed to Shim'on Bar Yoḥay, both of which quote this verse), see B. Lewis, "An Apocalyptic Vision of Islamic History," *BSOAS* (1950): esp. 313 (Hebrew trans. in his *On History, Collected Studies*, ed. R. Simon [Jerusalem 1988], pp. 194–214); cf. Crone and Cook, *Hagarism*, pp. 5, 17, 153, 166. See also the verse in both Hebrew texts in Even-Shmuel's edition, *Midreshei Ge'ula* (Tel Aviv 1954), pp. 188, 271–72. There was also a discussion among Muslim (and Jewish?) authors about the identity of the true "rider of the camel"—Moses or Muhammad? See for example, Abū Rayḥān al-Bīrūnī, *Al-Athār al-Bāqiya 'an al-Qurūn al-Khāliya*, ed. E. Sachau (Leipzig 1878), p. 19 (trans. E. Sachau, *The Chronology of Ancient Nations* [London 1879] pp. 22–23); and Aḥmad al-Qalqashandī, *Ṣubḥ al-A'shā* (Cairo 1918), 13:266. The whole problem of the (messianic?) riders of the ass and the camel in Muslim literature has yet to be clarified, including Ismā'īlī (and other) commentaries to Zech. 9:9. See also P. Kraus, "Hebraeische und Syrische Zitate," p. 255.

bal) has fallen and all its graven images." Ibn Qutayba adds:

> We and the Christians take the rider of the ass (*ṣāḥib al-ḥimār*) to be Jesus (*Al-Masīḥ*), and if he is Jesus, why can Muhammad, peace be upon him, not be the rider of the camel? Did not the idols of Babylon fall through him rather than through Jesus? In Babylon kings [continued to] worship idols since Abraham [until Muhammad]. And is he [Muhammad] not much better known as the rider of a camel than is Jesus as the rider of an ass?[84]

Earlier, Ibn Qutayba quoted another alleged Biblical verse based on this one: "Isaiah said to Ilyā [Aelia Capitolina], which is the city of Jerusalem [*Bayt al-Maqdis*] and her name is *Ūrshalīm*: Receive good tidings, oh *Ūrshalīm*, for here comes the rider of an ass, meaning Jesus, and the rider of a camel (*ba'īr*), meaning Muhammad, peace be upon him." Then follows a story about a Syrian Christian who told the ladies of Quraysh (including Khadīdja) to prepare themselves for the coming prophet Aḥmad.[85]

'Alī b. Rabban brings a longer, partly Qur'an-like translation of the passage "from the tenth chapter of Isaiah," and then adds:

> This, too, is a clear and obvious prophecy which only a man who deceives himself and throws away his intelligence can reject. As no reasonable man dares feign ignorance and say that there was in the world a rider on an ass more appropriate to this prophecy than Christ—peace be with him—so also no man with sound judgment and intelligence is allowed to say that there was in the world a rider on a camel more appropriate to this prophecy than the Prophet—may God bless and save him—and his nation. Are not the men of intelligence and science

[84] Ibn Qutayba/Ibn Al-Djawzī, pp. 66–67. See also Al-Māwardī, *A'lām al-Nubuwwa*, p. 103; Al-Qarāfī, *Al-Adjwiba al-Fākhira*, Bishāra 25; Ibn Taymiyya, Al-Djawāb al-Ṣaḥīḥ, 3: 304; and Ibn Qayyim al-Djawziyya, *Hidāyat al-Ḥayārā*, pp. 104–5.

[85] Ibn Qutayba/Ibn al-Djawzī, p. 60.

amongst the People of the Book ashamed to attribute such a clear and sublime prophecy to some rude and barbarous people?[86]

Ibn Ẓafar follows Ibn Qutayba's translation and interpretation and adds a story about a copper sculpture that stood at one of the gates of pre-Islamic Alexandria, representing an Arab camel-rider. People deprived of their rights would say to their oppressor: "Give unto me what belongs to me before this [rider] will come and take from thee what belongs to me—whether you agree or refuse."[87]

Isa. 9:6 (partly translated) is also understood by Muslim commentators to refer explicitly to Muhammad, especially the words "the government shall be upon his shoulder." Both ʿAlī b. Rabban and Ibn Qutayba (who follows ʿAlī b. Rabban in this case) translate the Hebrew word *ha-misrah* with *sulṭānuhu* (later translators also use *riyāsatuhu*), and take it to refer to Muhammad's bodily signs of prophecy (a mole between his shoulders).[88] Later Muslim authors read this explicitly into the verse (*wa-l-shāma ʿalā-kitfihi*) or stress that Jesus could not be meant by this verse as he had

[86] ʿAlī b. Rabban, *Kitāb al-Dīn*, text pp. 82–83, trans. p. 96.

[87] Ibn Ẓafar, *Khayr al-Bishar*, p. 17 (the passage is quoted by Kamāl al-Dīn al-Damīrī [d. 1405], *Kitāb Ḥayāt al-Ḥayawān* (Cairo 1887), 1: 251 (s.v. "*Djamal*"); see Schreiner, "Zur Geschichte der Polemik," pp. 627, 646, note 1; reprinted in *Gesammelte Schriften*, pp. 111, 130).

[88] See ʿAlī b. Rabban, *Kitāb al-Dīn*, text p. 81, trans. p. 95; Ibn Qutayba/Ibn al-Djawzī, p. 65. Ibn Qutayba here clearly follows ʿAlī b. Rabban, including his remarks about the difference between the Hebrew and Syriac versions of the verse and the numeration (*al-Faṣl al-Khāmis*) of the chapter, usually not to be found with Ibn Qutayba (but see Brockelman, Muhammedanische Weissagungen," p. 140). ʿAlī b. Rabban mentions in this context the term *Khātam al-Nubuwwa*, which Mingana translates (*Book of Religion and Empire*, p. 95) as "the seal of prophets." It is difficult to know whether ʿAlī b. Rabban already understood it thus. Cf. Y. Friedmann, "Finality of Prophethood in Sunni Islam," *JSAI* 7 (1986): 177–215. Al-Māwardī (*Aʿlām al-Nubuwwa*, p. 103) does not mention this term. Some Muslim commentators apparently understood Deut. 33:12 to refer to the same bodily signs of prophecy between Muhammad's shoulders. See also Zech. 13.

no such signs between his shoulders.[89] Ibn Qayyim al-Djawziyya adds that Jesus never ruled over his enemies but was oppressed by them, in clear contrast to Muhammad, whose rule is perfect and will never end.[90] It may be no coincidence that Saadia translated this part of the verse as "his authority [or leadership] will be upon his head" (*'alā ra'sihi*) rather than between his shoulders.

Perhaps the best-known of these verses is Deut. 18:18 (19,15), which has messianic connotations already in Qumran writings and early Christianity and has always played a role in Jewish-Christian polemics. Several scholars adduced this verse as an example of Muslim exegesis referring to Muhammad.[91] Indeed, many Muslim authors quote this verse, discuss at length Jewish and Christian interpretations of it, reject them, and interpret the verse to allude to Muhammad only.[92]

[89] See Al-Qarāfī, *Al-Adjwiba al-Fākhira*, Bishāra 35; Ibn Taymiyya, *Al-Djawāb al-Ṣaḥīḥ*, 2: 211, 3: 308. For the Christian explanation and its rejection by Jewish authors, see, for example, *Nizzaḥon Vetus* on the verse.

[90] See Ibn Qayyim al-Djawziyya, *Hidāyat al-Hayārā*, pp. 212–13, where a full translation of the whole verse is given; and see the subsequent discussion there about the various possible translations and about the fact that Muhammad is considered by Muslims to be only a servant of God, in spite of what the verse seems to imply (*Ilāh Qawiyy—El Gibbor* in Hebrew). In this context, Ibn Qayyim al-Djawziyya also says that many Jews and Christians (*Ahl al-Kitāb*) call their children by the name "Immanuel," which means only "God is with us" and no more.

[91] Cf. for example, Steinschneider, *Polemische und Apologetische Literatur*, p. 326; Schreiner, "Zur Geschichte der Polemik," p. 627; E. Ashtor (Straus), in *Memorial Volume for the Vienna Rabbinical Seminary*, pp. 191-92; Taeschner, "Die Alttestamentlischen Bibelzitate," pp. 30–31; Wansbrough, *Quranic Studies*, pp. 64ff.; Cook and Crone, *Hagarism*, pp. 17 and 167 n. 10.

[92] See, e.g., 'Alī b. Rabban, *Kitāb al-Dīn*, text pp. 73–74, trans. pp. 85–86; Ibn Qutayba/Ibn al-Djawzī, p. 63; Al-Bīrūnī, *Al-Athār al-Bāqiya*, p. 19; Ibn Ẓafar, *Khayr al-Bishar*, pp. 10, 13; Ibn Ḥazm, *Al-Faṣl*, 1: 111; Samau'al al-Maghribī, *Ifḥām al-Yahūd*, text pp. 29, 107–8 (autobiography), trans. pp. 45, 81; Al-Qarāfī, *Al-Adjwiba al-Fākhira*, Bishāra 3; Fakhr al-Dīn al-Rāzī, *Mafātīḥ al-Ghayb*, 1: 320; Ibn Qayyim al-Djawziyya, *Hidāyat al-Ḥayārā*, pp. 78, 82, 125–26.

Jewish medieval authors refuted the Muslim interpretation of the verse both explicitly and implicitly.[93] Muslim literature may have preserved some lost Jewish interpretations of the verse, which were perhaps invented ad hoc during oral theological discussions between Muslims and Jews. Ibn Qayyim al-Djawziyya describes in detail such a discussion, wherein he mentions different Jewish (and Christian) explanations of the verse (the verse refers to Joshua, to Samuel, or to Aaron; or it refers to Jesus; or it should be read with a question mark).[94] In the discussion described by Ibn Qayyim al-Dyawziyya, the Jews even quote verses from the Qur'an to the effect that "from among your brethren" may mean "from among yourselves," *in clear contrast to the Muslim interpretation.*[95] Of course, the real question behind the interpretation of the verse itself was whether Jews admit that true prophets may arise among Gentiles.[96] Other Jewish converts simply read

[93] See Jehuda Halevi, *Book of Kuzari*, 3: 40–41, Maimonides, *Epistle to Yemen*, ed. A. S. Halkin (New York 1952), p. 46ff. (English trans., B. Cohen, *Epistle to Yemen*, p. IX); cf. Jewish commentators to the verse, especially Ibn Ezra. See also *Ibn Kammūna's Examination of the Three Faiths*, ed. and trans. M. Perlmann (Berkeley 1967, 1971), text pp. 94–96, trans. pp. 138, 141–42.

[94] Joshua is mentioned by Ibn Ezra in his commentary on this verse. (See also Ibn Ẓafar, *Khayr al-Bishar*, p. 13). For Samuel, see Samau'al al-Maghribī, *Ifḥām al-Yahūd*, text pp. 29, 107–8, trans. pp. 45, 81; *Midrash Tehillim (Schocher Tob)*, Psalm 1:3 (ed. S. Buber [Wilna, 1891], p. 4). Perhaps there is some connection with Al-Shahrastānī's (d. 1153) statement that the Samaritans believe in the prophethood of Moses, Aaron, and Joshua. See his *Milal wa-Niḥal*, ed. W. Cureton (London 1846), p. 170 (German trans. T. Haarbruecker [Halle 1850–51], pp. 170, 258). Al-Rāqilī, *Ta'yīd al-Milla* (ed. and trans. L. J. Kassin, Ph.D., dissertation, Columbia University 1969), mentions also Hiob in the context of this verse (see text p. 28, trans. p. 156).

[95] See Ibn Qayyim al-Djawziyya, *Hidāyat al-Ḥayārā*, pp. 125–26; and see the Appendix below.

[96] Ibn Ezra, for example, denies this possibility in his commentary to Deut. 13:2, whereas Maimonides, following the Talmudic sages, admits it (see *Epistle to Yemen*, pp. 51ff.). This is why Al-Rāqilī (*Ta'yīd al-Milla*) quoted a Jewish interpretation according to which the verse alludes to Hiob and other (Gentile) prophets (but not to Muhammad).

into the text "from your brother Ismā'īl," or use Gemmatria to achieve the same effect.[97]

Epithets and Descriptions of Muhammad

Since 1861, when Sprenger wrote his famous Appendix "Hiess der Prophet Mohammed?"[98] every student of Islam has been aware of the possibility that some of the well-known epithets for Muhammad, including his names Muḥammad and Aḥmad, may have their origins in Hebrew and Aramaic verbs of praise and prayer. These names, as well as other adjectives and verbs from the root *Ḥmd*, were often interpolated by Muslim authors into their otherwise almost exact translations of Biblical verses. We have seen examples above, and Mingana has stressed the use of this root by leaving it always in Arabic in his English translation of 'Alī b. Rabban's book.[99] An unusual use of this root is made by the Jewish convert to Islam 'Abd-al-Ḥaqq. He concludes from 1 Kings 20:6 (and 22:35) and the words *maḥmad 'eyneykha* ("whatsoever is pleasant in thine

[97] See Sa'īd b. Ḥasan, *Masālik al-Naẓar*, text p. 327, trans. pp. 362–63; 'Abd-al-Ḥaqq, ms. Brit. Lib. Add. 9660, p. 17 (Perlmann, " 'Abd-al-Ḥaḳḳ al-Islāmī," p. 183).

[98] See A. Sprenger, *Das Leben und die Lehre des Mohammad* (Berlin 1961), pp. 155–61.

[99] See above, note 8; cf., for example, the part of Isa. 35:2 translated by some Muslim authors, in different versions, as "let them rejoice and flourish . . . because they will be given *by Aḥmad* the glory of Lebanon." (Muslim commentators knew that Lebanon and Carmel were taken by Jewish commentators to refer to Jerusalem and the Temple.) See 'Alī b. Rabban, *Kitāb al-Dīn*, text p. 85, trans. p. 99; Al-Māwardī, *A'lām al-Nubuwwa*, p. 103; Al-Qarāfī, *Al-Adjwiba al-Fākhıra*, Bishāra 31. Ibn Qutayba/Ibn al-Djawzī (p. 71) explains the verse in much the same way, but does not quote the direct interpolation. Neither does Ibn Qayyim al-Djawziyya (*Hidāyat al-Ḥayārā*, p. 106), who also offers this explanation, and who dwells at length several times (see, e.g., pp. 83, 91) on the use of the root *Ḥmd* in the Old and New Testaments. Muslim authors also translate Psalm 50:2 ("the perfection of beauty") as *Iklīl Maḥmūd*, and Isa. 52:7 ("him that brings good tidings") simply by "Muhammad." Cf. above, Chapter Two, note 76.

eyes") used there that the wicked King Aḥ'av was in fact an early believer in Islam. He may have based his speculation on the Midrashic explanation that those Hebrew words refer to the Torah scroll, which was deeply respected even by King Aḥ'av, who refused to turn it over to Ben-Hadad, king of Aram.[100]

Another name attributed to Muhammad, *Mushaffaḥ*, is, according to Muslim exegetes, also mentioned explicitly in the Bible (for example, in a paraphrase of Isa. 42:3–4, where it is interpolated), and is explained by Goldziher as derived from the Hebrew *Meshubbaḥ*, the "praised one."[101] Ibn Qayyim al-Djawziyya says that the name Muhammad is the Arabic equivalent of *Mushaffaḥ*.[102]

In this context, Gen. 17:20 is known to have been very popular even with early Muslim exegetes, who took the Hebrew words *bi-me'od me'od* ("exceedingly") to be names of the Prophet (*Mādh Mādh* or *Mūdh Mūdh*).[103] Some explained the names through Gemmatria (92 being the equivalent of Muhammad) and were explicitly refuted by

[100] See 'Abd al-Ḥaqq, ms. Brit. Lib. Add. 9660, p. 5 (Perlmann, "'Abd al-Haḳḳ al-Islāmī," pp. 180–81), and the Talmud, *Sanhedrin* 102 b.

[101] See I. Goldziher, "Ueber Muhammedanische Polemik gegen Ahl al-Kitāb," *ZDMG* 32 (1878): 374–75 (reprinted in *Gesammelte Schriften*, 3: 34–35).

[102] Ibn Qayyim al-Djawziyya, *Hidāyat al-Ḥayārā*, p. 114.

[103] See, for example, Ibn Qutayba/Ibn al-Djawzī, p. 61, where this verse is quoted literally without any explanation; 'Alī b. Rabban (*Kitāb al-Dīn*, text p. 67, trans. p. 78) quotes the same translation from "Marcus the translator," but gives also the version of the Septuagint. Cf. Al-Māwardī, *A'lām al-Nubuwwa*, p. 102; and Abū Rayḥān al-Bīrūnī, *Al-Athār al-Bāqiya*, p. 19. Ibn Ẓafar (*Khayr al-Bishar*, p. 7) quotes the two versions given by 'Alī b. Rabban. See also Motahhar el-Maqdisī, *Al-Bad' wa-l-Ta'rīkh* (*Livre de la création et de l'histoire*), ed. C. I. Huart (Paris 1916), 5: 30–31. Cf. a different translation in Al-Qarāfī, *Al-Adjwiba al-Fākhira*, Bishāra 1; and Sa'īd b. Ḥasan, in *Masālik al-Naẓar*, text pp. 325, 347, trans. pp. 361, 375. See also Kraus, "Hebraeische und Syrische Zitate," pp. 248ff. For lists of Muhammad's epithets and names, see, for example, Al-Qāḍī 'Iyāḍ al-Yuḥṣī, *Al-Shifā bi-Ta'rīf Ḥuqūq al-Muṣṭafā* (Cairo 1950), 1: 148, or Al-Nuwayrī, *Nihāyat al-Arab* (Cairo 1955), 16: 79. See also F. Taeschner, "Die Alttestamentlischen Bibelzitate," pp. 29–30.

Jewish authors,[104] whereas others explained the names phonetically and otherwise.[105]

Two somewhat contradictory descriptions of Muhammad were found by Muslim commentators in Psalm 45:4 and 5,[106] and in the verses about the "servant of God" in Deutero-Isaiah. The "mighty" (*djabbār*) who is called upon in the Psalm to gird his sword is taken to be Muhammad, yet so is the meek and powerless "servant of God." Some of the most typical descriptions of the "servant" (for example, Isa. 53) are not mentioned at all by Muslim commentators, however. Instead, they prefer to stress Muhammad's zeal and strength (Isa. 49:2) and his just rule (often Psalm 72 is quoted in this context), and especially his opening the eyes of the blind, the ears of the deaf, and the "uncircumcised" hearts to accept God's message.[107]

An interesting linguistic play is sometimes made between *aʿmā* ("blind") and *ummī* (understood to mean "il-

[104] See Wansbrough (*Quranic Studies*, p. 65), who quotes the commentaries of Al-Kalbī and Muqātil; cf. Samau'al al-Maghribī, (*Ifḥām al-Yahūd*, text pp. 31–33, trans. pp. 46–47), who combines Gemmatria with typology. See *Ibn Kammūna's*, *Examination of the Three Faiths*, text p. 95, trans. p. 139; Ibn Ezra's commentary on Exodus 1:7; and Maimonides, *Epistle to Yemen*, p. 40 (cf. also Halkin's introduction, p. xvii, and the English trans. p. ix).

[105] See Ibn Qayyim al-Djawziyya, *Hidāyat al-Ḥayārā*, pp. 82, 90, 114, 218, 219.

[106] See Steinschneider, *Polemische und Apologetische Literatur*, p. 329; Ibn Qutayba/Ibn al-Djawzī, p. 65; ʿAlī b. Rabban, *Book of Religion*, text p. 75, trans. p. 88; Ibn Taymiyya, *Al-Djawāb al-Ṣaḥīḥ*, 3: 300; Ibn Qayyim al-Djawziyya, *Hidāyat al-Ḥayārā*, pp. 102–3; Ṣāliḥ al-Djaʿfarī, in Al-Saʿūdī's *Muntakhab*, p. 141.

[107] See ʿAlī b. Rabban, *Kitāb al-Dīn*, text pp. 87ff., trans. pp. 101ff.; Ibn Qutayba/Ibn al-Djawzī, pp. 64, 66; Abū Nuʿaym al-Iṣfahānī, *Kitāb Dalā'il al-Nubuwwa*, p. 32. Later commentators, such as Al-Qarāfī, quote more the so-called "servant of God" verses from Deutero-Isaiah, with some changes, take them to refer to Muhammad, and even interpolate the names Aḥmad and Muḥammad into their translation. See, for example, Al-Qarāfī, *Al-Adjwiba al-Fākhira*, Bishāra 28 and 30 (referring respectively to Isa. 49:2–3 and 42:1ff.). See also Ibn Qayyim al-Djawziyya, *Hidāyat al-Ḥayārā*, pp. 106ff.

literate").[108] Abū Nuʿaym al-Iṣfahānī quotes Isa. 42:7 with other descriptions of Muhammad on the authority of the convert Wahb b. Munabbih, including the following: "I shall send therefore an *ummī* prophet, a blind (*aʿma*) one from among the blind, one who strayed (*ḍalla*) from among those who strayed [away from the right belief], who will open deaf ears, hardened hearts, and blind eyes."[109] The famous Qur'an commentator Al-Zamakhsharī (d. 1144) also quotes a *Ḥadīth Shaʿyā* in his commentary to Sūra 62:2, saying that God "will send a blind [messenger] to the blind, and an *ummī* [prophet] to the *ummī* people."

Deut. 33:2, too, is quoted by almost every Muslim author mentioned above, and many others, to the effect that the Bible foretells the religious history of humanity and the abrogation of Judaism (Sinai) and Christianity (Seʿir) by the final and perfect divine revelation of Islam to the son of Ishmael who dwelled in Paran.[110]

One could adduce more examples of this kind of Muslim

[108] See I. Goldfeld, "The Illiterate Prophet: An Inquiry into the Development of a Dogma," *Der Islam* 57 (1980): 58–67.

[109] See his *Kitāb Dalāʾil al-Nubuwwa*, p. 33.

[110] This explanation may be based in some ways also on early Jewish Midrash. (Cf. Steinschneider, *Polemische und Apologetische Literatur*, p. 308.) This verse and its different translations (some of which arose from copyists' errors) are mentioned in most of the sources and studies quoted above. Its most elaborate interpretation can be found in Ibn Taymiyya, *Al-Djawāb al-Ṣaḥīḥ*, 3: 284, where the Torah is compared to the break of the dawn, the Gospel to the rising sun, and the Qur'an to the shining sun in the sky. It is less well known that the Muslim interpretation of this verse gave rise to geographical and other speculation. Thus, for example, *Sāʿīr* is taken by Muslim authors to be a mountain or village near Nazareth. See, for example, Al-Māwardī, *Aʿlām al-Nubuwwa*, p. 102; and Yāqūt, *Muʿdjam al-Buldān* s.v. "*Sāʿīr*" (*Jacut's Geographisches Woerterbuch*, ed. F. Wuestenfeld [Leipzig 1868], 3:11). Jewish authors started to refute the Muslim interpretation of the verse at a rather early stage. See, e.g., Saadia Gaon, *Kitāb al-Amānāt wa-l-Iʿtiqādāt*, ch. 3, 8 (ed. G. Landauer [Leiden 1880], pp. 133–34; ed. J. Kafaḥ [1980], p. 137; English trans. S. Rosenblatt, *Saadia Gaon, The Book of Beliefs and Opinions* [New Haven 1948], pp. 164–65), whose interpretation disregards completely the Midrashic explanations of the verse. See also Maimonides, *Epistle to Yemen*, pp. 36, 38, 44ff. (English trans. p. ix), and the Jewish commentators to the verse.

Bible interpretation,[111] but it must be remembered that this exegesis never became a literary genre on its own, nor did it ever play an important role in Muslim medieval theology. Therefore it remained simplistic and unsophisticated, not only when compared to Christian typological and allegorical exegesis of the Bible, but also in comparison with Muslim mystical and other exegesis of the Qur'an.

[111] This type of Muslim Bible exegesis survives in modern linguistic studies of the Bible. See, for example, Ḥuṣām Arshad, *Al-Bishāra bi-Muḥammad fī-l-Tawrāt* (on Psalm 68) (Cairo[?] 1986).

CHAPTER FIVE

Muslim Authors and the Problematics of Arabic Translations of the Bible

THE HISTORY OF the translation of the Hebrew Bible into Arabic has yet to be written, even though many scholars have dealt over the years with different aspects of this subject, and have analyzed repeatedly the same bits of information found in Arabic literature with regard to translations of the Bible from Hebrew, Syriac, Greek, Coptic, or Latin into Arabic.[1] Here I wish only to draw attention to some neglected aspects of this history, which might be of some importance for further studies in this field, and to help discard some unverified assumptions held in it, such as the description given recently of early Muslim authors having "ready access to knowledge of the Bible and its commentaries through a flood of translations that were distributed by stationers and booksellers."[2]

[1] See most of the material and relevant bibliography in G. Graf, *Geschichte der Christlichen Arabischen Literatur* (Vatican City 1944), 1: 85–195. See also the studies of S. H. Griffith, esp. "The Monks of Palestine and the Growth of Christian Literature in Arabic," *The Muslim World* 78 (1988): 1–28, and "The Gospel in Arabic: An Inquiry into Its Appearance in the First Abbasid Century," *Oriens Christianus* 69 (1985): 126–67.

[2] See G. D. Newby, *A History of the Jews of Arabia* (Columbia, S.C., 1988), p. 67. Newby apparently never thought about the practical problems his description raises: scrolls containing the translation of the Pentateuch alone would be numerous, large, and heavy. Cf. Irfan Shahîd, (*Byzantium and the Arabs in the Fourth Century* [Washington, D.C., 1984], pp. 435ff.), who talks about Bible translations of pre-Islamic times (cf. A. Baumstark, "Das Problem eines vorislamischen christlich-Kirchlichen Schriftums in arabischer Sprache," *Islamica* 4 [1931]: 562–75; and see J. Blau, "Sind uns Reste Arabischer Bibelueberstezungen aus Vorislamischer Zeit erhalten geblieben?" *Muséon* 86 [1973]: 6–72). Cf. R. G. Khoury, "Quelques réflexions sur la première ou les premières Bibles ar-

Perhaps the most important point to be made in this context is the little-known fact that in the Islamic literature of *Tales of the Prophets* (*Qiṣaṣ al-Anbiyā*), which used most extensively Biblical and Midrashic material (*Isrā'īliyyāt*), exact literal Biblical quotations are extremely rare. Free and inexact paraphrases usually transmit in this literature (as in the Qur'an and early Ḥadīth literature) the Biblical, Midrashic, and other material mixed up together without distinction, perhaps partially following an ancient Targum-like (oral?) source. This is true for the well-known books of both Al-Kisā'ī and Al-Tha'labī (eleventh century; Al-Kisā'ī may have lived much earlier),[3] and to a great extent also for most of Islamic historiography, which was deeply influenced by Biblical tradition.[4] Thus, for example, the famous historian Al-Ṭabarī (d. 923), who devoted more than 100 pages to Biblical history at the beginning of his monumental work and was well versed in Biblical and Midrashic material, seldom quotes the Bible.[5] Later historians who

---

abes," in T. Fahd, ed., *L'Arabe preislamique et son environnement historique et culturel* (Strasburg 1987), pp. 549–61.

[3] See, for example, Al-Tha'labī, *Qiṣaṣ al-Anbiyā al-musammā 'Arā'is al-Madjālis* (Cairo, n.d.), pp. 214–15 (partial quotations of Num. 13–14). On Al-Kisā'ī, see A. Schussman, *Stories of the Prophets in Muslim Tradition, Mainly on the Basis of "Ḳiṣaṣ al-Anbiyā" by Muḥammad al-Kisā'ī* (in Hebrew) (Jerusalem 1981), ch. 1; but see also *EI*[2] s.v. "*Al-Kisā'ī, Ṣāḥib Ḳiṣaṣ al-Anbiyā*" (T. Nagel).

[4] See F. Rosenthal, "The Influence of the Biblical Tradition on Muslim Historiography," in *Historians of the Middle East*, ed. B. Lewis and P. M. Holt (London 1962), pp. 35–45, esp. 42.

[5] Some exceptions to this rule may be found in Al-Ṭabarī, *Ta'rikh al-Rusul wa-l-Mulūk (Annales)*, ed. M. J. de Goeje and I. J. Barth, 1st ser., repr. (Leiden 1964), 2: 636, 639–40, 658, where he gives shortened and slightly changed quotations of Ezek. 37:3–10 (twice) and Jer. 1:4–5 (including, however, several parts translated rather accurately). See also p. 167 there, a literal quotation of Gen. 4:19–22 (I owe this reference to F. Rosenthal). The story of Cain and Abel there, starting on p. 138, follows more the Midrash than the Bible, however. In his great commentary to the Qur'an, as well, Al-Ṭabarī usually does not quote the Bible directly. Again, one exception to this rule is the story of Hiob (and the first round of his discussion with his friends), from which he brings lengthy, sometimes almost exact quotations in his commentary to Sūra 21:83ff. See also

dwelled less on Biblical history only rarely cited exact Biblical quotations.[6]

Only if we assume that these authors had no direct access to a written Arabic translation of the Bible—although they knew much about its contents and about Judaism in general[7]—can we understand this strange phenomenon. They certainly could not have read the Hebrew original or an Aramaic Targum, and most of them had only a vague notion of the Biblical Canon.[8] Early exceptions to this rule were converts, like ʿAlī b. Rabban in the ninth century, who may have used a Syrian translation of the Bible (he mentions "Marcus the translator"—*tardjumān*—and his *Tafsīr*).[9] Most Muslim authors, however, seem to have relied mainly on oral transmission, and constantly quote as their sources of Biblical information Jews or early Jewish and Christian converts to Islam, like Kaʿb al Aḥbār and Wahb b. Munabbih.[10] Many Muslim scholars readily admitted to such contact with Jews and Christians in order to elucidate Qur'anic passages touching on Biblical material,

---

Ceza Kassem-Draz, "Texts' Generation and the Saturation of Meaning" (in Arabic), *Alif* 8 (Spring 1988): 31–81.

[6] Al-Bīrūnī (d. 1048), for example, quoted literally only very few verses (see above, Chapter Four). See also below.

[7] See, for example, R. Brunschvig, "L'Argumentation d'un théologian Musulman du Xe siècle contre le judaïsme," in *Homenaje a Millas y Valicrosa* (Barcelona 1954), 1: 225–41. See also G. Vajda, "Juifs et Musulmans selon le Ḥadīṯ," *JA* (1937): 57–127, and the many studies of I. Goldziher on this subject. Cf. also E. Straus (Ashtor), *History of the Jews in Egypt and Syria under the Mamluks* (in Hebrew, vol. 1) (Jerusalem 1944), ch. 4.

[8] See F. Rosenthal, "The Influence of Biblical Tradition," in *Historians of the Middle East* (on Ibn Kathīr [d. 1373]). E. Straus (Ashtor), on the other hand, assumes that "Ibn Kathīr had Arabic translations of the Bible before him" and knew it well (*History of the Jews*, p. 369). On Ibn Kathīr, See also below.

[9] See ʿAlī b. Rabban, *Kitāb al-Dīn wa-l-Dawla* (*The Book of Religion and Empire by ʿAlī Ṭabarī*), ed. A. Mingana (Manchester 1923), trans. A. Mingana (Manchester 1922). Cf. Graf, *Geschichte der Christlichen Arabischen Literatur*, 1: 44–48. On the term *Tafsīr*, see below.

[10] See *EI*² s.v. "Kaʿb al-Aḥbār" (M. Schmitz), and see above, Chapter Two. See *EI*¹ s.v. "Wahb b. Munabbih" (J. Horovitz).

a procedure that was condemned by others.[11] The fact that Jews usually felt no need to differentiate between the Biblical text and later Midrashic elaborations on it, and would have found it almost impossible to translate literally the Biblical text alone for their Muslim neighbors, may help to explain the combined material "quoted" by Muslim medieval authors. The ninth-century historian Al-Ya'qūbī, for example, gives in his "History" a general account of the Biblical stories mixed with many Midrashic details, most of which he must have obtained orally from Jews. He quotes Gen. 3:21 as: "Adam and Eve wore clothes of light" (*wa-kāna libāsu Ādama wa-Ḥawā thiyāban min nūr*), which no doubt reflects the mystical reading of Rabbi Meir (*or*, "light," instead of *'or*, "skin"; see *Bereshit Rabba*, Parasha 20:29). Such a version could have been transmitted and translated only orally by a Jew.[12]

The same assumption of oral transmission must underlie any attempt to understand the even stranger literary phenomenon, so common in Muslim medieval Arabic (and Persian) literature, of the many alleged quotations from the Bible, also termed *Isrā'īliyyāt*, and often cited on the authority of the same Jewish converts to Islam.[13] Even considering the wish of Muslim authors to reconstruct the true uncorrupted Biblical text (see Chapter Two), it is hard to imagine that the same alleged quotations would have become so widespread in Arabic literature if written Arabic translations of the Bible had been available to these authors. One may, of course, consider these quotations as a continuation of the Apocryphal literary tradition, but it is

[11] Cf. M. J. Kister, "Ḥaddithū 'an banī isrā'īla wa-lā-ḥaraja," *IOS* 2 (1972): 215–39.

[12] See Aḍmad b. Wāḍiḥ al-Ya'qūbī, *Tar'īkh*, ed. M. T. Houtsma (Leiden 1883), 1: 1. See, however, an almost exact literal translation of the Ten Commandments, 1: p. 26.

[13] See above, Chapter Two, and S. D. Goitein, "Isrā'īliyyāt" (in Hebrew), *Tarbiz* 6 (1934–35): 89–101, 510–22. Cf. Khoury, "Quelques réflexions sur les citations de la Bible dans les premières générations islamiques," *BEO* 29 (1977): 270–78.

unlikely that a literary genre that attempted not only to complement the Bible but also to reconstruct its true original would flourish in a society that had some knowledge of the Biblical text itself.

Bible translations into Arabic were usually made by Jews and Christians for the use of Jews and Christians. Muslim authors may not have had easy access to these written texts, most of which were kept in Christian monasteries—the eighth-century Basrian Sufi author Mālik b. Dīnār mentions explicitly the library of a Christian monastery in this context.[14] (The texts may not have been widespread even among Jews or Christians themselves!) The earliest existing manuscripts (apparently from the late eighth and ninth centuries) appear in the monasteries of Palestine, not in the great centers of Muslim culture, where Arabic replaced the Greek (for liturgical purposes) among the Melchites long before it did so in other places, among Syriac- and Coptic-speaking Christian denominations.[15] Dated manuscripts of Arabic translations of the Pentateuch made from the Coptic, for example, exist only from the thirteenth century on, though some undated ones may be earlier.[16] In general, remnants of Arabic translations of the Psalms, and especially of the Gospels, are much more abundant and apparently earlier than those of the Pentateuch or other books of the Hebrew Bible.[17] It is not known whether each mon-

[14] See Abū Nu'aym al-Iṣfahānī, *Ḥilyat al-Awliyā wa-Ṭabaqāt al-Aṣfiyā* (Beirut, 1985), 2: 375, and cf. p. 381—a literal translation of Psalm 1.

[15] See Griffith, "The Monks of Palestine," pp. 4–6, and cf. J. Blau, *A Grammar of Christian Arabic*, vol. 1, CSCO 267 (Louvain 1966), pp. 21–33. Christian Arabic literature of course, contains many Biblical quotations. See, for example, *Le Dialogue d'Abraham de Tiberiade avec 'Abd al-Raḥmān al-Hāshimī*, ed. G. C. Marcuzzo (Rome 1986). Cf. S. Pines, "Gospel Quotations and Cognate Topics in 'Abd al-Jabbār's *Tathbīt* in Relation to Early Christian and Judeo-Christian Readings and Traditions," *JSAI* 9 (1987): 195–278.

[16] See J. R. Rhode, *The Arabic Versions of the Pentateuch in the Church of Egypt* (Leipzig 1921), pp. 62, 36–38.

[17] Cf. Griffith, "The Gospel in Arabic." There exist some studies of the

astery had its own translation made (and the much-used manuscripts of such translations got lost) or whether there existed a tradition of translation shared by several monasteries or communities belonging to the same denomination. In case of the bilingual manuscripts (Coptic-Arabic), scholars still argue the point, and although some are convinced that the Arabic translation added to some Coptic manuscripts was made in each case from the Coptic version in each manuscript, others feel that it was a copy of a commonly shared existing Arabic translation.[18] The Arabic versions repeat misunderstandings common in the Coptic texts (not to be found in their source, the Septuagint); but only further studies will show what this evidence means in the general discussion.[19]

The existence of Saadia's translation was known to Muslim authors already in the tenth century. Ibn al-Nadīm in his famous *Fihrist* gives some general, fairly exact information about the Pentateuch, about the Biblical Canon in general, and even about the Mishna, which he received "from one of their [the Jews'] notable men." He was told about the division of the five Pentateuch books into *farāsāt*, which he takes to mean "Sūras," and about the division of every *farāsāh* into *absūqāt*, meaning "verses." He then adds: "Al-Fayyūmī [Saadia] was one of the most eminent of the Jews and of their scholars who were versed in the Hebrew language. In fact, the Jews consider that there was nobody else like Al-Fayyūmī. His name was Saʿīd, also said to be Saʿadiyā, and he lived so recently that some of our contemporaries were alive before he died."[20] (Ibn al-Nadīm

---

translations of different Old Testament books into Arabic, such as Judges, by B. Knutsson (Leiden 1974), or Daniel, by O. Loefgren (Uppsala 1936).

[18] These are the respective views of W. P. Funk (Quebec, Canada) and A. Shisha-Halevi (Hebrew University, Jerusalem). See also Graf, *Geschichte der Christlichen Arabischen Literatur*, 1: 51.

[19] See, for example, the Arabic translation of Gen. 1:29–30 in Ms. Paris Copt. 1 and Vat. Copt. 1 (Rhode, *The Arabic Versions*, p. 21), which connect v. 30 to v. 29 without the particle "to," as if God had also given man the beasts and fowls for food on the same occasion (I owe this reference to W. P. Funk).

[20] See Muḥammad b. Isḥāq al-Nadīm [Ibn al-Nadīm], *Kitāb al-Fihrist*,

then gives a list of book titles and translations [*Tafsīr*] with or without explanation [*Sharḥ*] by Saadia, not all of which are intelligible to us.) Saadia's Arabic translation of the Bible was transmitted by Jews in Hebrew characters, as was common practice among them, but there exist manuscripts of his translation of the Pentateuch in Arabic characters as well,[21] and he may have written it first in this way. The Jewish commentator Abraham ibn Ezra (d. 1164) says in his commentary to Gen. 2:11 that "to glorify God," Saadia translated the Pentateuch into "the language of Ishmael and their writing in order to show that the Torah contains nothing unintelligible." This may have facilitated the use of this translation also by the Samaritans and by some Christian denominations such as the Copts.[22] Contrary to some general assumptions by scholars, however, Muslim medieval authors usually do not follow Saadia's translation and often seem to have preferred Christian translations or other Jewish translations.[23]

Muslim and Karaite authors mention some earlier Jewish and Muslim translators other than Saadia,[24] but except for

ed. G. Fluegel and I. Roediger (Leipzig 1871), p. 23; (trans. B. Dodge, *The Fihrist of Al-Nadīm* [New York and London 1970], ch. 1 ["The Torah, Gospel and Other Scriptures"], 1: 43–45).

[21] See, for example, Ms. Vatican Ar. Borg. 129, whose date and provenance are obscure. Cf. below, the quotation from Al-Biqā'ī's *Tafsīr*, and see E. Algermissen, *Die Pentateuchzitate Ibn Ḥazms* (Muenster 1933), pp. 37–38. Cf. also J. Blau, *The Emergence and Linguistic Background of Judaeo-Arabic*, 2d ed. (Jerusalem 1981), pp. 39–41.

[22] See Ms. Vat. Libr. Ar. 2, and cf. Rhode, *The Arabic Versions*, pp. 94–97, texts pp. 37–49.

[23] See above, Chapter Four, p. 90 and note 44. Ibn Ẓafar rightly states that Jews used various Bible translations. See M. Steinschneider, *Die Arabische Literatur der Juden* (Frankfurt a.M. 1902), pp. 284ff. In Judeo-Arabic literature and in Genizah fragments, one can sometimes find Biblical quotations in Arabic that are very different from Saadia's translation. See, for example, the translation of Exod. 5:14 in the Jewish Theological Seminary Library ENA 3654/4, to which Dr. Sol Cohen from the Liebermann Institute for Talmudic Studies drew my attention.

[24] Ibn al-Nadīm (d. 995) in his *Al-Fihrist* (text pp. 21–22, trans. pp. 41–42) quotes Aḥmad b. 'Abdallāh b. Salām, "a protégé of Hārūn al-Rashīd," as having translated many books, among them the Torah and the Gospel (but his knowledge of Hebrew seems to have been extremely poor; see p.

their names we know nothing about them, a fact that did not deter some scholars from ascribing to such sources (for example, to Aḥmad b. ʿAbdallāh b. Salām) some early Biblical quotations of Muslim authors.[25]

The different translations of selected polemical verses (see Chapter Four) may also help to sustain the assumption that Muslim authors relied mainly on oral transmission from Jews and Christians, and later often copied the same verses from each other. Not only do these authors quote the same verses for generations, but they quote them totally out of their Biblical context and never show any knowledge of the verses immediately preceding or following the quotations. How could this have happened if the authors had actually read through the scrolls of fuller translations? It is hard to believe in any case that they would have been permitted to browse through or copy Arabic Biblical manuscripts existing either in synagogues or in the libraries of monasteries. Moreover, the different versions of the same verse quoted by the Muslim authors, who often mentioned that they had asked Jews (or Christians) about the exact translation of a word or verse,[26] seem to substantiate this.

---

120). Al-Masʿūdī mentions Abū Kathīr of Tiberias and perhaps confuses him with his famous pupil Saadia; see his *Al-Tanbīh wa-l-Ishrāf*, ed. M. J. de Goeje (Leiden 1843), pp. 112ff., where he also mentions the ninth-century Arabic translation of Ḥunayn b. Isḥāq and other Arabic translation of the Septuagint. Al-Qirqisānī speaks about Al-Ashkenazī, Al-Ramlī, and Ibrāhīm b. Nūḥ (*Kitāb al-Anwār wa-l-Marāqib*, ed. L. Nemoy, pt. 1 [New York 1939], p. 145). All these translations are lost. M. Zucker, in the Introduction to his *Saʿadya's Translation of the Pentateuch* (in Hebrew) (New York 1959), tried to prove that no direct translation from Hebrew into Arabic existed before Saadia. See also S. Baron, *A Social and Religious History of the Jews*, vol. 4 (New York 1957), pp. 265ff. (on Arabic translations of the Bible) and esp. p. 265 (including p. 458 n. 41).

[25] See, for example, D. M. Dunlop, "A Letter of Hārūn ar-Rashīd to the Emperor Constantine," in *In Memoriam Paul Kahle*, ed. M. Black and G. Fohrer (Berlin 1968), pp. 106–15.

[26] See, for example, Ibn Ḥazm, *Al-Faṣl fī-l-Milal wa-l-Ahwāʾ wa-l-Niḥal* (n. pl., 1329 Hg.) 1: 135 (where he explains that he asked Ibn al-Naghrīla for the meanings of the term "sister"—*Ukht*—with regard to Gen. 20:2, 12).

One should not imagine that these Muslim authors compared several different translations of the Pentateuch or other Biblical books, but rather that they consulted Jews and Christians orally and received different ad hoc translations of specific verses, even from the same person. Many mistakes, inaccuracies, and misunderstandings transmitted through generations of Muslim authors up to the fourteenth century (and even the bizarre Hebrew phonetical transcriptions of some of these verses into Arabic characters) would thus find plausible explanations.[27] Sometimes it is difficult to decide whether Muslim authors simply quoted a certain verse incorrectly or whether the translation of the verse was transmitted to them together with some lost Midrashic interpretation.[28] Of course, they could also have quoted Old Testament verses according to citations in the New Testament (and New Testament verses according to noncanonical Gospels or Manichaean sources).

That Muslim authors asked their Jewish and Christian neighbors for information and discussed religious issues with them is well attested by Muslim sources. Al-Bukhārī (d. 870), for example, quotes in his Ḥadīth collection a

[27] See, for instance, the translations of Gen. 17:20 in Ibn Ẓafar's *Khayr al-Bishar bi-Khayr al-Bashar* (Cairo 1863), p. 7. The end of the verse is quoted once (1.14–15) in an exact translation ("and I shall make him into a great nation"), as in both Ibn Qutayba and 'Alī b. Rabban. But it is also mistakenly translated there (line 12) as "and I shall give him a great nation" (*wa-u'ṭīhi sha'ban 'aẓīman*), apparently because of a literal misunderstanding of the Hebrew verb *natan*, a slip that could well stem from an oral ad hoc translation made by a Jewish informant. This mistaken translation is then repeated by later authors. See, for example, Al-Qarāfī, *Al-Adjwiba al-Fākhira 'an al-As'ila al-Fādjira*, ed. Bakr Zakī 'Awād (Cairo 1987), Bishāra 1.

[28] One such example is mentioned by Goldziher, who quotes a translation of Num. 20:10 by the early Qur'an interpreter Mudjāhid. The words "Hear now, ye rebels" are translated as "Hear now, ye asses," mistaking *ha-morim* for *ḥamorim* (*ḥamīr*), whereupon God forbids Moses to revile His creatures. See I. Goldziher, "Ueber Bibelzitate in Muhammedanischen Schriften," *ZAW* 13 (1893): 317. S. D. Goitein likely would have considered this mistake to be based on a lost Midrash on the verse!

well-known saying of the Prophet's companion Abū Hurayra (who is not considered to be a very reliable source) to the effect that "Jews and Christians (*Ahl al-Kitāb*) would read the Torah (*Tawrāt*) in Hebrew (*bi-l-ʿibrāniyya*) and translate and explain it (*yufassirūnaha*) in Arabic to the Muslims (*Ahl al-Islām*)," whereupon the Prophet instructed the believers neither to accept this information as true nor to consider it a lie, but to stick to their own belief.[29] A less well-known and much later source attributed to the third Caliph ʿUthmān the translation and explanation (*fassarahu bi-lisān* [sic] *al-ʿarabī*) of a fictitious Hebrew Davidic Psalm (*Zabūr*).[30]

One must carefully consider such statements in Muslim literature before accepting any part of them, even as reflecting later historical data. In the same way, I believe, we must carefully consider some modes of expression used by Muslim authors in this context, which, when taken literally, are bound to mislead scholars, and in fact have done so over the years. Thus, for example, the term *tardjama* does not necessarily mean only a translation of a text, but can mean also a compilation of a text; this is perhaps what was attributed to Wahb b. Munabbih with regard to the Psalms.[31] This meaning may also explain the strange statement of Aḥmad b. ʿAbdallāh b. Salām quoted by Ibn al-Nadīm in his *Fihrist*. He stated that he had "translated" (*tardjamtu*) the Torah and Gospel among many other books, and then gave examples of the way he chose to translate, which seem to prove that, like other Muslim authors, he

[29] Al-Bukhārī, *Al-Djāmiʿ al-Ṣaḥīḥ*, ed. L. Krehl, vol. 4 (Leiden 1908), bk. 97 (Kitāb al-Tawḥīd), p. 193. This saying is often cited in Muslim literature; see, for example, Ibn Ḥazm, *Al-Faṣl*, 1: 216.

[30] Ms. Chester Beatty 5492, p. 137 (according to my numeration). On this ms., see J. A. Arberry, *The Chester Beatty Library, A Handlist of the Arabic Manuscripts*, vol. 7 (Dublin 1964), p. 145. On the double meaning of the verb *fassara*, see below.

[31] See R. G. Khoury, *Wahb b. Munabbih*, Codices Arabici Antiqui 1 (Wiesbaden 1972), pp. 258ff. (As is well known, the term *tardjama* also means a compilation of biographical data.)

did not distinguish between Hebrew and Aramaic(?) and knew very little of either![32]

In the same way, when Muslim authors say something like, "I have found in the Torah" (*wadjadtu fī-l-Tawrāt*), or, "I have read in the Torah" (*qara'tu fī-l-Tawrāt*),[33] we do not have to depict them as literally reading through the Pentateuch and finding specific verses, but rather as collecting the information they needed with the help of people who knew these texts and quoted or read, translated, and explained them to the Muslims. Often these informants would correct themselves or add slight variations, which were taken by the Muslim authors to be different "versions" of Biblical translations (*nuskha ukhrā, tardjama ukhrā*).[34] Similarly, the verb *fassara* and the term *Tafsīr* must be understood not only as an interpretation of a text, but often as a translation of it, as the *Tafsīr* translation of Saadia proves.

The evidence presented thus far seems to indicate that Muslim authors until fairly recently did not use Arabic Bible translations on their own, and had no easy access to such translations as existed among Jews and Christians. They relied heavily on oral contacts, even in cases that may be considered in some ways to be exceptions to this rule.

One such early case is Ibn Qutayba (d. 889). At the be-

[32] See Ibn al-Nadīm, *Al-Fihrist*, text pp. 21–22, trans. pp. 41–42. Ibn Sarādj the Baghdadian Grammarian (d. 928) does not seem to have had any knowledge of Hebrew, either; see his remarks on the names Abraham, Sarah, and Isaac in his *Kitāb al-Uṣūl fī-l-Naḥw*, vol. 2 (Baghdad 1973), p. 96. (I owe this reference to A. Levin.)

[33] See, for example, Ibn Qutayba, *Kitāb al-Ma'ārif*, ed. 'Alī 'Abd al-Laṭīf (Cairo 1934), p. 6 ("I have read at the beginning of a book of the books of the Torah"), p. 9 ("I have read in the Torah" and "In the Torah it says"), etc.; Ibn Kathīr, *Al-Bidāya wa-l-Nihāya*, vol. 1 (Cairo 1932), pp. 95, 110 ("I have seen in the Torah"). On p. 281, however, Ibn Kathīr gives a literal translation of the greater part of the Ten Commandments.

[34] Cf., for example, Ibn Ẓafar, *Khayr al-Bishar*, p. 5 ("And I have read in another translation"), p. 7 ("And I have read in a translation of the Torah"), p. 9 ("And in another translation"), etc. He also mentions a Syriac translation in this context and seems to connect it with the corruption of the Hebrew text (pp. 9, 14).

ginning of his well-known book *Kitāb al-Maʿārif,* he quotes several paraphrases from Genesis mixed up with some Midrashic material, and a translation of Gen. 1–2, which Lecomte considers to be "sensiblement littérale" and copied directly from a translated text. Already G. Vajda and S. D. Goitein have expressed doubt, however, that Ibn Qutayba knew or had access to an Arabic translation of the Bible, or even of the Book of Genesis.[35] Ibn Qutayba must have relied on oral translations as well; this would explain his other Biblical quotations taken out of context (see Chapter Four) and the Midrash-like short paraphrases of Biblical stories in the *Kitāb al-Maʿārif* itself. Perhaps one of his informants started out translating for him the text of Genesis, to which Ibn Qutayba added some interesting comparisons with the Qur'an,[36] but the more literal beginning of this project soon gave way to shortened paraphrases of the Biblical stories.

Ibn Ḥazm (d. 1064) is another exception. It is difficult to establish the immediate sources of his lengthy quotations from the Pentateuch. In general, they are very different from Saadia's translation (although in at least one conspicuous [geographical] case he does follow him).[37] For exam-

[35] See G. Vajda, "Judaeo-Arabica 1, Observations sur quelques citations bibliques chez Ibn Qotayba," *REJ* 99 (1935): 68–80; G. Lecomte, "Les Citations de l'Ancien et du Nouveau Testament dans l'oeuvre d'Ibn Qotayba," *Arabica* 5 (1958): 34–46; Goitein, "Isrāʾīliyyāt," p. 90. Ibn Qutayba himself mentioned in another book of his (*Taʾwīl Mushkil al-Qurʾān*, ed. M. Saqar [Cairo 1954], p. 16) that the Pentateuch and the Psalms had been translated into Arabic, and the Gospel into several other languages, in contrast to the impossibility of translating the Qur'an. This was repeated by later Muslim authors.

[36] See, for example, *Kitāb al-Maʿārif*, pp. 6, 12, 17, etc.

[37] See above, Chapter Two, p. 28. Already Goldziher, Algermissen, and other scholars rejected the assumption that Ibn Ḥazm had used Saadia's translation. M. Schreiner assumed that he used some "Jewish translation"; see his "Beitraege zur Geschichte der Bibel in der arabischen Literatur," *Semitic Studies in Memory of A. Kohut*, ed. A. G. Kohut (Berlin 1897), p. 496 (reprinted in his *Gesammelte Schriften*, ed. M. Perlmann [Hildesheim 1983], p. 348). I. Goldziher apparently thought of a Christian translation; see "Ueber Muhammedanische Polemik gegen Ahl al-Kitāb,"

ple, the exact and full translation of Gen. 38 or Deut. 32, which he gives in *Al-Faṣl*,[38] and the lengthy quotations from the Pentateuch in his book against Ibn al-Naghrīla,[39] show clearly that he used another unknown Arabic Biblical text,[40] perhaps a Spanish Christian one. He knew the Gospel well, mentioned "the books of the Christians" and a Latin translation of the Bible (in at least one case he seems to have followed a version of the Vulgate), and used a slightly different enumeration of the Psalms he quoted (he starts with the second Psalm, as *Al-Mazmūr al-awwal*). This all seems to corroborate his use of a Christian Arabic Bible, as does independent information about early translations of the Bible into Arabic in Spain.[41] Yet even Ibn Ḥazm, whose knowledge of the Biblical text is attested in his books, relied upon oral contacts with Jews and Christians, perhaps in addition to the use he made of a partial written Arabic translation of the Bible.[42]

ZDMG 32 (1878). Algermissen in his *Die Pentateuchzitate* thought of some kind of a (Palestinian?) Arabic Targum.

[38] See *Al-Faṣl*, 1: 145–46, 200–201. In both cases Ibn Ḥazm states that he quotes the passages literally (pp. 148, 200).

[39] On this book, see Chapter Two, note 26 above, and see Hannah Shemesh's full translation of this book into Hebrew in *Muslim Authors on Jews and Judaism*, ed. H. Lazarus-Yafeh (Jerusalem 1992).

[40] Even when Ibn Ḥazm quotes "another version" (as for example, in *Al-Faṣl*, 1: 121 with regard to Gen. 3:24), this other version does not follow Saadia's either. In this case, Ibn Ḥazm scornfully adds: "If this is not a mistake made by the translator or commentator (*mutardjim*), I cannot understand this."

[41] See Algermissen, *Die Pentateuchzitate*, pp. 22–24. Already John Bishop of Seville is supposed to have translated the Bible into Arabic in the year 719 or 724, and there seem to exist ninth-century Andalusian manuscripts of Arabic translations of the Psalms. For the translations of Jewish texts, see D. Wasserstein, "An Arabic Version of Abot 1:3 from Umayyad Spain," *Arabica* 34 (1987): 370–74. (I. Goldziher, "Judeo-Arabes' Mélanges IX–XII," *REJ* 44 (1902): 63–72, and S. D. Goitein, "Isrā'īliyyāt," pp. 94–95 have already mentioned Arabic quotations from *Abot*.) See Ibn Ḥazm's quotations of the Psalms in *Al-Faṣl*, 1: 205–7 (above, Chapter Two, note 32.)

[42] Cf. *Al-Faṣl*, 1: 135, 150, and above, note 26. See, however, Algermissen (*Die Pentateuchzitate*, p. 30), who rejects the assumption of Ibn

Converts also constituted exceptions to the rule of oral transmission of the Biblical text. Often they still knew the Biblical text in the original Hebrew (Samau'al al-Maghribī) or in an earlier translation, such as Syriac ('Alī b. Rabban) or Coptic (Pseudo-Ghazzālī) and quoted it rather exactly.[43] This does not mean that all were reliable sources of information, however. In fact, some of them must be considered as the main channels of Biblical misinformation transmitted into Islam, either unintentionally or for polemical reasons. This is true of the early converts, like Ka'b al-Aḥbār and Wahb b. Munabbih, to whom Muslim sources attributed a multitude of alleged Bible quotations (see Chapter Two). It certainly is true of later converts, whose writings show a clear knowledge of the Bible and Midrash, but who purposely misquote certain verses. Thus, for example, Sa'īd b. Ḥasan of Alexandria, who converted to Islam in 1298, misquoted Balaam's prophecy in Num. 24:17 as: "Behold, a star appeared from the family of Ishmael and a tribe of Arabs sustained him. . . ." In this he followed earlier Jewish and Christian messianic interpretations of the verse, some of which (like that of Rabbi 'Aqiva) took the verse to allude to Ben-Kosiba (Bar Kochba), or perhaps to Jesus himself (as in the story of the Magi). He also interpolated Ishmael's name into the text elsewhere—for example, as one of the three Fathers, or in the much-discussed Deut.

Ḥazm's oral Jewish sources made already by H. Hirschfeld, "Mohammedan Criticism of the Bible," *JQR* 13 (1901): 226, and I. Di Matteo, "Le pretese contraddizione della S. Scrittura secondo Ibn Ḥazm," *Bessarione* 27 (1923): 88ff. No proof can be found for N. Roth's assumption in his "Forgery and Abrogation of the Torah" (*PAAJR* 54 [1987]: 204) that "Ibn Ḥazm was well versed in the Bible in Hebrew, as were numerous other Muslim writers both in Spain and elsewhere."

[43] Samau'al's Biblical quotations are sometimes slightly inaccurate; see, e.g., *Ifḥām al-Yahūd* (Silencing the Jews), ed. and trans. M. Perlmann, *PAAJR* 32 (1964): text p. 29, trans. p. 45. Pseudo-Ghazzālī, the author of *Al-Radd al-Djamīl li-Ilāhiyyat 'Īsā bi-Ṣarīḥ al-Indjīl* (ed. and trans. R. Chidiac [Paris 1939]), quoted mainly the New Testament. See H. Lazarus-Yafeh, *Studies in Al-Ghazzālī* (Jerusalem 1975), Appendix A.

18:18.[44] In a more sophisticated way, the Moroccan Jewish convert to Islam ʿAbd al-Ḥaqq gave a phonetical transcription of Hosea 9:5–6, but vocalized the Hebrew word *maḥmad* as Muhammad, as he did also with 1 Kings 20:6 and 22:35 (in the last case the change is slightly greater, from the Hebrew *moʿomad*).[45] Sometimes he also simply interpolated Muhammad's name into the Biblical text, claiming this to be the true original version—for example, at the beginning of Gen. 1:16, which according to him reads: "And God created the two great lights from the light of our lord Muhammad, blessed be he."[46] On other occasions, he gives an exact phonetic transcription of the Hebrew text, but translates differently; for example, Gen. 2:8: "And God put the lord Aḥmad into the Garden before mankind," or "before creation,"[47] and Gen. 12:2, which he translated as: "And I shall create Muhammad from you and I shall bless you."[48]

The mere fact that as late as the thirteenth or fourteenth century, Jewish converts misquoted the Biblical text (although they could always claim that this was the true, original version) may also be taken as further proof that among their readership, knowledge of the Biblical text was not widespread. Around that time, however, exact Biblical quotations become more common in Muslim literature, as the

[44] See Saʿīd b. Ḥasan, *Masālik al-Naẓar*, ed. and trans. S. A. Weston, *JAOS* 24 (1904): text p. 327, trans. p. 362, and see the interesting example there (text p. 326, trans. p. 362) where it is clear that Saʿīd knew the Midrash interpretations of Gen. 49:1–2 and used them in his polemical context (cf. *Bereshit Rabba* 98:1–2).

[45] Brit. Lib. Ms. Add. 9660, p. 8 (my numeration).

[46] Brit. Lib. Ms. Add. 9660, p. 11 (on p. 10 there he explained this Biblical text according to Gemmatria; see Chapter Four, p. 97 above). See also H. Lazarus-Yafeh, "The Contribution of a Jewish Convert from Morocco to Muslim Polemics against Jews and Judaism," *Peʿamim, Studies in Oriental Jewry* (in Hebrew) 42 (1990): 83–90.

[47] Already the Targum and the Vulgate understand the Hebrew word *mi-kedem* as referring to time and not to the east.

[48] Brit. Lib. Ms. Add. 9660, p. 15. See many more examples in the manuscript itself.

books of the Shi'ite author Ibn Tāwūs (d. 1266),[49] Al-Qurṭubī (d. 1273?),[50] and to a lesser extent Ibn Taymiyya (d. 1328) show.[51] Al-Qurṭubī also dealt critically with verses like "and no one knows his burial place to this day" (Deut. 34:6) and seems to differentiate between the Biblical text and later Midrashic additions *(laysa fī-l-Tawrāt)* not found in the text itself.[52]

Yet, even as late as the fourteenth and early fifteenth century, such Muslim authors as Ibn Qayyim al-Djawziyya (d. 1350) and Ibn Khaldūn (d. 1406), who were interested in the Bible and in Judaism, whether for polemical reasons (the former) or for scientific ones (the latter), did not consult written Arabic translations of the Bible. Ibn Qayyim al-Djawziyya mentioned translations of Biblical books such as Isaiah and Chronicles, but did not seem to trust their accuracy or exact transmission. Later Muslim historiographers, such as Abū-l-Fidā (d. 1331) and Al-Maqrīzī (d. 1442), did not yet consult written Arabic Bibles either.

Abū-l-Fidā stated explicitly that his history of the Israelite books of Judges and Kings might be full of mistakes be-

[49] Ibn Tāwūs was a prolific author. The Biblical quotations are to be found mainly in his *Sa'd al-Sa'ūd* (Nadjf, n.d.), where he quotes literal passages from an Arabic translation (the manuscript of which he apparently personally owned) of at least the Pentateuch, Psalms, and Gospels (pp. 32ff.). (I owe this reference to E. Kohlberg.)

[50] Al-Qurṭubī, *Al-I'lām bimā fī Dīn al-Naṣārā min al-Fasād*, ed. Aḥmad Ḥidjāzī al-Saqqā (Cairo 1980), pp. 263ff., 396ff. C. Brockelmann's assumption (in *GALS* 1 [New York 1938], p. 737, n. 7 to p. 416) that this author is identical to Shams al-Din al-Qurṭubī, author of *Aḥkām al-Qur'ān* (d. 1273) is hard to accept, although S. Pines apparently does ("Gospel Quotations and Cognate Topics," p. 265 n. 42). According to the colophon of one manscript of the book (Ma'had al-Makhṭūṭāt, Cairo), it was composed later as a response to a Christian work, with the title *Tathlīth al-Waḥdāniyya* (written in 1280/679 Hg.), and was finished only in the year 1325/726 Hg. In any case, the number and manner of Biblical quotations in this book are quite unusual and worth a separate study. (I owe this reference to J. Sadan.)

[51] See, for example, Ibn Taymiyya, *Al-Djawāb al-Ṣaḥīḥ li-man baddala Dīn al-Masīḥ* (Cairo 1905) 2: 41–42; and see Chapter Four above.

[52] See Al-Qurṭubī, *Al-I'lām*, pp. 188, 195.

cause the action in these books had taken place a long time ago and was written about in Hebrew. He mentioned the many contradictions he found between the various existing versions of this history with regard to the names, numbers, and years of rule of these people, and then added:

> And the Jews have twenty-four [holy] books, consecutive [or "well-transmitted" *mutawātira*], ancient, which have not yet been translated into Arabic (*lam tuʿrab ilā-l-ān*) but are in Hebrew. I have brought the two books of Judges and Kings and a man who knows Hebrew and Arabic and have let him read them, and have brought [for comparison] with them three versions and have written [in my book] what I thought to be true and have rendered the names as accurately as I could, letters and vowels, and God guides [us] to truth.[53]

Ibn Taymiyya remarks at approximately the same time that translations usually contain mistakes. So does "a contemporary translation of the Torah from Hebrew into Arabic, according to the testimony of truth-speaking experts who know both languages."[54]

One of the first Muslim authors to consult an Arabic Bible directly, though in a way similar to Abū-l-Fidā, was Burhān al-Dīn Ibrāhīm b. ʿUmar al-Biqāʿī (d. 1480), who also wrote a special treatise to defend his procedure.[55] In his commentary on the Qur'an, he quoted extensively from the Pentateuch and Gospels and compared their stories with those of the Qur'an. So far, only the first two chapters of his commentary on the Qur'an have been published,[56]

[53] See Abulfedae, *Historia Anteislamica Arabice*, ed. H. O. Fleischer (Lipsiae 1831), p. 34 and p. 50.

[54] Ibn Taymiyya, *Al-Djawāb al-Saḥīḥ*, 2: 17.

[55] See C. Brockelmann, *GAL*, vol. 2 (New York 1949), p. 142, and *GALS*, vol. 2 (New York 1938), p. 178; cf. Steinschneider, *Polemische und Apologetische Literatur*, pp. 389ff.

[56] *Nazmuddurar* [sic] *fi tanāsub-il āyāt was-suwar*, edited under the supervision of Dr. M. ʿAbdu'l Muʿid Khan (vols. 1, 3) and Mahamed Ali Abbasi (vol. 2) (Hyderabad 1969, 1970, 1971). I could not consult the existing manuscripts of the book.

but they leave no doubt that Al-Biqāʿī used a written Arabic translation of the Bible. He himself says:

> [So] it says at the end of the fourth book [of the *Tawrāt*], in the versions (*nusakh*) which are to be found among the Jews now in the ninth [Hidjri] century, which I have read in a translated version into Arabic, written also thus [in Arabic characters]. And on it there were signs of their readings and the times when each part is to be read. Then I have compared its meaning, as told before, with one of them and he read it thus. . . .[57]

A Jew, then, provided him with a translation of Num. 33:1–18 different (?) from the one he had found in the Jewish manuscript. These "other versions" Al-Biqaʿī often adduced are usually taken from Saadia's translation[58]; his main source, which according to him was also a Jewish translation, is (with some rare exceptions) very different from Saadia's, less islamized and more literally accurate.[59] Sometimes, however, Al-Biqāʿī's text is only a shortened version of the Biblical text. Often he skips repetitive verses, and sometimes he changes the wording.[60] Yet, on the whole, Al-Biqāʿī had a good knowledge of the text, and even compared Old and New Testament versions of the same verse.[61]

Al-Biqāʿī's commentary and sources have yet to be studied carefully.[62] But he seems to represent a turning point

[57] *Nazmuddurar*, 1: 422 ff.

[58] Cf. ibid., e.g., 1: 427, 3 (Exod. 14:6); 1: 429, 1–2 (Exod. 14: 21); 2: 169, 3 (Gen. 11:28); 2: 171, 2–3 (Gen. 13:28).

[59] For example, Moses, like Muhammad, is called *Rasūluhu* by Saadia, whereas Al-Biqāʿī uses *ʿAbduhu* (see ibid., 1: 430 [Exod. 14:31]).

[60] See, for example, ibid., 1: 427ff., where a literal translation of Exod. 14–15 is given, but some verses are skipped; or ibid., 1: 429, where Exod. 14:27 is translated as "and God punished the Egyptians on the sea and manifested their lies."

[61] See ibid., 2: 168.

[62] In his introduction, Al-Biqāʿī mentions many authors and the books he read and used. ʿAlī b. Aḥmad al-Hirālī, or Al-Harrālī (d. 1239), whom he quotes constantly, seems particularly important. Cf. C. Brockelmann, *GAL*, vol. 1 (New York 1949), p. 414, and *GALS*, vol. 1, p. 735.

in Muslim knowledge of the Bible. With a few exceptions (like Ibn Ḥazm), most Muslim authors up to Al-Biqāʿī had no direct knowledge of the Biblical text. Even after Al-Biqāʿī, many still quoted traditional polemical or fictitious verses. All of them needed help to find their way through the Biblical text. From the fifteenth century on, however, many more manuscripts of Arabic Bible translations seem to have been available to Muslim authors, until finally print took hold in the Arab world and changed it completely.

CHAPTER SIX

Conclusion: From Late Antiquity to the Beginnings of Modern Bible Criticism

In this small book, I have surveyed the attitudes of Muslim medieval authors toward the Hebrew Bible, their knowledge of it, and the use they made of it. I have tried to show that they developed a kind of Bible criticism very close in nature and detail both to earlier pre-Islamic Bible criticism and to the beginnings of later scholarly European Bible criticism. In all three cases, this critical literature could flourish because the text of the Hebrew Bible was not considered holy by the authors. There may be more here than phenomenological similarity, however.

If we look from a wider historical perspective at Muslim medieval Bible criticism, which flourished especially in the period between the eleventh (Ibn Ḥazm in the West) and the fourteenth century (Ibn Qayyim al-Djawziyya in the East), we may assume direct historical links between the literatures mentioned. It is plausible to suppose that Muslim scholars drew much of their material (for both higher and textual criticism) from earlier pre-Islamic literature. It is equally plausible to assume that Muslims later transmitted this material, which they had enriched and systematically elaborated, back to central Europe, where it may have helped to pave the way for modern European Bible criticism. Medieval Muslim literature on the Bible, then, would constitute another example of Islamic civilization playing the roles of both storehouse and creative transmitter for ancient heritage from late Antiquity to postmedieval Christian Europe.

Muslim authors could have drawn many of their arguments against the Bible (see examples in Chapter Two) from a variety of pre-Islamic sources: Samaritan, Jewish-Christian, Christian, Gnostic, Hellenistic anti-Christian, Manichaean, and others, all of which dealt with some sort of Bible criticism[1] based on their respective theologies as well as on the classical tradition of textual studies. Classical Islamic literature has kept records about many such groups and individuals; these records are proving to be much more reliable than scholars previously thought. Some are now lost, or are preserved only in partial quotations, such as those by Abū ʿĪsā al-Warrāq (d. 861). Others are well preserved, edited, and translated—for example, Ibn al-Nadīm's tenth-century *Fihrist*, which contains a detailed chapter on the "Ṣabians, Manichaeans, the Daiṣāniya, Ḥurramiya, Marcionites, Mazdakites, and Other Sects."[2]

Muslim heresiographies, often known by their later common titles as *Milal wa-Niḥal* books ("Books on Religions and Sects"), are especially important to the preservation of materials concerning pre-Islamic sects, which may have been sources for Muslim Bible criticism. This literature started very early in Islam and was probably influenced by Christian works on this theme, like John of Damascus's *De haeresibus*. Yet it developed in Islam more fully than it ever did in Christian literature, and the study of comparative religion became, according to G. von Grunebaum, "the research acumen of the Muslims shown at its best."[3] Al-Ashʿarī (d. 935), Al-Malaṭī (d. 977), Al-Baghdādī (d. 1037), Ibn Ḥazm (d. 1064), and Al-Shahrastānī (d. 1153) wrote some of this genre's most famous existing books, which

[1] See, for example, E. Stein, *Alttestamentlische Bibilkritik in der Spaethellenistischen Literatur* (Lwow 1935) (*Collectanea Theologica*, Societas Theologorum Polonorum 16).

[2] See W. Madelung, "Abū ʿIsā al-Warrāq ueber die Bardesaniten, Marcioniten und Kantaeer," *Festschrift A. Spuler* (Leiden 1981) pp. 210–24 (reprinted in W. Madelung, *Religious Schools and Sects*, Variorum Reprints 20 [London 1985]); C. Colpe, "Anpassung des Manichaeismus an den Islam," *ZDMG* 109 (1959): 81–92; and Ibn al Nadīm, *Kitāb al-Fihrist*, ed. G. Fluegel and I. Roediger (Leipzig 1871) (trans. B. Dodge, *The Fihrist of Al-Nadīm* [New York and London 1970]), ch. 9.

[3] G. von Grunebaum, *Medieval Islam*, 2d ed. (Chicago 1953), p. 337.

contain a wealth of information about non-Islamic religions and sects. Muslim historiographers, Qur'an commentators, and theologians also often dealt with the same subjects, and their important remarks are scattered throughout the many books they composed.

We know now not only that Arabic literature kept records of ancient sects and religions, and may have preserved (unknowingly?) even lengthy quotations of their texts in Muslim treatises,[4] but also that these sects were much longer-lived than we used to think; some might have existed well into the tenth century. This would mean, for example, that Marcionite or Manichaean ideas of Bible criticism could have reached Muslim and heretic authors like Abū ʿĪsā al-Warrāq, the later Ibn al-Rāwandī (d. 865 or 912), or the ninth-century Jewish author Ḥīwī al-Balkhī directly, so that specific literary links need not be established.[5] Similarly, the anti-Christian arguments of Porphyrius, Celsus, or Julianus, including their Bible criticism, could easily have become known to Muslims through Christian neighbors, even those who knew their Church Fathers only slightly. The same holds true for Zoroastrian ideas, although here we may face other methodological problems. For example, the ninth-century Zoroastrian Martān Farūkh wrote, in Pahlavi, his *Škand Gūmānīk Vičar*,[6] wherein he criticized harshly the major religions of his

[4] See, for example, S. Pines, "The Jewish-Christians of the Early Centuries of Christianity According to a New Source," *Proceedings of the Israel Academy of Sciences and Humanities* 2 (1966); cf. below, note 14.

[5] See, for example, ʿAlī-Masʿūdī (d. 956), *Murūdj al-Dhahab* (Maçoudi, *Les Prairies d'or*, ed. and trans. C. Barbier de Meynard and P. de Courtille, Société asiatique [Paris, 1863], 2: 319), where a Coptic disputant with Jews tells about regular meetings held by Muslim theologians and philosophers with Dualists, Manichaeans and members of other sects and religions in the court of the Egyptian ruler Aḥmad b. Ṭūlūn. See below.

[6] Cf. J. P. de Menasce, ed. and trans., *Une Apologétique mazdéene du IXème siècle, Škand Gūmānik Vičar (La Solution decisive des doutes)* (Fribourg 1945). See also S. Baron, *A Social and Religious History of the Jews*, vol. 5 (New York 1957), pp. 105–7; J. Neusner, *A History of the Jews in Babylonia*, vol. 4 (Leiden 1969), App. 1.

time, including Manichaeism, and their respective Scriptures. He may have used ancient Zoroastrian motifs against the Hebrew Bible, but he may also have been influenced already by early Muslim Bible criticism. It will be difficult to establish his sources directly.

Muslim and other Arabic authors were particularly fascinated with religious issues, as the vast corpus of Arabic literature clearly shows. Their literary discussions must echo, at least in part, the many personal encounters between followers of different religions and sects, in which ideas were exchanged orally. In spite of the evolving orthodoxy of Sunni Islam, religious curiosity remained great, and in certain places and periods of time even Muslim orthodox authors remained quite open-minded. They often asked non-Muslims for information about their beliefs and Scriptures, though this was frowned upon by some, especially when related to the Jewish or Christian material (*Isrā'īliyyāt*) found in the Qur'an.[7] The meaning of Hebrew words or phrases was often discussed ("Hebrew is the closest of all languages to Arabic," says Ibn Qayyim al-Djawziyya[8]), and Qur'anic verses were compared to alleged or true Biblical ones and their similarities pointed out, not always in a negative polemical manner. Tenets of belief were analyzed rationally in an almost free, intellectual atmo-

[7] See I. Goldziher, "Ueber Muhammedanische Polemik gegen Ahl al-Kitāb," *ZDMG* 32 (1878): 341–87; M. J. Kister, "Ḥaddithū 'an banī Isrā'īla wa-lā-ḥaraja," *IOS* 2 (1972): 215–39. Jews and Christians also asked members of other faiths for information. Hai Gaon (d. 1038), for example, sent one of his disciples to the "Catholikus" to ask for the explanation of Psalm 141:5, but his act was criticized. See S. Abramson, *Problems in Gaonic Literature* (in Hebrew) (Jerusalem 1974), p. 245 n. 2.

[8] Ibn Qayyim al-Djawziyya, *Hidāyat al-Ḥayārā fī-l-Radd 'alā-l-Yahūd wa-l-Naṣārā* (Beirut, n.d.), ch. 7, p. 90. This book, which is usually printed in the margin of 'Abd al-Raḥmān Bek Bechaji Zāda's *Kitāb al-Farq bayn al-Maklūq wa-l-Khālıq*, contains a wealth of information about, and comparisons with, Jewish and Christian material. Some of it was copied from earlier authors, a fact unknown to I. Goldziher; see, for example, M. Perlmann's remark B33 on p. 96 of his edition and translation of Samau'al al-Maghribī's *Ifḥām al-Yahūd* (Silencing the Jews), *PAAJR* 32 (1964). Further examples can be easily adduced.

sphere, about which some theologians even complained.[9] Islam, of course, always had the last word, and it was always dangerous (and strictly forbidden) to express any criticism of Muhammad or the Qur'an; yet these discussions were very different from the later enforced court disputations between Jews and Christians in medieval Europe. The very fact that members of so many different sects and religions could participate in such discussions among theologians, sectarians, philosophers, mystics, freethinkers, and heretics opened up minds, and made arguments easily change forms and places and traffic freely from author to author, from religion to religion, or from civilization to civilization, sometimes exposing their origins explicitly, at other times disguising themselves cautiously.

In this manner, and often through converts to Islam, Greek anti-Christian material, Karaite arguments against the Rabbanites, interdenominational Christian disputes, Shiʿi, Ismaʿili, and other Muslim sectarian material entered the Islamic pool of arguments against other holy Scriptures.[10] They were widely used by Muslim authors who could not, or perhaps did not wish to, distinguish clearly between orthodoxy and heterodoxy in religions

[9] See, for example, Baron, *A Social and Religious History*, 5: 83, and cf. R. Dozy, "Sur l'Averroisme," *JA*, 5th ser., 1 (1853): 93. In philosophical circles, unlike the religious *ʿUlamā* mentioned here, this open-mindedness was the rule, perhaps especially so in the tenth and eleventh centuries. See J. L. Kraemer, *Humanism in the Renaissance of Islam* (Leiden 1986). In Jewish and Christian literary descriptions of such discussions, this open-mindedness is also clearly reflected. See, for example, Jehuda Halevi's *Book of Kuzari*, or *Le Dialogue d'Abraham de Tiberiade avec ʿAbd al-Raḥmān al-Hāshimī à Jerusalem vers 820*, ed. G. C. Marcuzzo, Textes et études sur l'Orient Chretien 3 (Rome 1986).

[10] The Jewish convert to Islam Samau'al al-Maghribī (d. 1175), for example, used several Karaite arguments and Biblical interpretations in his Muslim polemics against Judaism, some of which were known already, in a more general way, to Ibn Ḥazm. See *Ifḥām al-Yahūd*, text pp. 20–21, 52–53, 68ff.; trans. pp. 40–41, 55–56, 62ff. On polemical interaction between Jews, Christians, and Muslims, see also, e.g., S. H. Griffith, "Theodore Abū Qurrah's Arabic Text on the Christian Practice of Venerating Images," *JAOS* 105 (1985): 53–73.

other than their own. Only a small part of what must have been happening in these oral discussions has been preserved for us in writing,[11] and an even smaller part refers directly to the critical study of the Bible, the topic that concerns us here. But this polemical atmosphere provides the intellectual setting for this literature, without which the literature cannot be fully understood.

Given that in the West, in Muslim Spain, and especially in Cordova, literary contacts and translations, as well as disputes between members of different religions and sects, may have been even more common than in the Muslim East, it is not unlikely that Ibn Ḥazm of Cordova (d. 1064) was the true founder of Muslim polemics against the Bible. He has been described by scholars as "the first scholarly critic of the Bible," or the one "who anticipated much of modern Bible criticism,"[12] but his possible pre-Islamic sources are never mentioned.

In spite of his language and tone, there can be no doubt that Ibn Ḥazm's systematic scrutiny of the Bible text is a rare scholarly achievement, unparalleled in medieval Arabic literature. He had a deep impact on subsequent medieval Muslim polemics, and his arguments of Bible criticism (for example, his idea that Ezra the Scribe was the composer or falsifier of the Biblical canon; see Chapter Three)

[11] Cf. above, and see, for example, the Genizah fragment in the Jewish Theological Seminary Library 3734/12, which mentions literati, theologians, philosophers, doctors (*udabā, mutakallimīn, mutafalsifīn, atibā*), and others who used to attend meetings in which various religions were discussed (*majdlis al-kalām 'alā-l-sharā'i'*), apparently in the presence of the Fatimid wazir Ibn Killis (d. 991), himself a former Jew who converted to Islam. See M. R. Cohen and S. Somekh, "In the Court of Ya'qūb ibn Killis: A Fragment from the Cairo Genizah," *JQR* 80 (1990): 283–314. Cf. S. D. Goitein, *A Mediterranean Society*, vol. 5 (Berkeley 1988), pp. 444, 447.

[12] See E. Algermissen, *Die Pentateuchzitate Ibn Ḥazms* (Muenster 1933), p. 20; Goldziher, "Ueber Muhammedanische Polemik," p. 370; I. Di Matteo, "Le pretese contraddizione della S. Scrittura secondo Ibn Ḥazm," *Bessarione* 27 (1923): 77–123; and H. Hirschfeld, "Mohammedan Criticism of the Bible," *JQR* 13 (1901): 222–40.

may have been transmitted, through Jewish and Christian literary links, to modern European writers.

Ibn Ḥazm had contacts and discussions with well-educated Jews such as Ibn al-Naghrīla[13] and must have known and used Christian and anti-Christian materials for his book. He came from a family of Christian origins (a fact that he tried to hide), and his polemic against Christianity has been defined as containing "Jewish-Christian" materials.[14] He is one of the first Muslim scholars who knew the Pentateuch well, but he was less well versed in other parts of the Bible.[15] He is the first author in Arabic literature to give lengthy paraphrases and even exact literal translations of whole chapters of the Bible (for example, Gen. 38 or Deut. 32), but it is difficult to establish his exact sources. He knew much less about later Jewish literature, but he mentioned, for example, the anthropomorphic book *Shiʿur Qomah* (in print erroneously: *Shiʿr Toma*), which he believed to be part of the Talmud, as well as other details that may have reached him through Jewish Merkabah mystics in Spain, or perhaps through Karaite or Christian sources (see Chapter Two). The anthropomorphic theme looms large in his polemics against Judaism and Christianity. This may have been one reason why he apparently preferred Christian Arabic translations of the Bible to that of Saadia Gaon (d. 942), with which he was also acquainted (see Chapter Five). But whereas Saadia tried to avoid systematically all anthropomorphic terminology,[16] Christian literal translations of the Bible gave Ibn Ḥazm more opportunity to attack the crude anthropomorphic beliefs of Jews

[13] Cf. Ibn Ḥazm, *Al-Faṣl fī-l-Milal wa-l-Ahwā wa-l-Niḥal* (n. pl., 1329 Hg.), 1: 135, 152; Goldziher, "Ueber Muhammedanische Polemik"; and M. Perlmann, "Andalusian Authors on the Jews of Granada," *PAAJR* 18 (1948–49): 268–69.

[14] S. Pines, "Judaeo-Christian Materials in an Arabic Jewish Treatise," *PAAJR* 35 (1967): 187–217, esp. 213ff.

[15] Perlmann, "Andalusian Authors," pp. 277ff.

[16] In contrast to earlier Targumim, who did so only sporadically. See M. Klein, *Anthropomorphism and Anthropopathism in the Targumim of the Pentateuch* (Jerusalem 1982).

(and Christians) and to use ancient anti-Christian material against the Bible. Often he attacked Jewish and Christian readings of the Bible together—as he did, for example, for the opening verses of Gen. 18. He criticized the anthropomorphism of these verses, and the language shifts from singular to plural that seem to confuse God with the angels and the angels with men. He also stated, however, that he "had seen in the books of the Christians" their (well-known) attempts to prove the Trinity from these verses—and that this was even worse in his eyes.[17]

Ibn Ḥazm did not know Hebrew, but he knew about the Septuagint (which was already mentioned by earlier Muslim authors, for example, Al-Masʿūdī [d. 956])[18] and about Latin translations of the Bible.[19] He stressed that there are at least three different versions of the Bible with discrepancies between them—the Jewish version (the text of Ezra), the Christian version (the Septuagint), and the Samaritan Pentateuch[20]—and he drew from this far-reaching

[17] Ibn Ḥazm, *Al-Faṣl*, 1: 130–31. See also C. H. Becker, *Islamstudien*, vol. 1 (Leipzig 1924), p. 449; and D. Berger, *The Jewish-Christian Debate in the High Middle Ages* (a critical edition of *Nizzaḥon Vetus* with an introduction, translation, and commentary), Jewish Publication Society (Philadelphia 1979), App. 4.

[18] See *Al-Tanbīh wa-l-Ishrāf*, ed. M. J. de Goeje (Leiden 1843), p. 112.

[19] See Ibn Ḥazm, *Al-Faṣl*, 1: 50, where he mentions Latin in general, without knowing it, and 1: 152, where he quotes an Arabic translation of Gen. 49:10, apparently following the Vulgate. He also mentions that he had to ask for the meaning of certain Hebrew words (for an example, see Chapter Five, note 26 above).

[20] Ibn Ḥazm, 1: 117, 198; 2: 7–10. This was a widespread theme already in early Muslim polemics. See Al-Masʿūdī, *Murūdj al-Dhahab* (Les Prairies), 2: 219; Al-Bīrūnī (d. 1048), *Al-Athār al-Bāqiya ʿan al-Qurūn al-Khāliya*, ed. E. Sachau (Leipzig 1878), pp. 20–21 (trans. E. Sachau, *The Chronology of Ancient Nations* [London 1879], p. 24); ʿAbd al-Malik al-Djuwaynī (d. 1085), *Šifāʾ al-Ġalīl fī-l-Tabdīl*, ed. and trans. M. Allard, *Textes apologétiques de Ǧuwainī* (Beirut 1968), pp. 45ff.; cf. Algermissen, *Die Pentateuchzitate*, pp. 21ff. See also Ibn Kammūna's reply to this (the Christians do not have the Torah in the original language of revelation, but in Syrian and Greek). See *Ibn Kammūna's Examination of the Three Faiths*, ed. and trans. M. Perlmann (Berkeley 1967, 1971), text p. 31, trans. pp. 51–52. Muslim authors not only considered the "Christian"

conclusions about the reliability of the transmission of the original text (see Chapter Two).

Sometimes Ibn Ḥazm seems both to echo Christian arguments and to predict modern Bible criticism—for example, when speaking of the historical development of Judaism. He mentions in several places the new "synagogue Judaism" of the Second Commonwealth and "the prayer that their Rabbis invented . . . instead of Temple sacrifices, thus creating for them a new religion," very different from the one given to them by God on Mt. Sinai.[21] This polemical motif, like many others, was taken up a hundred years later by Samau'al al-Maghribī (d. 1175), the Jewish convert to Islam, who denounced in much detail the fabrication of the new prayers, new fasts, as well as the new dietary and other laws by the "Rabbanite legists."[22] Indeed, Ibn Ḥazm and Samau'al, who followed him in many details but also added much new material of his own, must be considered the two basic sources for medieval Muslim polemics against Judaism and the Bible. (They may have used the same sources, or there may have been a literary mediator between them that has not yet been found.) Other Muslim authors followed them closely, only rarely trying new approaches or adducing new material. Among those who did so, to some extent at least, we have mentioned Ibn Ḥazm's contemporary Ibn Ẓafar (d. 1169), who in his book "The Good Message about the Best of Mankind" (*Khayr al-Bishar bi-Khayr al-Bashar*)[23] showed special interest in different translations of Biblical verses; Al-Qarāfī (d. 1285),

Greek translations of the "originally" Hebrew Gospels to be proof of their falsification, but also dwelt at length on the inner contradictions between the four Gospels. (See, for example, Ibn Ḥazm, *Al-Faṣl*, 2: 10–69.)

[21] Ibn Ḥazm, *Al-Faṣl*, 1: 197.

[22] Samau'al al-Maghribī, *Ifḥām al-Yahūd*, text pp. 20–21, trans. pp. 40–41.

[23] The printed copy of this book (Cairo 1863) is rarer than the manuscript. The author seems to have spent some time in Sicily (see C. Brockelmann, *GAL*, vol. 1 [New York 1949], p. 325, and *GALS*, vol. 1 [New York 1938], p. 595) and may have been engaged there in polemics with Christians. See Chapter Four.

who devoted his main efforts to polemic against Christians and Christianity, especially in his book "The Glorious Answers to Wicked Questions" (*Al-Adjwiba al-Fākhira ʿan al-Asʾila al-Fādjira*);[24] Ibn Kammūna (d. 1285), the rationalistic philosopher, who examined all three revelational religions with the same detachment in his *Examination of the Three Faiths* (*Tanqīḥ al-Abḥāth li-l-Milal al-Thalāth*)[25]; and Ibn Qayyim al-Djawziyya (d. 1350), who furthered the scholarly aspects of Muslim polemics against Judaism and Christianity through his vast knowledge and original comparisons. Among his many books, the "Guidance of the Perplexed" (*Hidāyat al-Ḥayārā*) is the most relevant to our subject here.[26] Thereafter only very simple popular writings seem to have been written in Arabic by Muslim authors, who reiterate earlier polemical arguments,[27] but do not live up to the high scholarly standards set by Ibn Ḥazm, Samau'al al-Maghribī, and Ibn Qayyim al-Djawziyya.

The non-Muslim authors who may have transmitted Ibn Ḥazm's and Samau'al's critical approach to the Bible would have linked medieval Muslim Bible criticism with the beginning of modern European Bible research. We can men-

[24] Ed. Bakr Zakī ʿAwād (Cairo 1987). This book is also often printed on the margin of Bechaje Zāda's above-mentioned book (note 8).

[25] The author wrote under the Mongols' rule before their conversion to Islam, and tried therefore to approach critically even the Qur'an (*Ibn Kammūna's Examination*, ch. 4), but had to pay a high price for his audacity. See Perlmann's introduction to the English translation.

[26] See *EI*[2] s.v. "Ibn Qayyim al-Djawziyya" (H. Laoust), and see below, Appendix. (For the title "Guide to the Perplexed" in Arabic, cf. A. Gileadi, "A Short Note on the Possible Origins of the Title *Moreh Ha-Nevukhim*," *Le Muséon* 97 [1984]: 259–61.)

[27] See, for example, L. J. Kassin, "A Fourteenth Century Polemical Treatise Adversus Judaeos" (Al-Rāqilī's *Ta'yīd al-Milla*), diss., Columbia University, 1969; or the above-mentioned (Chapter Two, note 9) Cambridge Arabic ms. Qq 29, *Tafhīm al-Djāhilīn Dīn al-Yahūd al-Maghḍūb ʿalayhim wa-l-Naṣārā al-Ḍāllīn* (Enlightening the Ignorant about the Faith of the Jews with Whom God Is Wrathful and of the Christians Who Are Astray) by ʿAlī al-Munayyar al-Shāfiʿī (d. c. 1520). This manuscript is a very popular work, which makes confused use of Ibn Ḥazm's arguments.

tion here only some well-known figures and some general points of contact. The Jewish Bible commentator and author Abraham ibn Ezra (d. 1164) knew Arabic very well, travelled much, and may have had personal contacts with philosophical rationalistic circles in Baghdad, to which Samau'al al-Maghribī also belonged (see Chapter Three). He is mentioned (though only once) and praised explicitly by Spinoza for his critical remarks about the composition of the Bible and about Ezra,[28] but he must have known much more about the Muslim critical approach to the Biblical text. The Spaniard Petrus Alfonsi, who converted to Christianity from Judaism in 1106, was also quite familiar with polemical writings in Arabic, such as Ibn Ḥazm's, as many details in his writings seem to imply.[29] The Spanish Dominican Friar Raimundus Martini (d. 1285) may have served as another link between civilizations, charging in his *Pugio Fidei* that Ezra the Scribe and his collaborators corrupted the Biblical text through their emendations (*Tikkunei So-*

[28] See Spinoza, *Tractatus Theologico-Politicus*, ch. 8, and see Chapter Three above. (Ibn Ezra does not mention Ezra specifically.)

[29] See Ch. Merhavia, *The Church versus Talmudic and Midrashic Literature* (Jerusalem 1970), ch. 3; and see M. Orfali, "Anthropomorphism in the Christian Reproach of the Jews in Spain," *IMMANUEL, A Journal of Religious Thought and Research in Israel* 19 (1984–85): 60–79. Recently, A. H. and C. E. Cutler have suggested that Petrus Alfonsi is Peter of Toledo, who translated Arabic writings into Latin—for example, the *Apology* (Risāla) of 'Abd al-Masīḥ al-Kindī. See their *The Jew as Ally of the Muslim: Medieval Roots of Anti-Semitism* (Notre Dame 1986), ch. 3. See also G. Monnot, "Les Citations coraniques dans le 'Dialogus' de Pierre Alfonse," in *Islam et Chrétiens du Midi*, CNRS, Cahier des Fanjoux 18 (Toulouse 1983), pp. 262–77. For a more general approach see also A. Funkenstein, "Changes in the Patterns of Christian-Jewish Polemics in the 12th Century" (in Hebrew), *Zion, Quarterly for Research in Jewish History* 33 (1969): 125–44; R. Chazan, "The Condemnation of the Talmud Reconsidered," *PAAJR* 55 (1988): 11–30; H. A. Wolfson, "The Veracity of Scripture from Philo to Spinoza," *Alexander Marx Jubilee Volume* (New York 1950), pp. 603–30 (reprinted in his *Religious Philosophy, A Group of Essays* [New York 1965], pp. 217–33).

frim). The expulsion of Jewry from Spain and their movement into Europe and Turkey at the end of the fifteenth century, and the subsequent flourishing of the Jewish community in the Ottoman Empire,[30] may have aided the transmission of Arabic sources or ideas to Europe as well.

Many more points of contact doubtless could be found to trace the movement of pre-Islamic ideas of Bible criticism into Islam, and from there to the beginnings of modern Bible criticism. Here I have only pointed out the general directions of this chain of transmission, the middle link of which is to be found in medieval Muslim Bible criticism. The details of this transmission have yet to be studied assidously in each of the three civilizations concerned. At this point, one can only state that these different worlds are indeed interdependent and intertwined: there seems to be no real basis for the commonly accepted belief among scholars that they are phenomenologically totally different from each other and that there is no historical or literary evidence that could establish a link between them.[31]

[30] Cf. the recent studies of the literary activity of this community (in Hebrew) by J. Hacker. See also R. H. Popkin, "A Late Seventeenth-Century Gentile Attempt to Convert the Jews to Reformed Judaism," *Israel and the Nations, Essays in Honor of Shmuel Ettinger* (Jerusalem 1987), pp. xxv–xlv, esp. p. xxxiii, where one can discern clearly Muslim polemical motifs against the Bible, in the *Letters Writ by a Turkish Spy at Paris*.

[31] See, for example, M. Haran, "Midrashic and Literal Exegesis and the Critical Method in Biblical Research," *Studies in Bible, Scripta Hierosolymitana* 31 (Jerusalem 1986), pp. 19–48.

Appendix: Jewish Knowledge of, and Attitudes toward, the Qur'an

THE JEWISH PHILOSOPHER Ibn Kammūna (d. 1285) says in his *Examination of the Three Faiths*:

> The Jews may say: if the contacts of non-Jews with us were as close as our contacts with the Muslims, this [our belief in the perpetuity of Jewish law] would be known concerning our faith. But the contact of Muslims with Jews does not necessitate a Muslim inquiry into what the Jews assert, especially since the Jews are prevented from declaring their creed, and their books are in a tongue the Muslims do not understand. The contact of a minority with a majority affects the majority and the minority differently. Thus, when a linguistic minority (*al-aqall min ahl lugha*) is in contact with a linguistic majority, the minority learns the language of the majority whilst the majority does not learn the language of the minority or, at best, learns it much later. Moreover, despite numerous contacts of the bulk of the Jews with the Muslims, many Jews still do not know the basic Islamic tenets known by the rank and file Muslims, let alone the elite. It is even more natural that a similar situation should obtain on the Muslim side, or, at the very least, that both sides should be equal [in mutual ignorance].[1]

I have attempted in this book to describe what Muslims knew about the Hebrew Bible and how they may have acquired this knowledge. Here, I try briefly to describe how much Jews knew of the Qur'an and how they used their knowledge.

The restrictions imposed by Islam on its "Protected People" (*Ahl al-Dhimma*, mainly Jews, Christians, and Samar-

[1] *Ibn Kammūna's Examination of the Three Faiths*, ed. and trans. M. Perlmann, Arabic text (Berkeley 1967), p. 50; Eng. trans. (Berkeley 1971), pp. 76–77.

itans), known usually as the "Pact of 'Umar" (*'Ahd 'Umar*), often prohibit those people from studying the Qur'an, and even the Arabic language, as well as from using Arab by-names and engraving Arabic inscriptions on their seals.[2] Early Muslim jurists—for example, Abū Yūsuf (d. 798), Al-Shāfi'ī (d. 820), and Al-Māwardī (d. 1058)—usually do not mention these specific prohibitions, but Al-Ṭabarī (d. 923) tells in his historiography that in the year 236 Hg. (850), the 'Abbasid Caliph Al-Mutawakkil forbade the Dhimmis (more especially the Christians) to send their children to Muslim boy-schools (*katātīb*) or to hire a Muslim teacher for them.[3] Al-Māwardī added that *Ahl al-Dhimma* were forbidden to criticize the Qur'an, the Prophet, or the religion of Islam.[4] In later versions of the "Pact of 'Umar," these prohibitions appear in more detail, but few scholars have paid attention to them,[5] perhaps because it seems obvious that these specific restrictions, such as one forbidding use of the Arabic language, could never have been enforced effectively, as both Jews and Christians became thoroughly arabicized under Islamic rule.

The study of the Qur'an may have been a different matter, as a story from the Genizah about a well-known Egyptian Jewish banker and administrator by the name of Abū-l-Munadjdjā Solomon b. Sha'yā shows. Abū-l-Munadjdjā copied the Qur'an while in prison and sent it to the bazaar with the signature "written by Abū-l-Munadjdjā the Jew."

[2] See, for example, Muḥammad b. Walīd al-Ṭarṭūshī (d. 1126), *Sirādj al-Mulūk* (Cairo 1935), pp. 252–53 (Eng. trans. in B. Lewis, ed. and trans., *Islam, from the Prophet Muhammad to the Capture of Constantinople*, vol. 2 [New York 1974], pp. 217–19).

[3] Cf. Al-Ṭabarī, *Ta'rīkh al-Rusul wa-l-Mulūk* (*Annales*), ed. M. J. de Goeje, M. T. Houtsma, and S. Guyard, 3d ser., repr. (Leiden 1964), p. 1389.

[4] See 'Alī al-Māwardī, *Al-Aḥkām al-Sulṭāniyya* (Cairo 1909), p. 129 (trans. E. Fagnan, *Mawerdi, les statuts gouvernementaux* [Alger 1915], p. 305).

[5] A. S. Tritton, *The Caliphs and Their Non-Muslim Subjects* (London 1930), does not mention this subject at all, and A. Fattal, *Le Statut legal des non-Musulmans en pays d'Islam* (Beirut 1958), mentions it only briefly (p. 111).

When asked why he had done this, he explained that he wanted to be liberated from prison, by death (as punishment for copying the Qur'an). Instead, he was set free by the Ayyubid viceroy Al-Malik al-Afḍal (1094–1121).[6]

There can be little doubt, however, that both Jews and Christians, who were well acquainted with Arabic Muslim religious literature and were deeply influenced by it, had some knowledge of the Qur'an. There exists literary evidence to this effect, but part of this evidence may simply derive from what used to be common parlance in medieval Arabic. Jews (and Christians) who used the Arabic language often included—consciously or unconsciously—Qur'anic idioms and phrases from the Ḥadīth in speech and writing, as well as in amulets and talismans.

A good example of such a case is the recurring Qur'anic phrase *Al-Amr bi-l-Ma'rūf wa-l-Nahy 'an al-Munkar* (to enjoin right conduct and forbid evil), which is mentioned several times in the Qur'an[7] but was used in a much wider context in Arabic in general. Jewish authors often used this phrase, and the Spanish eleventh-century author Baḥya b. Paquda, for example, seems to have been especially fond of it.[8] He connected it with the Biblical command "to rebuke your neighbor" (Lev. 19:17) and with its traditional exegesis—from which, in fact, the Islamic enjoinder may have been derived in the first place.[9] Nevertheless, Baḥya may

[6] See Ibrāhīm b. Muḥammad ibn Douqmāq, *Description de l'Egypte*, ed. K. Vollers (Cairo 1893), 2: 46–47; S. D. Goitein, *A Mediterranean Society*, vol. 2 (Berkeley 1971), pp. 356, 605 n. 6 (where the reference to Ibn Douqmāq [vol. 5] is erroneously quoted). See also J. Mann, *The Jews in Egypt and Palestine under the Fatimid Caliphs*, vol. 1 (New York 1970), p. 215. (I owe the reference to this story to M. A. Friedman.)

[7] See, for example, Sūra 3:104, 110, 114; Sūra 7:157; Sūra 9:67, 71, 112.

[8] See *Al-Hidāya 'ilā Farā'iḍ al-Qulūb des Bachja ibn Jōsēf ibn Paqūda aus Andalusien*, ed. A. S. Yahuda (in Arabic characters) (Leiden 1912), text, e.g., pp. 172, 196, 219, 248–49, 272, and esp. 330; cf. Y. Kafaḥ's edition, *Torat Ḥovot ha-Levavot le-Rabbenu Beḥayye ben Joseph ben Paquda* (in Hebrew characters) with a Hebrew translation (Jerusalem, n.d.), pp. 182, 209, 266–67, 293, 342, and esp. p. 357.

[9] The idea is expressed in the Talmud; see, for example, *Shabbat* 54a,

not have been aware that he was quoting a Qur'anic phrase.

The evidence is less clear with regard to another Qur'anic simile that Baḥya used, of "an ass carrying books." In the Qur'an (Sūra 62:5), it is used in a polemical manner against the Jews, who do not know or adhere to the contents of their own Scriptures, whereas Baḥya used it to describe the lowest of ten categories of students of the Torah.[10]

Jews using Arabic also used the term *Qur'ān* to denote the Bible,[11] and *Sūrat al-Tawḥīd* to denote the first portion of the Recitation of the Shemaʿ.[12]

Some Jewish authors had a more direct knowledge of the Qur'an[13] and quoted the Qur'an explicitly—for example,

---

and in a more detailed way, connected with the same Biblical verse, *'Arakhin* 16b.

[10] See Bachja, *Al-Hidāya* (ed. Yahuda), text p. 144; and Kafaḥ's edition, *Ḥovot ha-Levavot*, p. 148. Yahuda does not remark on the Qur'anic use of this idiom, although elsewhere he refers to other Qur'anic parallels; see, e.g., text p. 82 n. 2 (Sūra 89:13). (Kafaḥ never mentions Qur'anic parallels.) See also G. Vajda, *La Théologie ascétique de Baḥya ibn Paquda* (Paris 1948), p. 42. This simile also seems to be pre-Islamic and appears, for example, in the sixth-century *Book of Asaf Harofe*; see E. Ben Yehuda's *Complete Dictionary of Ancient and Modern Hebrew* (Tel Aviv 1948), 3: 1617 (s.v. "*Ḥamor*"). Bachja also quotes, perhaps unconsciously, Sūra 42:11 ("Nothing is as his likeness"); see Bachja, *Al-Hidāya* (ed. Yahuda), pp. 72, 181 (without any remark), and cf. Kafaḥ, *Ḥovot ha-Levavot*, pp. 76, 192. Of course, in Hebrew translations these quotations are totally lost.

[11] See, for example, Saadia's introduction to his *Siddur*, in *Siddur R. Saadja Gaon*, ed. I. Davidson, S. Assaf, and B. I. Joel, 3d ed. (Jerusalem 1970), frag. 3 (Cambridge *T.-S.* Ar.18[1]23) p. ד • line 20; cf. H. Lazarus-Yafeh, *Some Religious Aspects of Islam* (Leiden 1981) pp. 81–82; David b. Abraham al-Fāsī, *Kitāb Jāmiʿ al-Alfāẓ* (Agron), ed. S. L. Skoss, Yale Oriental Series 20 (Philadelphia 1936), 1: 34, 52, and passim. (I owe this reference to A. Dotan.)

[12] Thus, in a Genizah fragment (in Cambridge *T.-S.* Misc. 28.7), in a passage attributed to Rav Joseph Rosh Haseder. (I owe this reference to L. Ginat.)

[13] M. Steinschneider already drew attention to this fact. See his *Polemische und Apologetische Literatur in Arabischer Sprache* (Leipzig 1877), pp. 313ff. Cf. J. Blau, *The Emergence and Linguistic Background of Judeo-Arabic* (Jerusalem 1981), pp. 36–37.

the Karaite author Al-Qirqisānī, or Jehuda ibn Quraysh, Moses ibn Ezra, Nethanel al-Fayyūmī,[14] and (in a more indirect manner) Maimonides.[15] The Jewish rationalist philosopher Ibn Kammūna (d. 1285) had an especially wide knowledge of the Qur'an and its different *Qirā'āt* versions, as well as of Muslim theology in general.[16]

Other Jewish authors tried to disguise the fact that they were quoting the Qur'an. The thirteenth-century Spaniard Abraham bar Ḥisday did this in his Hebrew translation of Al-Ghazzālī's *Mīzān al-'Amal*. He quoted an almost exact Hebrew translation of *Sūrat al-Fātiḥa* as a "prayer of one of the sages" in his *Moznei Zedeq*,[17] where the Arabic original apparently had only the first verse of the same Sūra (perhaps because every Muslim knows this Sūra by heart).

One of the translators of Al-Ghazzālī's *Mishkāt al-Anwār*

[14] See Al-Qirqisānī, *Kitāb al-Anwār wa-l-Marāqib*, ed. L. Nemoy, pt. 3 (New York 1941), ch. 15, pp. 292–301 (cf. I. Friedlaender, "Qirqisānī's Polemik gegen den Islam," 26 (1912): 93–110; Dan Becker, *The "Risāla" of Judah ben Quraysh: A Critical Edition* (in Hebrew) (Tel Aviv 1984), p. 35 n. 17 (Becker mentions there two other eleventh-century Jewish authors who quoted the Qur'an: Ibn Djanāḥ and Ibn Barūn); Moshe ben Ya'akov ibn Ezra, *Kitāb al-Muḥāḍara wal-Mudhākara* (Liber discussionis et commemarationis), ed. A. S. Halkin (Jerusalem 1975), pp. 4, 92, 112, 117; Nethanel al-Fayyūmī, *Bustān al-'Uqūl*, ed. D. Levine (New York 1908), text pp. 18, 66–67, 69, trans. pp. 29–30, 105, 109 (Y. Kafaḥ's edition, *Bustān al-'Uqūl, Gan Ha-Sekhalim le-Rabbenu Nethanel* (Jerusalem 1954), pp. 32, 116–17). See also R. Kiener, "Jewish Ismā'īlism in Twelfth-Century Yemen: R. Nethanel ben Al-Fayyūmī," *JQR* 74 (1983–84): 249–66. See also Joseph ibn 'Aqnīn's explicit statement that Saadia and Rav Hai Gaon both quoted the Qur'an and Ḥadīth, in his Arabic commentary to the Song of Songs, *Inkishāf al-Asrār wa-Ẓuhūr al-Anwār* (Divulgatio mysteriorum luminumque apparenta), ed. A. S. Halkin (Jerusalem 1964), pp. 493–94.

[15] See, for example, Maimonides, *Epistle to Yemen*, ed. A. S. Halkin (New York 1952), p. 38; and W. Z. Harvey, "Ibn Rushd and Maimonides on the Commandment of I'tibār" (in Hebrew), *Tarbiz* 58 (1989): 75–83, esp. 80–81.

[16] See Perlmann, *Ibn Kammūna's Examination of the Three Faiths*, e.g., chs. 1 and 4, Arabic text pp. 20, 67, 69, 71–74, 86–87; Eng. trans. pp. 37, 101, 103, 106–10, 126–27.

[17] See Abraham bar-Chasdai Barcinonensi, *Compendium Doctrinae Ethicae*, by Al-Gazali Tusensi, ed. J. Goldenthal (Leipzig and Paris 1830), p. 96.

into Hebrew (*Sodot ha'Orot ha'Elohiyot*) quoted many Qur'anic verses in his translation, sometimes very accurately, sometimes with slight omissions, misunderstandings, or changes.[18] When he mentioned their source, he quoted them very generally as divine prophecies; once (ms. p. 78) he even explained, following the Arabic original, that the text (which is an almost full and literal rendering of the short Sūra 112) was revealed to the Messenger of God (*Shli'aḥ ha'El a.h.*) as a response to the questioning of some Arabs (the Arabic text has *Al-Aʿrāb*, namely Beduins). This translator also quoted Ḥadīth sayings by "the Prophet" (or "our Prophet, peace, be upon him") and his companions and mentioned some of them by name (for example, ʿAlī, ʿAbd al-Raḥmān b. ʿAwf, ʿAbdallāh b. Masʿūd, and Ubayy b. Kaʿb) but omitted others (ʿAbdallāh b. ʿAbbās).[19] But the same translator (or one of his later copyists) sometimes omitted explicit references to the Qur'an as such, often rendering his translation unintelligible. (Most of these Hebrew translations, which have not yet been edited and published, still await thorough investigation.)

Qur'anic phrases also appear in unexpected places in Judaeo-Arabic literature. Thus Saadia translated "red heifer" (Num. 19:2) with *baqara ṣafrā*, the Qur'anic term for it (see Sūra 2:69ff., where it is mixed up with the heifer mentioned in Deut. 21). Yet Saadia usually translated "red" with *aḥmar* and other derivatives of the root *ḥmr* rather than with *aṣfar*.[20]

[18] See *Bibliothece Apostolicae Vaticane*, cat. 1, Codices Ebraicos et Samaritos (Rome 1756), p. 170, ms. no. 209, 5, e.g., pp. 69 (Sūra 24:35), 72 (64:8; 4:174; 7:179), 73 (78:38; 37:165–66), 74 (28:88; 40:16), 75 (11:61; 24:55; 27:62; 2:30), 76 (41:53). Cf. M. Steinschneider, *Die Hebraeischen Uebersetzungen des Mittelalters* (Berlin 1893), pp. 346, 196b.

[19] See *Bibliothece Apostolicae Vaticane*, ms. no. 209, 5, e.g., pp. 78, 80 ("the Prophet"), pp. 77, 79, 80 (his companions).

[20] See, for example, his translations to Gen. 25:25, 30; Exod. 28:17 (where *aṣfar* is also used); Lev. 13:18, 42, 43, 49, or Isa. 1:18, 63:2. Cf. J. Blau, "Between Judaeo-Arabic and the Qur'ān" (in Hebrew), *Tarbiz* 40 (1971): 513–14; but Blau does not mention the fact that Saadia usually

Of course most Qur'anic quotations in Judaeo-Arabic literature are lost when translated into Hebrew. The Qur'an itself is rarely mentioned explicitly in Hebrew; on the few occasions when it is mentioned, the derogatory Hebrew term *Qalon* is used.[21] To discern possible influences of Qur'anic exegesis on Jewish literature is even more difficult.[22]

The study of the Qur'an also served polemical purposes for the Jews. Jewish authors attacked the concept of the inimitability of the Qur'an and the claim that it is the perfect book, as well as the idea of abrogation;[23] but it is hard to believe that they ever composed polemical treatises pointing out the inner contradictions of the Qur'an, as the one attributed to Samuel Hanagid supposedly did.[24] Very

---

uses the word *aḥmar* for "red." The translation of colors is, of course, very tricky.

[21] Steinschneider (*Polemische und Apologetische Literatur*, p. 316) doubted that Jewish authors like Maimonides (see his *Epistle to Yemen*, p. 38 and n. 52) termed the Qur'an *Qalon* even when writing in Arabic, but Karaite authors did so. See H. Ben Shammai, "The Attitude of Some Early Karaites towards Islam," in *Studies in Medieval Jewish History and Literature*, ed. I. Twersky, vol. 2 (Cambridge, Mass. 1984), p. 16; cf. Samau'al al-Maghribī, *Ifḥām al-Yahūd* (Silencing the Jews), ed. and trans. M. Perlmann, *PAAJR* 32 (1964): text p. 67, trans. p. 62, and note B66 on p. 99. For the Islamic dimension lost in Hebrew translations, see M. Gottstein, "Translation and Translators in the Middle Ages" (in Hebrew), *Gotthold E. Weil Jubilee Volume* (Jerusalem 1952) pp. 74–80.

[22] S. Pines, for example, thought that one line of Ibn Gabirol echoed Qur'anic exegesis to Sūra 113:1–2. See his "And He Called Out to Nothingness and It Was Split—A Note on a Passage in Ibn Gabirol's *Keter Malkhut*," *Tarbiz* 50 (1981): 339–47. Y. Liebes, who drew my attention to this item, contested Pines's view in his "The Kabbalistic Myth of Orpheus," *Shlomo Pines Jubilee Volume*, ed. M. Idel, W. Z. Harvey, and E. Schweid, Studies in Jewish Thought (Jerusalem 1988), p. 446 n. 64.

[23] See, for example, Friedlaender, "Qirqisānī's Polemik," p. 105; cf. Samau'al al-Maghribī, *Ifḥā al-Yahūd*, text p. 65, trans. pp. 61–62; Steinschneider, *Polemische und Apologetische Literatur*, p. 103. See also above, Chapter Two, p. 37 and note 52. Cf. R. Brunschvig, "L'Argumentation d'un theologien musulman du Xe siècle contre le Judaisme," in *Homenaje a Millas y Valicrosa*, vol. 1 (Barcelona 1954), pp. 225–41.

[24] See above, Chapter Two, p. 27 and note 26.

seldom did Jews hint that the Qur'an also might have been tampered with and falsified.[25] This was probably the result not only of fear, but also of the simple fact that since the Qur'an was a later Scripture than the Bible, it posed no real theological problem for Jews, in contrast to the problem the Bible posed for Muslims. Nevertheless, the problem of gentile (late) prophecy remained a serious issue for Jews.

Sometimes we hear about Jews supposedly quoting Qur'anic verses in their discussions with Muslims about the proper interpretation of Biblical verses. According to Ibn Qayyim al-Djawziyya (d. 1350), Jews quoted the Qur'an in order to refute the Muslim claim that Deut. 18:15, 18 actually predicted the coming of Muhammad.[26] The discussion concerned the words describing the future prophet "from the midst of thee, of thy brethren like me," and "from among their brethren." In a discussion that, according to Ibn Qayyim al-Djawziyya, took place (if ever) in North Africa *(bi-bilād al-Maghrib)*, Muslims argued that this verse could not refer to any Jewish prophet such as Joshua, because "at the end of the Torah" it is stated explicitly that in Israel there arose no prophet like Moses. Also, the brethren of Israel are either the Arabs (the sons of Ismāʿīl) or the Byzantine Christians (*Al-Rūm*), sons of Esau (*Banū-al-ʿĪṣ*). The latter had only Hiob for a prophet—before Moses. Therefore the Biblical verse must necessarily refer to the Arabs and to Muhammad, whose grandfather Ismāʿīl "built his camp (*fusṭāṭa*) among his brethren." According to Ibn Qayyim al-Djawziyya, one of the Jewish discussants then retorted:

> You have in the Qur'an the verses: "And to [the tribe of] Midyan [we sent] their brother Shuʿayb" [Sūra 7:85]; "And to [the tribe of] ʿĀd [we sent] their brother Hūd" [Sūra 7:65]; "And to [the tribe of] Thamūd [we sent] their brother Ṣāliḥ" [Sūra 7:73].

[25] See, for example, H. Hirschfeld, "Ein Karaer ueber den von Mohammad gemachten Vorwurf Juedischer Torahfaelschung," *ZA* 26 (1912): 111–13.

[26] Cf. above, Chapter Four, pp. 105–6.

And the Arabs say, "O brother of Banū Tamīm" to one of them [of Banū Tamīm]. Therefore, the [Biblical] verse "I shall raise [a prophet] to the Children of Israel—from their brethren" is to be understood in the same way [namely, as referring to an Israelite prophet].

The Muslim discussant then answered that there was a clear linguistic difference between the Qur'anic and Biblical verses, and that it would be impossible to use the term "brother"—meaning one of their own sons—other than in the singular. It is impossible to say, for example, that the Banū Isrā'īl are the brethren of Banū Isrā'īl, or that Banū Tamīm are the brethren of Banū Tamīm. In the singular, however, it is perfectly right to say (as the Qur'an does) that Zayd is the brother of Banū Tamīm, Hūd the brother of 'Ād, Ṣāliḥ the brother of Thamud, and so on, meaning he is one of their kinsmen.[27] The Jews then tried to use the common polemical motif that Muhammad was never sent to the Children of Israel, but to the Arabs alone (they even mentioned the Jewish 'Īsāwiyya sect in this context), but, naturally, their argument was rejected by the Muslims. The Jewish participants, of course, did not change their minds, but (according to the Muslim author) were at a loss how to save themselves from the Arab discussant and decided that the least they could do was to refrain from speaking ill of Muhammad.[28]

Oddly, while relating this (imaginary?) story, Ibn Qayyim al-Djawziyya, does not show any sign of resentment that Jews knew and quoted the Qur'an. Yet he himself was the author of a detailed study of the laws concerning the Dhimmis, wherein he mentioned explicitly that they were not allowed to study the Qur'an.[29]

Christians, of course, also quoted the Qur'an, even more

[27] The legal definition of "brother" is a much-discussed issue among Rabbanites and Karaites as well. (See Chapter Two above, note 44.)

[28] See Ibn Qayyim al-Djawziyya, *Hidāyat al-Ḥayārā fī-l-Radd 'alā-l-Yahūd wa-l-Naṣārā* (Beirut, n.d.), p. 126 and cf. p. 78.

[29] Ibn Qayyim al-Djawziyya, *Kitāb Aḥkām Ahl al-Dhimma* (Damascus 1961), 2: 775.

so than Jews, in polemical contexts. They also tried to interpret Qur'anic verses about Jesus, Mary, and the Holy Spirit in a Christian manner.[30]

In spite of all that has been said so far, actual translations of the Qur'an into Hebrew, are rare and late. They are inaccurate and include polemical material about Muhammad.[31] Further, they were made not directly from the Arabic original but from earlier Latin, Italian, and Dutch translations. Three such Hebrew Qur'ans exist in the Bodleian Library at Oxford, the British Library in London, and the Library of Congress in Washington, D.C.,[32] The first two seem to be identical, as S. D. Goitein has already remarked,[33] and include a Hebrew translation of the Qur'an made from an Italian translation, which in turn was made from an earlier Latin one. The translator was Yaʿaqov b.

[30] See, for example, *The Apology of el-Kindī* (London 1911), pp. 27, 65–66, 115ff.; L. Cheicho, *Vingt Traites théologiques* (Beirut 1920), pp. 115ff. (Paul Rāhib); cf. D. S. Sahas, *John of Damascus on Islam* (Leiden 1972), pp. 89–93; S. H. Griffith, "Theodore Abū Qurrah's Arabic Tract on the Christian Practice of Venerating Images," *JAOS* 105 (1985): 66–67; idem, "The Monks of Palestine and the Growth of Christian Literature in Arabic," *The Muslim World* 78 (1988): 21. Cf. P. Cachia's introduction to his edition of the *Kitāb al-Burhān* of Eutychius, CSCO 20 (Louvain 1960), pp. iii–iv. The same holds true for Christians in the Spanish West. See, for example, G. Monnot, "Les Citations coraniques dans le 'Dialogus' de Pierre Alfonse," and A. Cortabarria, "La Connaissance des textes arabes chez Raymond Martin," in *Islam et Chrétiens du Midi*, CNRs, Cahiers des Fanjoux 18 (Toulouse 1983), pp. 261–77, 285–91. Christians also used verses from the Qur'an in their polemics against Jews. See N. Daniel, *Islam and the West* (Edinburgh 1966), pp. 174–75.

[31] Curiously Al-Djāḥiẓ (d. 869) had already stated that if the Jews were to translate the Qur'an they would certainly mistranslate it. See his *Al-Radd ʿalā-l-Naṣārā*, in *Three Essays of Al-Jahiz*, ed. J. Finkel (Cairo 1926), p. 29.

[32] See A. Neubauer, *Catalogue of Hebrew Mss. at the Bodleian Library*, vol. 2 (Oxford 1906), no. 2207, Ms. Michael 113; Brit. Mus. Ms. Or. 6636; LC Heb. Ms. 99. (In EI^2, s.v. "Ḳur'ān" 9, 5, it is stated erroneously—by J. D. Pearson—that one of these translated Qur'ans is in Cambridge, instead of London.

[33] See *Encyclopaedia Judaica* s.v. "Koran" (S. D. Goitein), translated from the German edition.

Israel ha-Levi from Salonica, who wrote in Venice in the year 1547.[34] This translation of the Qur'an comprises 124 chapters (instead of 114 Sūras), following R. Ketton (d. 1143) and others who, in their Latin translation of the Qur'an, divided the long second Sūra and other parts into several subchapters. M. M. Weinstein discussed the problematics of these translations, and especially of the third Qur'an translation in Washington, D.C. (which was apparently written in Cochin by David Cohen [d. 1772] and translated from the Dutch), in a detailed study that is also important for the nineteenth-century history of the Jews in Iran.[35]

Modern Hebrew translations of the Qur'an from Arabic were made by H. Reckendorf in the middle of the last century, and more recently by J. J. Rivlin and A. Ben-Shemesh. The Muslim Aḥmadiyya movement published in 1988 a Yiddish translation of selected Qur'anic verses from Arabic.[36]

There exist also transcriptions of the Qur'an into Hebrew characters, most of them late, except for several Genizah fragments, which are difficult to date.[37] Steinschnei-

[34] See ibid., s.v. "Levi, Jacob b. Israel" (J. Hacker), and cf. J. Hacker, "Patterns of the Intellectual Activity of Ottoman Jewry in the 16th and 17th Centuries" (in Hebrew), *Tarbiz* 53 (1984): 569–601.

[35] M. M. Weinstein, "A Hebrew Qur'ān Manuscript," *Studies in Bibliography and Booklore* 10, *Hebrew Union College*, Cincinnati (1971–72): 19–52. Partial Hebrew translations of the Qur'an are to be found also in Mss. B 234 and 659 of the Institute of the People of Asia in Leningrad. (I owe this reference to M. Weinstein.)

[36] *Selected Verses of the Holy Quran in Yiddish*, Islam International Publications Ltd. (Islamabad 1988).

[37] These include fragments such as Cambridge *T.-S.* Ar. 51.62 (*Sūrat al-Fātiḥa* and the beginnings of Sūra 2) and Saltykov-Shchedrin Ebr.—Arab. (Firk.) 2, 1731 (Sūra 2:1–21 and Sūras 97, 110, 93, 82, 81). I am very grateful to P. Fenton, who first drew my attention to this fragment, and to V. Lebedef, who provided me with a microfilm of it. Some fragments seem to have been lost, for example, Jewish Theological Seminary Library, ENA 499. See also Weinstein, "A Hebrew Qur'ān Manuscript," p. 45 n. 21. For Genizah fragments with Qur'anic verses written in Arabic characters (and in reverse order of the Sūras), cf. G. Khan, "The Arabic

der mentioned three such transcriptions,[38] parts of which still exist: *Vatican 357b.* is incomplete, inaccurate, and difficult to read with a partial Latin translation between the lines.[39] *DMS Ms. Arab 5* (Halle) was described by Roediger in 1860 as very unusual.[40] (Steinschneider answered that Qur'an transcriptions into Hebrew characters were not so unusual.) This transcription seems to originate in Crimea and may have been made by Karaites. Its handwriting is not fluent, and the Arabic is very inaccurate, with some partial vocalization. The fragment goes from Sūra 42:13 to Sūra 43:45—some eighty verses in all.[41] Only the third manuscript (*Bodl. Hunt. 529*) is a full transcription of the whole Qur'an, very accurate, in an easily readable handwriting with partial Hebrew and Arabic vocalization and Masoretic accents.

According to M. Beith-Arié from the Hebrew University in Jerusalem, this third manuscript was written in either the fourteenth or fifteenth century, in any case before 1600, in the East, perhaps in Iraq or Iran. (Southern Iraq is a strong possibility; see below.) M. Steinschneider remarked that although the handwriting in this manuscript is definitely Jewish, there are signs of three crosses at the beginning (apparently at the lower end of p. 2). If these are

---

Fragments in the Cambridge Genizah Collections," *Manuscripts of the Middle East*, vol. 1 (Leiden 1986), p. 58.

[38] See *Hebräische Bibliographie*, vol. 3 (Berlin 1860), p. 113, and Steinschneider, *Polemische und Apologetische Literatur*, p. 315; cf. E. Mainz, "Koranverse in Hebræischer Schrift," *Der Islam* 21 (1933): p. 229. There exists also an early print (1688) of Sūras 30 and 48 in Hebrew characters, apparently for the polemical and scholarly use of Christian readers. See M. F. Beckii (Beckius), *Al-Corani*. (I owe this reference to B. Z. Kedar.)

[39] *Bibliothece Apostolicae Vaticane*, cat. 1, p. 336 ("Liber Alcorani Mahometis pseudoprophaetae").

[40] E. Roediger, "Mitteilungen zur Handschriftenkunde in Hebraeischer Schrift," *ZDMG* 14 (1860): 485–89 (see also *ZDMG* 13 [1859]: 341, no. 271).

[41] See E. Roth, *Verzeichniss der Orientalischen Handschriften in Deutschland* (Wiesbaden 1965), p. 110 (the former nomenclature of this ms. was DMG B. 271). I am very grateful to S. Schreiner for the microfilm of this fragment.

in fact crosses, they may have been added by a later hand. At approximately the same time that this Qur'an seems to have been transcribed into Hebrew, there was an attempt made in Istanbul to re-enforce the restrictions of the "Pact of ʿUmar," and instructions were given to confiscate all copies of the Qur'an found with Jews.[42] This might be indirect proof that Jews did in fact study, transcribe, or translate the Qur'an in this period.

The Bodleian Hebrew transcription of the Qur'an is indeed unique, especially because of the unusual remarks on its margin, which were misunderstood by Neubauer.[43] It contains an Arabic Muslim prayer in Hebrew characters at the end, and a quotation from what seems to be a Shiʿite Arab poem in Arabic characters on the margin of page 172. The manuscript is 200 double pages long. On its first page are drawings of two double (or four) candlesticks or cups; on the left side of the same page are two lines of instructions on how to read the "vocalization of the Ishmaelites"—for example, *qālā̄* should be read *qālān* and *qāl* ـه should be read *qālūn*. The transcription starts on the following page with the whole of *Sūrat al-Fātiḥa* and the beginning of *Sūrat al-Baqara*, but without any headings, unlike the following Sūras, which all start (like in the Qur'an) with headings containing their names and the number of their verses. This second page has also floral decorations, which appear nowhere else in the manuscript; on the lower left side are some drawings, in which Steinschneider saw the signs of the cross. At the end of the manuscript, on the margin of page 199 (which is also slightly decorated), the above-mentioned Muslim Arabic prayer is written in Hebrew characters, vocalized with mixed Hebrew and Arabic signs. It starts with *Ṣadaqa Allāh al-ʿAẓīm* ("God the Almighty spoke the truth"—usually said after a quotation from the Qur'an), *waṣadaqa rasūluhu-l-karīm* ("and his

[42] See M. A. Epstein, *Ottoman Jewish Communities* (Freiburg 1980), p. 38.

[43] See A. Neubauer, *Catalogue of the Hebrew Mss. in the Bodleian Library*, vol. 1, (Oxford 1896), p. 432, no. 121; cf. below.

noble messenger spoke the truth"), then apologizes for any mistakes made while reciting the Qur'an (*fī tilāwat al-Qur'ān*) and asks God for help against the unbelievers. The Qur'an is recited in the hope that it will help people both in this world and in the world to come, and God is asked to make the Qur'an a companion for man both in his grave and on the day of resurrection, as well as a shield protecting him from eternal fire.

The manuscript ends with a detailed list of contents, containing the names of all Sūras, and the pages and sides of pages on which they begin (the page numbers and side "a" or "b" are indicated in Hebrew letters). This list makes a distinctive late or "modern" impression, but it seems to have been written in the same handwriting as the whole Qur'an and the prayer at the end. Only the remarks in the margin, or at least some of them, could have been written by one or more other people. The whole transcription is very accurate and in classical Arabic, and there are no apparent deviations from the language of the Qur'an, nor are there intentional changes of the kind (mentioned by M. Weinstein in his article) that were added, in either Arabic or Persian, in Hebrew characters to the Washington, D.C. manuscript of the Hebrew translation of the Qur'an.[44]

Parts of the manuscript contain an unusually full Hebrew vocalization and some partial Arabic vocalization. The vocalization is not always accurate, and sometimes the Hebrew and Arabic vocalizations within the same word contradict each other. The vocalized parts include *Sūrat al-Fātiḥa* and *Sūrat al-Baqara* up to verse 249, all of *Sūrat Maryam* (Sūra 19), and the first verses of *Sūrat Ṭaha* (Sūra 20), as well as some single verses, such as Sūras 5:42, 9:30, 21:33, 22:25, and the last twelve Sūras.[45] It is hard to find the common denominator, but at least some of these verses deal with anti-Christian (and anti-Jewish) polemics.

There are other signs in the manuscript that seem to re-

[44] See Weinstein, "A Hebrew Qur'ān Manuscript," pp. 29, 41.

[45] On Sūra 9:30, see above, Chapter Three, pp. 51ff..

semble Biblical Masoretic (and Qur'anic) accents, but some are totally unknown, though they look very familiar (Q on *h* at the end of a word; the Q looks like a *Telishah ketanah* but seems to signify a stop; ∞ looks like a closed *Zarqa*). Also in the margin are numbered Qur'anic *Adjzā* (divisions) and some other sporadic divisions, such as a recurring enumeration of ten verses, as if for the sake of study or liturgic purposes. Arabic words denoting prayer time, such as morning (*fadjr*) or, less often, evening (*'ishā*) are sometimes added.[46]

The margin sometimes has words or parts of verses that are omitted in the text, some of which are written in Arabic characters. Other words found in the margin are in Arabic characters as well, although they exist in Hebrew characters in the text.[47] In the margin of Sūra 50:28–38, there are two lines in Arabic characters of a poem about the love of 'Alī, which saves from eternal fire. 'Alī is called "the real successor (*Wasī*) of the Prophet" and "*Imām* of the people and genii[?]." This poem may point to the Shi'ite milieu of the person who wrote the transcription and/or the remarks on the margin. A remark in Hebrew on page 112 may furnish us with further geographical details. It seems to relate to Sūra 21:85, which mentions Dhū-l-Kifl with Ismā'īl and Idrīs among the righteous (prophets). It says: "I have seen this verse written on the entrance [of the tomb] of Ezekiel, peace be on him" (the blessing is given in both Hebrew and Arabic initials). Indeed, one of the prophets with whom Muslim authors identify the mysterious Dhū-l-Kifl is Ezekiel, and one of the places where they show his tomb is in the Shi'ite area of southern Iraq, between Karbalā and Nadjf. This tomb was holy both to Jews and to Muslims, who tried to prevent Jews from visiting it.[48]

[46] See, e.g., pp. 9, 15, 17, 22, 23, 27, 30, 35, 43, 47, 69, 95; a cf. Weinstein, "A Hebrew Qur'ān Manuscript," p. 24.

[47] See, e.g., pp. 7, 9, 12, 14, 17, 30 (where *wa-khālātikum* is added in Arabic and *'arayoth* in Hebrew), 105, 195.

[48] See *EI*² s.v. "*Dhū-l-Kifl*" (G. Vajda); cf. Suleiman Sasson, *Massa' Bavel* (in Hebrew), ed. M. Benayahu (Jerusalem 1955), pp. 158–60. See

Most interesting are the marginal remarks in Hebrew (very seldom the remarks are in Judaeo-Arabic—as on page 41, for example). They relate to the contents of the Qur'anic verses and are scattered all over the book, but they seem to be concentrated in the first long Sūras. A. Neubauer in his *Catalogue* inaccurately described these remarks as Hebrew translations of some Qur'anic passages and "references to corresponding passages of the Bible or the Aggadah."[49] Some of these remarks do indeed summarize the Qur'anic material in Biblical Hebrew, but they are not translations, and they contain no clear reference to Hebrew sources. Thus, for example, it says on page 3 regarding Sūra 2:30: "When God, blessed be he, created the first Adam he consulted the angels, but they did not know"; regarding the following verse, it says: "And Adam gave names to all cattle" as in Gen. 2:20; on page 18, regarding Sūra 3:130, it says: ". . . One does not heed those who take interest"; on page 39, regarding Sūra 5:6: "Concerning their [!] prayer—how [they] wash," and regarding 5:12: "Concerning the twelve spies"; on page 59, regarding Sūra 7:142: "The forty days and forty nights which Moses [see the curious Hebrew spelling of the name][50] went up high" and "concerning the calf which Israel made and later their sin was forgiven"; and so on. These remarks stop after twenty Sūrahs. From the Hebrew language (*Parasha*, "their" prayer, etc.) it seems clear that these remarks were written by a Jew (or a former Jew?), unlike the Muslim prayer at the end.

Most unusual are the polemical remarks, which Neu-

---

also S. D. Goitein on Ezekiel's tomb, in *Studies in the History of the Iraqi Jewry and Their Culture* (in Hebrew) vol. 1, ed. S. Moreh (Tel Aviv 1981), p. 20. Cf. J. L. Kraemer, *Humanism in the Renaissance of Islam* (Leiden 1986), p. 80.

[49] Neubauer, *Catalogue*, 1:432, no. 121.

[50] As suggested by Weinstein with regard to the translators of the Qur'an into Hebrew. See his "A Hebrew Qur'ān Manuscript." The same spelling *Mīsha* (instead of Moshe) also occurs on p. 130 of the manuscript.

bauer does not mention at all, and which were apparently written by the same person. They raise difficult questions about the whole manuscript. They may have been directed primarily against Christians, so that we have here Hebrew anti-Christian polemics based on verses from the Qur'an! On page 8, for example, Sūra 2:120 is mistakenly (or purposely?) explained "as saying that Israel is good but he who is uncircumcised is no good, and if you want to convert, the law of Israel is better than the law of the uncircumcised." In fact, the Qur'anic verse talks about the Jews and Christians who refuse to follow the new religious message of Islam. On page 21, Sūra 3:50 is explained "as saying that the Torah is true and I am a witness upon you concerning what the Torah has said." In the same vein, on page 36: "He says that the Torah which was revealed first is true . . . whoever denies it will have no future part [in the world to come] and is an unbeliever." On page 38, regarding Sūra 4:171: "He says that Jesus son of Miryam the messenger of God, who was His word[?] . . . came to Miryam; believe in him but do not say three concerning Father, Son, and Spirit." On page 43, about Sūra 5:72–73: "He proves false the answer of the Christians who believe in three, Son, Spirit, and Father"; verse 82 is explained as "concerning the uncircumcised who hate Israel, those who have *Qasīsīn* [priests] and *Ruhbān* [monks] and *Asāqif* [bishops]—be they accursed[?]." This explanation must have been made intentionally, because the well-known verse states explicitly that the Jews (and idolaters) hate the (Muslim) believers more than anybody else, whereas the Christians are their friends "because they have priests and monks [*Qasīsīn* and *Ruhbān*] and are not proud."

Some rare marginal remarks (made by somebody else?) are anti-Muslim. For example, on page 142, regarding Sūra 33:40: "The *Pasul* [a Hebrew nickname for Muhammad reconstructed after the Arabic *Rasūl*] had no son."

It will take a separate study of these remarks to establish their purpose, as well as to understand for whom the manuscript was intended. If we accept the supposition that the

Qur'an is simply used here in Jewish anti-Christian polemics, the Muslim prayer in Hebrew characters at the end of the manuscript (and in the same handwriting) is totally out of place. It also would not fit the manuscript's Jewish-Christian attitude, which accepts the Qur'anic view of Jesus but rejects the Trinity. On the other hand, to think of Jews converted to Islam but still harboring a positive attitude toward their former Jewish heritage will raise other difficulties, for example with regard to such derogatory terms as *Pasul* for Muhammad. This holds true also for any suggestion of a Jewish Muslim sect.[51] Also, one must keep in mind that sometimes a single Jewish author (like the Karaite Al-Qirqisānī) polemicized against both Christianity and Islam or copied Hebrew translations of both the New Testament and the Qur'an.[52] In any case, there is certainly a great need to study further every fragment of a Hebrew translation or transcription of the Qur'an to be found. Though rare, such fragments may help not only to shed light on the extent of Jewish knowledge of the Qur'an, but also to elucidate the deep influence Islam exerted on some Jews.

[51] Prof. B. Lewis suggested the possibility of a Doenmeh Jewish-Muslim environment, but then 1600 cannot be the terminus ad quem, nor Iraq the place of origin.

[52] See examples in Weinstein, "A Hebrew Qur'an Manuscript," and J. Hacker, "Patterns of the Intellectual History of Ottoman Jewry." Cf. also A. H. Cutler and C. E. Cutler, *The Jew as Ally of the Muslim: Medieval Roots of Anti-Semitism* (Notre Dame 1986), pp. 245–46.

List of Biblical Verses Cited

New Testament

List of Qur'anic Verses Cited

Index

Lightning Source UK Ltd.
Milton Keynes UK
UKHW020146270620
365635UK00005B/267